Language, Discourse and Power in African American Culture

D1036490

African American language is central to the teaching of linguistics and language in the United States, and this book, in the series Studies in the Social and Cultural Foundations of Language, is aimed specifically at upper-level undergraduates and graduates. It covers the entire field – grammar, speech and verbal genres – and it also discusses the various historical strands that need to be identified in order to understand the development of African American English. The book deals with the social and cultural history of the American South, urban and Northern black popular culture as well as policy issues. Morgan examines the language within the context of the changing and complex African American and general American speech communities, and their culture, politics, art and institutions. She also covers the current heated political and educational debates about the status of the African American dialect.

MARCYLIENA MORGAN is Associate Professor of Afro-American Studies at Harvard University and Associate Professor of Anthropology at the University of California, Los Angeles. Her research has focused on language, culture and identity, hip hop and rap, sociolinguistics, and discourse and interaction. She is the editor of *Language and the Social Construction of Identity in Creole Situations* (1994).

Studies in the Social and Cultural Foundations of Language

The aim of this series is to develop theoretical perspectives on the essential social and cultural character of language by methodological and empirical emphasis on the occurrence of language in its communicative and interactional settings, on the socioculturally grounded "meanings" and "functions" of linguistic forms, and on the social scientific study of language use across cultures. It will thus explicate the essentially ethnographic nature of linguistic data, whether spontaneously occurring or experimentally induced, whether normative or variational, whether synchronic or diachronic. Works appearing in the series will make substantive and theoretical contributions to the debate over the sociocultural-function and structural-formal nature of language, and will represent the concerns of scholars in the sociology and anthropology of language, anthropological linguistics, sociolinguistics, and socioculturally informed psycholinguistics.

Editors
Judith T. Irvine
Bambi Schieffelin

Editorial Advisers
Marjorie Goodwin
Joel Kuipers
Don Kulick
John Lucy
Elinor Ochs
Michael Silverstein

Language, Discourse and Power
in African American Culture

Marcyliena Morgan

University of California, Los Angeles

CAMBRIDGE
UNIVERSITY PRESS

PUBLISHED BY THE PRESS SYNDICATE OF THE UNIVERSITY OF CAMBRIDGE
The Pitt Building, Trumpington Street, Cambridge, United Kingdom

CAMBRIDGE UNIVERSITY PRESS
The Edinburgh Building, Cambridge CB2 2RU, UK
40 West 20th Street, New York, NY 10011-4211, USA
477 Williamstown Road, Port Melbourne, VIC 3207, Australia
Ruiz de Alarcón 13, 28014 Madrid, Spain
Dock House, The Waterfront, Cape Town 8001, South Africa

http://www.cambridge.org

First published 2002

Printed in the United Kingdom at the University Press, Cambridge

Typeface Plantin 10/12 pt.   *System* LaTeX 2$_\varepsilon$ [TB]

A catalogue record for this book is available from the British Library

Library of Congress Cataloguing in Publication data
Morgan, Marcyliena H.
Language, discourse and power in African American culture /
Marcyliena Morgan.
     p.   cm. – (Studies in the social and cultural foundations of language; no. 20)
Includes bibliographical references (p.   ) and index.
ISBN 0 521 80671 2 – ISBN 0 521 00149 8 (pbk.)
1. Black English.   2. English language – Social aspects – United States.
3. Speech and social status – United States.   4. Power (Social sciences) – United
States.   5. African Americans – Social conditions.   6. English language –
Discourse analysis.   7. Language and culture – United States.   8. African
Americans – Languages.   I. Title.   II. Series.
PE3102.N44 M67   2002
427′.973′08996073 – dc21   2001043689

ISBN 0 521 80671 2 hardback
ISBN 0 521 00149 8 paperback

To Lawrence Douglas Bobo

Contents

Maps, figures and tables

Acknowledgments

Throughout the writing of this book I have been influenced by the insight of many. And I cannot conceive of having completed this project without their support and generosity. First I would like to thank the women and youth who directed me to people and locations in Chicago and Mississippi and whose warmth, wariness and wisdom fueled this project. They include Juliette Morgan, Ruth Skinner, Ruth Murray, Mary Ann Corley, Stephen DeBerry, Anderine Jones, Diann Washington and Donna Moore. I also owe a debt of gratitude to all those who worked with me in Philadelphia, especially Deborah White, who will always be in my heart. My work at Project Blowed would not have been possible without the generous support and friendship from Ben Caldwell.

A number of research assistants worked on this project and many of their ideas and concerns are included. They are: Devery Rodgers, Lanita Jacobs-Huey, Kesha Fikes, Uma Thambiaya, Sumeeya Chishty Mujahid, Lauren Ferguson, Danielle Beurteaux, Jenigh Garret, Jessica Norwood, Stephen DeBerry, Tarek Captan, Brendesha Tynes and Dionne Bennett. Ben Caldwell, Geneva Smitherman, John Rickford and John Baugh have provided valuable comments on this project. Funding for the research and writing of this book have been provided by the Humanities Institute of the University of California, the Ford Foundation, Harvard University Graduate School of Education and the DuBois Institute at Harvard University.

The UCLA DIRE (Discourse Identity and Representation) Collective Patricia Baquedano-Lopez, Dionne Bennett, Kesha Fikes, Lanita Jacobs-Huey, Soy Kim, Adrienne Lo, and Steve Ropp provided a space to present these ideas and receive feedback from some of the brightest scholars I know. I am forever grateful for their support. Over the years, I have been fortunate to receive comments and support from numerous scholars including Olga Rubio, Salikoko Mufwene, Dell Hymes, Gillian Sankoff, William Labov, Elinor Ochs, Alessandro Duranti, Marjorie Goodwin, Lorene Cary, Paul Kroskrity, Shirley Heath, Valerie Smith, Henry Louis Gates Jr., Ana Celia Zentella, Judith Irvine and Bambi Schieffelin.

Colleagues in numerous places and associations have also assisted me in completing this volume. They include Gerlin Bean, Stella Dadzie, Lorene Cary, Dorinne Kondo, Linda Dessner, Nancy Sander-Best, Irene Maksymujk, Deborah Wafer, Brenda Sykes, Sophia Gael-Valenzuela, Abel Valenzuela and Frank Funk.

Dionne Bennett has been instrumental in my completing this project and has inspired me with her love of black culture and her critical and persistent engagement of ideas. I thank my husband, Larry Bobo, for his vision of me successfully completing this project, his unfaltering love and support, and amazing intellect. Finally, I thank all the wonderful men and women in the African American community who have shared a culture and history that they have held so close to their heart for so long. Yours is truly a love supreme.

"The Death of Emmett Till": lyrics reprinted by kind permission of the Bob Dylan Music Company, New York.

"Speak Out Against Ebonics," Ketchum Advertising. *New York Times*, October 9, 1998, A19 (National Edition). Reprinted by kind permission of Lee St. James.

Notes on the transcriptions

CAPITAL LETTERS indicate some form of emphasis which may be signaled by changes in pitch or amplitude.

BOLD CAPITAL LETTERS indicate loud-talking.

Italics indicate a change in the quality of speech.

. A period indicates a stopping fall in tone, not necessarily the end of a sentence.

, A comma indicates a continuing intonation, not necessarily between clauses of sentences.

: Colons indicate that the sound just before the colon has been lengthened.

↑ An upward arrow indicates a rising inflection.

! An exclamation mark indicates an animated tone, not necessarily an exclamation.

— A single dash can indicate (1) a short untimed pause, (2) halting, abrupt cutoff, or, when multiple dashes hyphenate the syllables of a word or connect strings of words, the stream of talk so marked has (3) a stammering quality.

[All overlapping utterances, including those which start simultaneously are marked with a single left bracket.

] The point where overlap stops is marked with a single right bracket.

= When there is no interval between adjacent utterances, the second being latched immediately to the first, the utterances are linked together with equal signs. They are also used to link different parts of a single speaker's utterance when those parts constitute a continuous flow of speech that has been carried over to another line to accommodate an intervening interruption.

(.) A period within parentheses indicates a one-second pause.

( )   When intervals in the stream of talk occur, they are timed in tenths of a second and inserted within parentheses either within an utterance or between.

(())   Double parentheses provide description of quality of talk and activity related to talk.

Introduction

The study of African American language is the study of how people of African descent use language as a cultural resource that in turn represents, constructs and mediates social reality. I learned this truth as I was growing up on Chicago's segregated South Side in the late 1950s. When people in my childhood neighborhood talked about language and communication, as they frequently did, they referred to racial, social and regional differences and the importance of style and ambiguity in conversing with those in positions of power, especially under white supremacy. They also expressed great love and respect for conversations that were deeply ambiguous. Everyday conversations were always filtered through proverbs, references to past events and people. The past was never a concept about time but about perspective, the type of perspective that meant that even young children were told the truth about life in America – "All you *have* to do is stay black and die."

There were always people "passing through" our home. My family included my grandfather, father, mother, aunts, uncles and five sisters. Together we lived on the top two floors of a three-story apartment building – with our apartments separated by sixteen stairs in the front and fourteen in the back. To us kids this separation meant little, as we proved daily when we jumped (or flew), in one fell swoop, from our place at the top of the back steps to the rest of my family at the bottom. From my perspective, whoever visited the family visited me, and I always tried to find a comfortable spot under a table or out of the way so that I could hear the fantastic stories told by our many guests. They included jazz musicians like Hazel Scott, Billy Eckstine and Sarah Vaughn, Pullman porters, politicians, laborers, underworld dealers, dancers and various representatives from the "respectable" middle class. One of my most vivid memories of these times is of an extraordinary woman named Mrs. Jackson.[1]

Mrs. Jackson always walked slowly, dragging her feet and shifting her weight from one hip to the other – as she carried two enormous weathered leather bags. She seemed to be hidden under layers of deeply hued fabric. When she completed her greetings, which included hugging and teasing adults and children alike, Mrs. Jackson would collapse onto a chair. Breathing a sigh of relief, but holding onto her bags, she would look at my sisters and me as though she knew everything about us. We thought she was a strange woman, and we liked that about her. We would sit in a row on the couch and wait for her to catch her breath. Once she was settled she would look at us, as though she could see deeply within, and ask in a sonorous voice: "What do you know about slavery?" She would lean close and whisper; "Do you know who Paul Robeson is?" "Have you heard of Harriet Tubman, Frederick Douglas, the Harper's Ferry?" I'm not sure whether we knew any of the names and events before she spoke them but one thing was certain. When those names came across her lips we knew that we were about to learn something that was not just an important and great secret, but that was also the best secret of all! She was prepared to guide us through history to knowledge of what it meant to be black in America – and we knew that some of the answers were in her bags.

As she spoke, Mrs. Jackson would reach deep into her sacks and pull out her "special treasures" of tattered books and pamphlets. She would whisper the word *special* as though her books' very existence depended on our valuing them. Mrs. Jackson would then perform dramatic readings of slave narratives that were both enlightening and frightening. Then she would have us reenact our escape from slavery to freedom on the Underground Railroad!

My sisters and I competed for roles that included the slave catcher, evil overseer, the evil plantation owners, the benevolent yet complicit plantation wife, the sell-out and scared slave, the knowing survivor and, finally, the brave warrior on the way to freedom! It was never clear who would get to hold the whip and who would be on the receiving end under the evils of slavery as reenacted through sibling rivalries. No matter when Mrs. Jackson arrived, I always wanted to be the warrior slave on the way to freedom. Mrs. Jackson would exhort us to get the "real feel" of slavery. She insisted that in our respective roles, masters should talk like masters – "speak direct, enunciate, sound cold!" She also insisted that slaves should talk like slaves. She'd say, "You're slaves, so speak slowly – like you don't know nothing! Bow your heads to the white people! If they notice what's on your mind they'll catch you, give you the whip and take you back!"

We encountered evil in all forms on our escape from slavery. We reveled in our walk and flight to freedom and mourned those who never made it. We learned to laugh and cry about slavery and racism in America. We learned how to live with both the truth and the lie with humanity, dignity and resolve. Until my Underground Railroad experience, I never understood why my mother would get so angry when I said, "OK, I hear you" in response to an order or advice she gave. I thought she was irritated because she knew I intentionally didn't respond immediately and directly. After my walk to freedom, I understood that my mother meant much more when she said, "I know you hear me – But girl, you'd better start listening!" She was warning me that words not only describe – they reflect and construct cultural experience. And hearing is only the beginning.

My childhood memories about language and wisdom in the black community remain vivid not only because they are about family, but also because they are recalled in everyday interactions. And participating in them not only brings me home, but it rekindles the joy of a community that strongly believes that the most difficult aspect of communication is figuring out what someone actually means, and why they said it the way they did. And this is tied to the importance of character – something you can't claim yourself, but has to be verified by those around you. Whether one's character is good or bad is not the point. What matters is that you must be able to express who you are and be able to determine who you are dealing with. And the analysis of people is through social relations, language and the presentation of self. That's why people who don't respect African American English (AAE) scare me, especially if they're black. I mean, how will they know when they've been told the secret? What if they "miss that train?"

America's fascination with the language and interaction styles of African Americans has arguably resulted in it being the most studied and best-known dialect in the world. It shows no sign of abating. This is remarkable for several reasons. First, African Americans are only 12 percent of the US population and not all people of African descent speak varieties of AAE.[2] Second, there are competing and often contradictory arguments over its status as a language or dialect. Similarly, there are numerous social, political, cultural and linguistic arguments concerning its development and continued use.

Accordingly, this book explores African American language, verbal style and discourse in African American culture in particular and American culture in general. In this sense, I focus on language as both a cultural production and social construct. It is a cultural production because it is based on values and norms that exist throughout African American communities. It is also a social construct because it is the vehicle by means of which much social activity occurs and through which roles, relationships and institutions are negotiated. Consequently, this text reviews but does not dwell on purely linguistic arguments and the proofs and debates typical in linguistic science. Rather, one aim of this text is to place much of the linguistic discussion within the changing and complex African American and general American speech communities and within their significant cultural, public, artistic, political, institutional and social contexts.

The community where African American speech is employed is rich and diverse in terms of members, contexts for usage and attitudes toward it. A cursory glance at television programs, movies, music videos, news broadcasts and popular publications gives some indication of the contradictory attitudes toward black language and discourse style. Americans hypocritically want to get rid of it, speak it, keep it, regulate it, stereotype it, write it, call it a language, call it a dialect, rename it, claim it and blame it for the problems of black youth!

The extent of the conflicted attitude toward African American English erupted on December 18, 1996, when the Oakland, California, Unified School District Board of Education approved a language education policy for speakers of African American English that – they argued – affirmed Standard English language development for all children. The policy included a training program to enable "teachers and administrators to respect and acknowledge the history, culture, and language that the African American student brings to school." In referring to the children's speech, the school district wrote, "This language has been studied for several decades and is variously referred to as Ebonics (literally 'black sounds'), or 'Pan-African Communication Behaviors,' or 'African Language Systems.'" The Oakland plan incorporated African American history and culture and Ebonics in the language arts curriculum. The popular response was swift and akin to hysterical outrage. With few exceptions, progressive African American politicians and public figures like the political leader Jesse Jackson and novelist and poet Maya Angelou rushed to decry Oakland's proposal and express their anguish. The immediate rejection of the Oakland plan aligned heretofore-progressive politicians and artists with political conservatives who derided the decision as one more example of liberal political correctness gone awry. The media circus that ensued was a surreal American replay of cultural critic Kobena Mercer's (1994) analysis of the strange bedfellows that have also emerged in Black British politics. Though to some, Oakland was simply a case of "déjà vu all over again," for many linguists who study African American language and communication, it was much more than that.

The debates surrounding the declaration were similar to the acrimony that followed two earlier proposals concerning African American English. The proposals were the Ann Arbor legal case on Black English in education, which was settled in 1979, and a later study in 1985 by William Labov on the divergence of African American and white urban dialects

(Labov and Harris, 1986; Morgan, 1994b; Smitherman, 1981a, b). In the Ann Arbor case (also known as the King case), parents successfully sued their children's school because it consistently placed poor African American children in remedial classes. In the divergence studies scholars found that black and white children's language varieties were growing further apart and predicted that the black children's continued use of Black English would lead to further failure in school. These two highly publicized events concerning language education and socialization remain of great interest for several reasons. First, they both raised and politicized questions concerning what is African American English, who speaks it and why it exists. They also revealed that AAE research often conflicts with language and education policy and planning. The arguments also embodied the intricacies and webs of social and cultural life that entangle arguments of language and identity. Thus, the African American community's response to the various plans and proposals exposed the existence of a well-integrated ideology regarding language, culture and education. Perhaps surprisingly to linguists, popular culture's interest in and response to the plan highlighted the contradictions and festering antagonisms between the pervasiveness of African American culture and language in mass cultural production and resentment toward it. Finally, despite the fact that each proposal incorporated different views on the function of AAE in education, all plans were rejected by significant segments of the African American community. Thus in many respects the furor that followed the Oakland decision was not simply about education, or African Americans. Rather, it was about language as a symbol of culture, politics, nationalism, identity and power.

In the late 1960s, when linguists began to analyze what had been highly subjective depictions of black speech, they recognized the social importance of their work within a politically charged climate. What they could not predict was that AAE would continue to be central to African American identity in particular and the fields of sociolinguistics and cultural studies in general. For those who study language ideology and politics, it is not surprising that in the process of critiquing AAE, the larger society at times succumbs – albeit dazed and confused – to its charms. This has been in the form of caricatures like the white rapper Vanilla Ice, who attempted to invent a hard-core ghetto identity, to white rapper Eminem who, as black female rapper Missy Eliot put it, "knows he's white" because he focuses on his circumstances and his own perspective while demonstrating knowledge of urban African American cultural values. In either case, vexing questions of authenticity and exploitation abound within the reality of whites getting rich as they perform appropriated and well-circulated stereotypes of black youth behavior.

This appropriation, coupled with criticism, has led to more complex concerns from an African American community that is challenged by the following elaborate question: "What happens to identity when language styles, which constitute a group's culture, are removed from their cultural context and cast out onto film, novels, electronic networks, videos, police dramas, comic formats and so on?" This type of inquiry tends to unify the African American community, eliding social class conflicts, while provoking analyses of marginalization, power, racism, sexism, exploitation and cultural imperialism in American society. And it leads to the question that often throws black middle-class youth, who are socialized within African American culture but do not fit popular stereotypes, into unfathomable contortions: *Will the* real *and* authentic *intellectually defined black person please stand up?*

The ethical concerns inherent in these questions were highlighted in April 1998, when *Boston Magazine* referred to Harvard University's chair of the Department of Afro-American Studies and the W. E. B. Du Bois Institute for Afro-American Research as the "Head Negro in Charge" (HNIC). HNIC is a term created by African Americans that deconstructs and critiques white privilege and its effects. As such, it has multiple and often contradictory references. HNIC can be used to refer to African Americans who have assumed a position from which blacks have previously been excluded because of their race. And in this case it is a cultural high-five.[3] It can also be used to refer to blacks in positions of responsibility that are adored by whites in particular, but doubted by many blacks. In this instance, it is employed as a critique of collaboration with white privilege, implying that the black leader is following someone else's orders. So HNIC can be a direct compliment. It can also indirectly signify on the black person and is an admonishment. And it signifies on white people, who believe that they know and can select the one black person to represent all African Americans. Thus the referential meaning of the expression is contextually sensitive and politically laden.[4] Yet, the white editor of *Boston Magazine* confidently placed it on the cover and defended his use of the expression because "black people use it." But he neither questioned nor seemed to understand how black people used it and why the black perspective should have been addressed for the sake of all concerned. These types of popular incidents attach urgency to the question of "what to do" and demonstrate that language and verbal style, as products and instruments of cultural practice, which are simply "out there," without their cultural framework and social context are actually "somewhere" and susceptible to another culture's interpretive machinery.

This book is concerned with all of the issues described above and focuses on cultural beliefs and practices, social life and institutions, as well as linguistic and historical information related to the African American experience in the US. That is, its aim is to identify and analyze the attitudes, norms, changes, developments and innovations of language and verbal form and function within society. In this respect, this book is one of many multidisciplinary bodies of work in African American studies. It is based on cross-generational qualitative and quantitative analyses that address gender and socioeconomic status and their impact on language and identity. While it includes diverse sectors of the population, it adds to the growing body of scholarship on women's language and interaction. It incorporates language and communicative practices within social and cultural frameworks as well as interpretations in the arts, popular culture and education.

The analysis presented here is the result of fieldwork, interviews and research I conducted with African American women, youth and families over the past fifteen years in Chicago, Philadelphia, Los Angeles and Mississippi. It has involved the collaboration of many men and women who rejected the role of informer and became collaborators and contributors. In order to participate in these communities, I also explored the material culture typical in the homes and neighborhoods. This has included reading neighborhood newspapers, numerous magazines, watching television programs, going to movies in black theaters, listening to radio programs and exploring all the materials that speech community members deemed valuable.

African American English is important to African American people. Whether they celebrate or criticize it, it is the evidence of what they have been through. The speaker who relies on its most vernacular form represents his or her social world and the encroachments of racism and class inequities. The successful adult who claims an allegiance to standard, "good" speech uses language as proof that the escape from racism is successful and over. The teenager who confronts and confounds the world with language games and verbal usage that celebrates the dialect is recognizing its power. And the college student and computer specialist who uses elite speech when working and AAE when theorizing and plotting to overtake the world evokes home. African American English is part and parcel of social, cultural and political survival. It is about ideas, art, ideology, love and memory.

Despite the many changes that have occurred within the black community, African Americans remain central to national discourses about identity, culture and representation. Yet many of these discourses, even at the highest levels of power, are organized around misinformation, misconceptions, and, at times, vicious stereotypes about African Americans. By presenting more accurate portrayals of African American values and cultural practices, based on thoughtful and committed research, I believe that black scholars can and must do their part in transforming these discourses into more meaningful and productive exchanges of information, experiences and possibilities.

The book is organized into six chapters. Each chapter begins with an analysis of field notes that frames issues within conversation and daily life. The first chapter, "The African American speech community: culture, language ideology and social face," focuses on the role of local knowledge and history in the development of the urban speech community. Within this chapter, many sociological and psychological descriptions of African Americans and concepts such as social face and double consciousness are discussed within a theory of language and social interaction.

The second chapter, "Forms of speech: verbal styles, discourse and interaction," explores African American interaction and verbal style within a complex system of social face and character representation that incorporates hearers, overhearers and others who may be in a position to evaluate an interaction. In particular, it explores communicative practices indicative of African American interaction including the verbal game of "the dozens," conversational signifying, indirectness, turn taking, strategic overlap and timing.

Chapter 3, "Language norms and practices," focuses on the symbolic and practical functions of African American English (AAE) and General English (GE). It explores the relationship between language, race and social class and issues of code switching, style shifting and identity "reading dialect" and grammar. It incorporates data from Philadelphia to explore the use, role and status of AAE and GE in narratives. Chapter 4, "When women speak," is an analysis and critique of the current scholarship on African American women's speech. This chapter uses ethnographic observations and reviews the current literature to describe and analyze discourse, conversation and verbal styles of African American women across generations. It looks at women's language socialization and how girls grow from instigating to incorporating conversational signifying and other styles of interaction.

Chapter 5, "Urban youth language: black by popular demand," explores the language ideology and practices of urban youth affiliated with the social organization, culture and politics of hip hop music. Hip hop's impact on adolescent social networks and value systems is discussed in relation to crew and speech community formation, style, identity and language. Chapter 6, "Language, discourse and power: outing schools," provides a comprehensive review of how African American English scholarship has been employed in educational policy and how the African American community responds to planning that incorporates

AAE usage. It reviews arguments concerning dialect readers and other planning instruments. In particular it examines the educational, political and cultural forces and issues behind the 1996 Oakland School District decision and other cases that affected the education of African American children.

The burgeoning arguments and discourses about texts, signs and signifiers have thrust linguistic anthropology, sociolinguistics and linguistic philosophy into a more public arena. With this new recognition and audience has come an urgency to resist the separation of language and meaning from society and culture. This historical moment is therefore not simply the erasure or merging of boundaries, but the introduction of analyses which consider the complex, multilayered lives of people who have established, sustained and continue to maintain their communities and who live and work with others. Not surprisingly, while one aim of this book is to describe and analyze contemporary language and communication among African Americans in the US, its main focus is on language as an aspect of culture and the ways in which it mediates identity across cultural and social contexts. So in many respects this book is also an exploration and analysis of African American language ideology. It is about why and how a variety of language and a way of talking – whether denigrated or celebrated – remains something precious and worth preserving.

1 The African American speech community: culture, language ideology and social face

One hot, humid evening in August 1992, after about a month of fieldwork in Mississippi, I was driving alone on a desolate highway from Magnolia to Lexington. The car radio was blaring as a caller explained that she had ended her relationship with a man who had "done her wrong!" The deejay was in fine form as she kept playing "Drop that Zero," a song about a woman who could "do bad all by herself!" As I sang along with the fifth broadcast of the tune in one hour, I suddenly noticed something in the night that paralyzed me with fear. It was a road sign that read, "Crossing the Big Black River."

During my stay in Jackson and Magnolia, people would give me the names and locations of family and friends who lived near the Black River. These names were offered whenever talk turned to the times when "You had to *know your place* in front of white people!" And "You could get into trouble for *speaking* like a grown man or woman!" These statements were often punctuated with ironic laughter, knowing nods and tense smiles. Invariably, someone would quietly ask me: "Have you been to the Black River yet? You need to go." Or begin their story: "There was a store..." or "You remember when Booker T went to that juke joint near the Black River and..." Their voices would trail off, never completing the story, and they would say earnestly, "You need to go there." At first I thought the name was a joke. It wasn't. While I knew that I would understand their past and present lives much better if I visited the Black River, I also sensed that they were cautioning me.

Later, a friend confirmed my worst fears. Countless black people had disappeared near that river. The names were an offering and a way to remember loved ones who were killed "for trying to be a man." The name offering was also a warning and test to see if I knew better than to go asking questions about black life and racism in those parts. I wrote in my notes, I have to learn to hear their warning – "Cousin Joe who 'wasn't never afraid of nobody'" The country store that was "always full of white people!" The bar and fish and chicken shack that they were never allowed to enter from the front – and the Black River. I had heard them.

10

And I put my foot on the gas pedal until the Big Black River was safely behind me.

The first time: language and the contact zone

Though this book is not about the South, it begins there. For many African Americans in the North, the South is a sort of homeland. My people came from Mississippi or thereabouts. Where my people's people came from is a question that I've never heard anyone in my family answer. My grandfather just used to say, "They were Africans." That was all we knew and somehow that said it all. And when my grandfather talked about olden times, it was often impossible to tell whether he was talking about Mississippi at the end of slavery or stories of Africa. The connections between Africa, Mississippi and Chicago were obvious. They were everywhere and came in the form of folktales, language and family history. These stories were records of how African American communities survived, thrived and changed. Surviving the horrors of slavery was a badge of honor to the older generation around me, as they talked of the hypocrisy of Jim Crow and segregation in Chicago. Their tales raised innumerable questions but perhaps the most beguiling was the time they actually picked for their beginning. From a child's perspective, it was always mysterious when our questions about great-great grandparents or how somebody died or – as they would say – "came up missing" were immediately suppressed as though our curiosity was itself an egregious act. To make matters worse, there was little public discourse about what life was like during slavery and neither schoolbooks nor teachers offered a clue about the atrocities our families suffered. Still, the older generation persisted in their contorted dance around family history as well as the moment(s) when stories about family and friends – that could be recounted and contested – actually began as *our* stories. They just never answered. And they had good reason.

Questions of the beginnings of nations, a people, a family and so on are "first-time" narratives. These are often tales of desire, exploration, loss and awakening. That is unless the "first time" is also an instance of violence, subjugation and exploitation. In that case, the awareness of the "first time" is disturbed and disturbing because regardless of how horrific the circumstances, it was still the "first time." It remains a passage that belongs with other stories of new beginnings. But how does one tell the story so that all can appreciate a narrative of rebirth and death and truth and suspicion? The story of African American English is embedded in the story of the first time and laden with layers of significance because it is not simply about a contact language or variety. Rather, the question wrestles with an epochal moment in American history – the beginning and confirmation of African American culture and society. It is in this sense that the existence of African American English (AAE) is much more than about the "first time" – it is proof of it. It is the evidence that something has been silenced – and the only possibility of resolution is through language as a symbol of collective recognition that slavery, white supremacy and racism happened – whether we talk about it or not. This moment is not exclusively about the politics and power of contact through the slave trade and plantation slavery – that would be complicated enough. Rather, it is also about how the contact changed everything. It is about how it spawned endless revisionist histories of American and African American culture.

Contact situations are often catastrophic events and include conquerors and the conquered, oppressors and the oppressed, intermediaries, onlookers, and many, many, more. As Mary Louise Pratt explains:

A "contact" perspective emphasizes how subjects are constituted in and by their relations to each other. It treats the relations among colonizers and colonized, or travelers and "travalees," not in terms of separateness or apartheid, but in terms of copresence, interaction, interlocking understandings and practices, often within radically asymmetrical relations of power. (Pratt, 1992)

For African Americans, the importance of the first time and the nature of contact is not only to describe historical circumstances, but to contest the notion that the only way to describe African American culture is as a problem – through the interpretation and supposed benevolence of the oppressors, intermediaries and onlookers and their descendants. Thus any study of the contact zone, whether from scholars or laypersons, includes the critical analysis and interpretation of historical occurrences and narratives. This interpretation of contact occurs as an "historical trauma of an inaugural event and our collective memory of it" (Scott, 1991: 261). It also occurs within the less political terms of linguistics as in "when two or more previously existing languages come together" (Sebba, 1997).

The fact is, when two or more languages come together, two or more peoples have come together and the result is always about power and identity. If the result is that one language becomes the lingua franca, it means that the ideology of a dominant language/people has overwhelmed the other languages/peoples and the conquered must deal with that marginalization. If the result is a pidgin – a language that is nobody's mother tongue, where there is no recognizable grammatical structure associated with a particular language – then there is a desperate need to communicate, whether for trade or survival after conquest. If children use the pidgin language and they expand the vocabulary, introduce grammar and so on until it becomes a creole language, then that means that they were conquered people who never got back home. So if the history of a language speaks volumes, the history of African American English is deafening.

Irrespective of the political focus, the test of scholarly accuracy can seem extreme in language study – where history and historical linguistics often spar over both major and minor points. While many issues loom large within linguistic circles, the debate over the nature of the African American contact situation always returns to how to characterize the most basic factors that constituted the beginnings of African American English. It is a question about the nature of the language contact situation and the transcendence from individual captivity to collective identity. It is a question about the representation of life and death and truth and betrayal.

This point and the improbability of trying to fix one moment or linguistic influence is revealed in Richard Price's (1983) ethnography of the collective narratives of the Saramaka Indians of modern-day Suriname: *First-Time: The Historical Vision of an Afro-American People*. These narratives focus on the struggle against the Dutch colonial army and the ongoing struggle for autonomy. They represent the harrowing and epochal points when the present began. David Scott (1991) argues that for the Saramakas, "'first-time'" knowledge:

marks out for them a temporal and even a spatial break . . . first-time knowledge is embedded in a variety of other, disparate sorts of discursive or rhetorical forms: as Price describes them, they include "genealogical nuggets," personal epithets, commemorative place-names, proverbs, songs, etc. And this knowledge is pre-eminently knowledge of "events." (Scott, 1991: 266)

Thus for Saramakas, these narratives are chronotypes (Bakhtin, 1981b; Bender and Wellbery, 1991) in which time and the moments and nature of the contacts assume practical and conceptual significance. These narratives incorporate not only information about the past, but knowledge of the present and how those within the cultural and social present interpret history (Ochs and Capps, 1996; Bender and Wellbery, 1991). Thus narratives are constantly evolving "at multiple individual, social, and cultural levels . . . They change over time and therefore have a history or histories, the construal of which itself is an act of temporal construction. . . they are improvised from an already existing repertoire of cultural forms and natural phenomena" (Bender and Wellbery, 1991: 4). It is thus for both political and structural reasons that "first-time" narratives of those of African descent are routinely contested and contradicted, especially regarding the historical sources of language and communication style. They are not linear narratives neatly packaged with temporal structure and moral tale intact. There is no one source, one moment or looking back without being aware of "now."

Race and culture in the social sciences

American anthropological theories on the "first time" and beginnings of African American culture, while effectively arguing against racial determination of culture, have also argued that differences between African Americans and other Americans are not cultural (Boas, 1945, 1963). Instead, as Szwed (1974) and others (Mintz, 1970; Willis, 1970) report, the theory that persisted in both anthropology and sociology was that slavery deprived African Americans of any significant cultural roots (e.g. Benedict, 1934/1959). E. Franklin Frazier (1934) commented on what he considered to be the conspicuous lack of culture for African Americans. Similarly, Kenneth Clark (1965) described Harlem culture as self-hating and destructive with dialect and speech style that "suggests mental disorder." Ruth Benedict (Benedict, 1940/1959, 1934/1959) argued that African Americans in the cities adapted the behavior of their white counterparts. In explaining the process of culture loss she wrote, "Their patterns of political, economic, and artistic behavior were forgotten – even the languages they had spoken in Africa" (p. 86). All of the above scholars were respected in their fields and considered proponents of racial equality. Yet, when it came to language and culture, they consistently supported arguments that trans-Atlantic slavery left African Americans with no cultural roots worth mentioning and they laid the foundation for later beliefs that aligned blackness with pathology and whiteness with progress.[1]

The fall-out from these social science theories proved devastating. Anthropology interpreted these theories as indicative of self-hate (or low self-esteem) and proof that African Americans are ashamed of their African and slave heritage (e.g. Nelson, 1993; Willis, 1970). Some sociologists (e.g. Glazer and Moynihan, 1963; Myrdal, 1944) interpreted the anthropological view to mean that African American behavior that did not mirror white behavior was pathological or deviant, while others (e.g. Clark, 1965; Frazier, 1934, 1939) considered attempts to mimic white behavior pathological.

Though these perspectives represent the dominant view of anthropology and sociology until the late 1960s, there were, in fact, competing views concerning African American culture and language. Melville Herskovits

(1925, 1935, 1941) introduced the notion of African continuity along with Zora Neale Hurston (1935/1993) and later Sterling Stuckey (1971, 1987), Lawrence Levine (1977) and others. Though Herskovits is a major proponent of this position, Sidney Mintz and Richard Price (1992) contend that the African continuities may have been overstated since Herskovits focused on specific cultural traits that were not widespread throughout the African continent. They write, "Treating culture as a list of traits or objects or words is to miss the manner in which social relations are carried on through it – and thus to ignore the most important way in which it can change or be changed" (p. 22). Instead, they suggest that the areas of culture that may reveal widespread continuities are in African language and cultural values (see also Alleyne, 1980). They consider historical arguments about the origins of African American English to be one element of proof of African continuities. More importantly, they argue for cultural and social analysis that might reveal "by what social processes such a language became standardized, was taught to newly imported slaves, could be enriched by new experiences, invested with new symbolic meanings, and attached to status differences" (Mintz and Price, 1992: 21).

Though providing analyses of how language reflected and helped shape the culture and social order is of fundamental importance, it was first necessary to prove that aspects of African languages survived slavery. Lorenzo Turner (1949/1973) presented conclusive evidence of Africanisms in the Gullah language. Turner's work was followed later by creolists who identified features of African American English that are similar to those in African or creole languages (e.g. Dalby, 1969, 1972; Dillard, 1972; Stewart, 1967). Since disputes about the speech of African Americans often concern political and social statements about African American culture, politics and history in general, linguistic arguments likewise involve the entire gamut of possibilities. These include the origins of AAE, the social, cultural and political conditions from which it emerged and whether it is a language or dialect. There are also questions about its identifying features, the context in which information about it is gathered, why it exists, the social and political implications of its continued existence, its orthographic representation and the role of African American activism in the scholarly representation of culture and language.

Great language expectations: Paul Lawrence Dunbar

The fact that scholarly work on African American language behavior and culture would always embody the issues described above was firmly established at the dawn of the twentieth century with the publication of poetry by Paul Laurence Dunbar (1893). Dunbar was one of the first American authors of "pure" African ancestry and the son of ex-slaves. He was born in Ohio and graduated from Central High School in Dayton, was editor of a student newspaper, class poet, and president of the literary society. He was a celebrated and prolific writer of essays, short stories, novels, librettos, plays and poetry. Because it had been illegal to teach slaves to read, Dunbar wrote at a time when there was still a limited black readership and he could not reach a wide black audience through his writings. Thus his success was the result of a mainly white readership (Rauch, 1991).

In spite of his accomplishments, the achievements of Paul Lawrence Dunbar were plagued by debate within and between black and white America over the communicative and linguistic norms and values of Americans of African descent. Dunbar was treated as a "novelty" of his time because few African Americans possessed advanced literacy skills, and it was routinely argued that only "mixed" African Americans with discernable European ancestry were capable of such skills (Rauch, 1991). Additional irony accompanied the work of Dunbar because, though well educated, he wrote many of his poems in plantation "dialect" – the early twentieth-century literary version of the vernacular. According to James Weldon Johnson (1922), Dunbar wrote in plantation dialect because he believed it was the only variety in which he could write that a white readership would find acceptable.[2]

Dunbar's writings are often cited as the first example of a culturally rich and insightful portrayal of typical black life during and immediately following slavery. At the same time, African American writers and critics have vilified his writings as generally sentimental, humorous, childlike, absurdly optimistic and agonizingly uncritical of slavery (e.g. Johnson, 1922; Locke, 1974; Wright, 1957). This harsh assessment occurred because Dunbar's cultural portrayals were constructed with categorically stereotypical language, which, according to the above writers, confirmed and reconstituted racist stereotypes of African Americans as possessing childlike dependency and low cognitive ability. The contrasts between the variety of language used and content are apparent in his classic poem "We Wear the Mask" and excerpts from "The Party" (Dunbar, 1940).

> *We Wear the Mask*
> We wear the mask that grins and lies,
> It hides our cheeks and shades our eyes, –
> This debt we pay to human guile;
> With torn and bleeding hearts we smile,
> And mouth with myriad subtleties.

Why should the world be over wise,
In counting all our tears and sighs?
Nay, let them only see us, while
We wear the mask.

We smile, but O great Christ, our cries
To Thee from tortured souls arise.
We sing, but oh, the clay is vile
Beneath our feet, and long the mile;
But let the world dream otherwise,
We wear the mask.

"We Wear the Mask" explicitly highlights the dignity of the African American experience and indignity suffered under white supremacy. It also highlights the importance of a social face – with its subtleties – that does not express the agony to those who either inflicted or were spared the experience of slavery and its aftermath. In contrast, "The Party" is about celebration.

> *The Party*
> Dey had a gread big pahty down to Tom's de othah night;
> Was I dah? You bet! I nevah in my life see sich a sight;
> All de folks f'om fou' plantations was invited an'dey come,
> Dey come troopin' thick ez chillun when day hycahs a fife an'drum.
> Evahbody dressed deir fines' – Heish yo' mouf an' git away.
> Ain't seen sich fancy dressin' sence las' quah'tly meetin' day;
> Gals all dressed in silks an'satins, not a wrinkle ner a crease,
> Eyes a-barrin', teeth a-shinin', haih breshed back ez slick ez grease;
> Skut's all tucked an' puffed an' ruffled, evah blessed seam an' stitch;
> Ef you'd sen 'em wif deir mistus, couldn't swahed to which was which.
> Men all dressed up in Prince Alberts, swallertails 'u'd tek you' bref!
> I cain't tell you nothin' 'bout it, yo' ought to seen it fu' yo'se'f.
> Who was dah? Now who you askin'? How you 'spect I gwine to know?
> You mus' think I stood an' counted evahbody at de do'.

For Dunbar's largely white audience, "The Party" may mistakenly be viewed as a minstrelsy blackface portrayal of happy-go-lucky black people. But it is an example of what happens behind the mask where people assume they are intelligent and capable – so they can speak their dialect among themselves, adorn their bodies, play their music and dance the night away – knowing that having a party is also one aspect of who they are and what makes them people trying to live a full life. In this sense, "The Party" signifies the urgent need of emotional concealment.

I begin with this brief review of the polemics surrounding Paul Lawrence Dunbar's work because it embodies nearly every issue that has emerged concerning African American language over the last thirty years. The intellectual and critical ideas of Dunbar are regularly framed as grammatically and phonologically educated speech, while irresponsible and childlike behavior is associated with plantation dialect. Since dialect variety and cognitive ability are inextricably linked in this case, it was unheard of that any educated person would freely admit that he or she spoke and respected both. In fact, as in sociology and anthropology, some linguists have considered the phenomenon of educated African Americans using AAE subversive to the extent that they have argued that these varieties were fabrications and never existed at all (e.g. McDavid, 1963; Williamson, 1970). Others suspected that educated African Americans who criticized linguists promoting AAE suffered from self-hate (e.g. Stewart, 1975). Fortunately, scholarly research and public attitudes concerning the language behavior of African Americans continued to evolve throughout the twentieth century. Nevertheless, the initial depiction of Africans as primitive, the belief that African culture was completely lost during the middle passage and the belief that contact with Africans who spoke different languages meant the eradication of all vestiges of people's native language meant that AAE was destined to be endlessly stigmatized and evaluated. But before it was seriously scrutinized, it was dismissed as not existing at all.

Dialectologists were especially prone to dismiss any African influence in the speech of African Americans since their research focused exclusively on migration and influence from the British Isles (Dillard, 1972). The result was that AAE was described in relation to various types of US speech spoken by those of British descent (e.g. McDavid, 1963; McDavid and McDavid, 1951; Mencken, 1977; Williamson, 1971). In fact, George Krapp (1924) did not believe that there were any aspects of speech that could not be traceable to England. Moreover as Dillard (1972) reports, Raven McDavid Jr., who abridged H. L. Mencken's *The American Language*, suggested that AAE was a contrived variety developed for use among white patrons and dropped once out of their presence (p. 478 fn 4)!

In contrast to dialectologists who either ignored the presence of AAE or focused on British influences, sociolinguists and creolists attempted to develop comprehensive descriptions and analyses of AAE. This included efforts to describe its historical origins, lexicon, grammatical and phonological features, use and function within and among members of the African American speech community (Dillard, 1972; Smitherman, 1977; Tolliver-Weddington, 1979; Turner, 1949/1973) irrespective of other varieties of American English. At the same time, others (e.g. Labov, 1969, 1972a; Wolfram, 1969) focused on the systemic nature of AAE in relation to the system of American English.

After the mid 1980s, scholars of AAE expanded linguistic, historical and descriptive theories to reflect African American history and culture and connect it to other parts of the English-speaking African diaspora (Alleyne, 1980; Bailey, 1965; Baugh, 1980; Dillard, 1972; Mufwene, 1992a; Turner, 1949/1973). Still others have provided insight into its function, style and role and implications in education (e.g. Smitherman, 1977, 1981a,b; Ball, 1992; Baugh, 1999; Lee, 1993; Rickford, 1999; Rickford and Rickford, 1995; van Keulen, Tolliver-Weddington and DeBose, 1998). Even though some of these perspectives address the multicultural language contact first experienced by Africans and their descendants – who were both sold and born into US slavery – several questions remain.[3] How have African Americans used language to address political and social concerns and identities in the face of white supremacy and pervasive poverty? How was an African American culture that was influenced by but distinct from the African, Euro-American and (in some cases) Native American languages and cultures brought together by the contact? And how do we interpret the role and constitutive elements of African American culture and language in American society today?

The slave community

In linguistics, the question of the "first time" for African Americans is necessarily framed within the question of how the language and culture of African societies in contact with each other as equals under slavery, and subjugated under the rule of European travelers, traders, adventurers and exploiters, came to communicate with each other. Though there remain numerous unanswered questions regarding specific language backgrounds of Africans brought to the New World, there are several factors that are known. First slavery, and the development of African-origin communities in the US, occurred in two waves (Morgan, 1989).

The first occurrence was represented by the upper colonies' demand for domestic and manufacturing work and the lower colonies' for agricultural production of rice, indigo and tobacco (Johnson and Campbell, 1981).[4] The majority of the Africans were brought directly to the mainland ports and the Atlantic slave trade did not stop in the Caribbean (Mannix and Cowley, 1962).[5] During this first stage, language contact was with coastal West Africans as well as those from countries between Angola and Senegal.[6] Several historians (e.g. Berry and Blassingame, 1982) regard this period as one of both isolation and ongoing contact. For example, those who were sent to the Carolinas were geographically isolated on the Sea Islands and formed very different speech communities from those

Table 1 *Expansion of the slave population in the United States, 1790–1860*

Census year	1790	1800	1810	1820
Number	697,624	893,602	1,191,362	1,538,0022
Decennial increase		28.1	33.3	29.1
Census year	1830	1840	1850	1860
Number	2,009,043	2,487,355	3,204,313	3,953,760
Decennial increase	30.6	23.8	28.8	23.4

Source: Negro Population in the United States 1790–1860 (1915: 53)

involved in domestic and manufacturing labor (Berry and Blassingame, 1982; Fields, 1985).

The second stage emerged around 1793 with the introduction of the cotton gin. This invention's entry into the Southern economy was followed by the official cessation of the Atlantic slave trade in the early 1800s, though it continued years after (Franklin and Moss, 1988). In order for the cotton gin to realize its promise to increase the production of cotton, intensive slave labor was demanded. During this period of slavery the plantation system of the Gulf States and the Mississippi Valley expanded. By 1815, internal slave trading was a major activity within the US and between 1830 and 1840, nearly 250,000 slaves were transported over state lines. During 1850–60, over 193,000 were transported and by 1860, the slave population had reached over 4 million. Maps 1–4 and table 1 suggest that between 1790 and 1820 the language contact situation was such that many of the African slaves retained their first languages, a contact variety (see below) and some version of English (cf. Dillard, 1972).[7]

Once the internal slave trade became the dominant character of US slavery, and individuals within extended families, clans and national groups were forced to move to other states, it became increasingly difficult to determine one's country of origin whether originally from Africa or born into slavery.[8] The internal slave trade lasted over sixty years and was followed by eighty years of Jim Crow laws. What remains uncertain is how the plantation system and white supremacy after the period of Reconstruction, when national citizenship included those of African descent (roughly 1865–77), affected the linguistic development of African American English.

The concentration of African Americans in Southern regions formed what was known as the Black Belt South because it seemed to extend

Map 1.1   Expansion of the slave
population in the USA, 1790

Map 1.2   Expansion of the slave
population in the USA, 1800

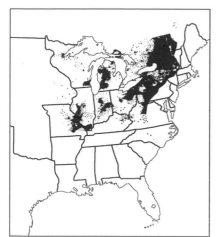

Map 1.3   Expansion of the slave
population in the USA, 1830

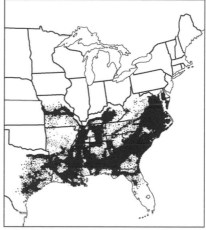

Map 1.4   Expansion of the slave
population in the USA, 1860

across the South when highlighted on a map. Though the speech community remained geographically concentrated and largely intact after slavery
officially ended in 1865, gradual splintering and expansion began to take
shape after the turn of the century. This change occurred in a population
movement known as the Great Migration (1900–60). Blacks moved out

of the South in search of work and to flee lynching and white supremacy. During this period, over a million people fled to the North. As Carole Marks (1989) writes:

The great Migration represents a "watershed" in the experience of blacks in the United States because it was the first mass movement out of the South, the beginning of significant industrial employment, and the initial exercising of the rights of citizenship. (p.1)

The availability of jobs in the North was partly due to World War I, which effectively halted European migration to the US and led to the loss of menial and factory labor in the North. At the same time, thousands of white men left their jobs to fight in the war – and in a segregated military. This was followed by the decimation of the Southern cotton crop by the boll weevil, leaving many blacks jobless. The final assault was the 1929 depression that devastated an already struggling black community, which did not reassert itself again until World War II.

World War II represents the second phase of mass movement from the South and resulted in vacancies of thousands of jobs in the city that had been traditionally held by white men. It also revealed the presence of urban African American communities where the demand for labor presented renewed hope for black Southerners (Adero, 1993; Drake and Cayton, 1962; Johnson and Campbell, 1981; Marks, 1989). As a result of the urban period, three forces can be identified that helped to transform black culture and the nature of the community: (1) migration and urbanization, (2) creation of the black economic and social class structure and (3) commercialization. On the one hand, there was a concentration of blacks into urban areas. On the other hand, urban life was less intimate than rural life since the population changed more frequently. The result was a greater variety in attitudes, beliefs and practices. The population was transformed from mainly agricultural workers and families to individual workers within factories, often with white workers who performed similar labor.[9] As the African American population moved throughout urban centers, they encountered emigrants from Eastern and Western Europe, Asia, and the rest of the Americas. And as a black American culture and identity continued to evolve, so did a language ideology that reflected and represented all aspects of an ever-changing "first time."

Counterlanguage and power in discourse

Contact situations that result in subjugation and marginalization often lead to diverse speech communities that share geographical space but represent different language ideologies. Depending on the relationship of the groups, the ideology of those in power can include denigrating the language and speech style of others. This is especially true for US plantation slavery where all behavior as well as speech and style of speaking were greatly regulated. Total institutions (Goffman, 1961) such as plantation slavery often lead to antisocieties and underground institutions where people resist subjugation (Goffman, 1961; Halliday, 1978). These antisocieties typically emerge when those who dominate individuals require that the subjugated display an attitude that reaffirms the dominator/dominated relationship – in the presence of others – by verbal or physical confirmation (e.g. bowing heads or saying, "Yes sir/ma'am"). However, antisocieties should not be viewed solely as underground institutions. They are in response to control from those with power and are only underground in the sense that disempowered or marginalized groups rely on and participate in them. Consequently, from the perspective of the non-dominant group, antisocieties are very much above the ground and a significant aspect of everyday speech. These institutions are cloaked and unseen by those in power. Thus they allow people a form of agency found in face-to-face encounters so that they can construct a system of communication that incorporates social face (Goffman, 1967), the image and impression that a person conveys during encounters, along with others' evaluation of that image.

It is important to remember that until the 1960s, Southern segregationists could, without consequences, control and regulate the verbal interactions of blacks, and especially interactions between blacks and whites (see chapter 3). These policies, which were protected by the legal system, considered certain forms of direct talk by African Americans to constitute claims regarding rights and status (cf. Gwaltney, 1981; Morgan, 1980, 1994a). Thus "talk" and "interaction" were constitutive elements of a system of inequity and participants' social roles were partially constructed through conversation. The resulting unwritten – but enforced – policy meant that in order to participate in the average black/white interaction, a black person minimally had to abide by language and communicative rules which functioned to mark a presumed belief in the superiority of a white audience/hearer. Goffman also mentions this type of restriction where the act of making a statement is viewed as a symptom of the problem (Goffman, 1961: 45). He uses the term "looping" to refer to instances where a person cannot distance him or herself from "the mortifying situation" (1961: 36) by any face-saving action. Instead, they lose any aspect of positive social face and must behave as though they comply with the assessment.

Some rules of how blacks were to communicate with whites included: (a) talking only when permission was granted; (b) never having direct eye contact with a white person; (c) never using educated speech (unless told to perform); (d) determining and then saying whatever the person wanted to hear; (e) never asking a question about a white person's intention; (f) never contradicting what someone says; (g) bowing heads and (h) saying "Yes sir/ma'am"; and (i) never receiving respectful forms of address in return (cf. Morgan, 1994b). The harsh consequences that might result when the communicative dictums described above were ignored have been brilliantly illustrated in many slave narratives and literature about lynching and black cultural life under segregation (e.g. Brent and Jacob, 1973; Gwaltney, 1981; Johnson, 1982; Morrison, 1987; Simonsen, 1986; Stevenson, 1997; Walker, 1982; Whitfield, 1988; Williams, 1986).

In response to the demand that they have the "attitude" of someone who should be oppressed, African American culture and antisociety undermined the values, attitudes and beliefs that the dominant society held toward them (cf. Bryce-Laporte, 1971) through the use of existing African systems of indirectness (Morgan, 1989, 1991, 1993). Indirectness occurs when cultural actors recognize talk as symbolic of ideas, values and occurrences that are not directly related to the present context. African American adult indirectness includes an analysis of discourses of power since these adults know that their cultural practices, beliefs and values are generally not shared by the wider society who may not be aware that they exist at all. Once the phenomenology of indirectness operated both within white supremacist encounters and African American culture and social encounters, interactions, words or phrases could have contradictory or multiple meanings beyond traditional English interpretations. Thus a counterlanguage emerged that was based on indirectness and functioned to signal the antisociety (e.g. ideological black audience) and provided a means for a speaker to reveal a social face (Goffman, 1967) that resisted and contested the practice of racial repression.

Though based on norms of African interaction, the counterlanguage developed in ways that reflected the social, cultural and political experience of African Americans. Thus in stark contrast to the cross-racial rules of interaction outlined earlier, black interactions embodied and highlighted an exacting sense of speaker agency (Morgan, 1993). This intense focus on speaker agency was co-constructed with a black audience for whom language forms and styles signal that content or speaker intent is being camouflaged. In other words, within the system of repression, the counterlanguage provided a vehicle for face-work (Goffman,

1967) and protected and confirmed the existence of the antisociety. Its function in instantiating speaker agency was so great that the "act" of talking was potentially political and highly symbolic.

Within the counterlanguage, the basic concept of audience included all black hearers and potential hearers, as well as the likelihood that there were spies and overhearers/reporters. Thus the audience and hearer, whether immediately present or presumed present through gossip, spies, etc., were socially and culturally constructed entities. As a result, speakers were also expected to exhibit their conversational prowess and manage to direct what was said to a black audience who, in turn, held him or her responsible for what was said as well as possible interpretations. Thus in many profound ways, a speaker's social face, status and standing were always at stake (Morgan, 1991; Smitherman, 1977).[10]

From slavery until the 1960s, these principles continued to function as counterlanguage in the Southern United States within white supremacy dictums of interaction between blacks and whites, which were enforced by state-sanctioned policies. These policies considered certain forms of talk by African Americans to constitute and index claims regarding citizenship rights and status. Thus "talk" and "interaction" were constitutive elements of the system of inequity and participants' social roles were partially constructed through conversation (see chapters 2 and 4 for discourse and linguistic rules). The counterlanguage included multiple audiences, layers of understanding and concomitant multiple subjectivities. It may not have survived and been adapted were it not for dominant Southern society's relentless monitoring of African Americans' communication and language. Irrespective of the reason for its continued significance in African American interactions, the counterlanguage is the foundation of all African American discourse (see chapter 2). Following are two narratives about life and injustice in the South that employ counterlanguage and local knowledge as described above.[11]

John Henry was a hard-working man

The narrative of John Henry Martin illustrates life as a sharecropper, the difficulty in expressing rights and the desire to own property. This difficulty is embedded in the language ideology of white supremacy and that of African American counterlanguage. The art of telling a story, trying to fully represent "what happened," is a monumental task which most "everyday people" accomplish with authority, style and wit. Narratives do not simply relate human experience but culturally fashion it so that stories are constitutive of everyday life. In the lives of many older African

Americans like my grandfather, narratives were how children learned that their questions represented the truth about black life and their answers could only be understood within life's ironies and complexities. He taught that only fools (and perhaps children) are satisfied with simple answers. It is in this sense that narratives embody social reality and, in the case of marginalized groups, both deconstruct and interrogate life under hegemony. It is thus apropos that US African American narratives both embody and contest the multiple realities that emerge in the process of mediating identity and citizenship rights while functioning both within and in opposition to mainstream control (Griffin, 1995; Smith, 1987).[12]

John Henry Martin's narrative is one of work and independence. It is based on knowing the social and language rules of white supremacy.[13] It focuses on the significance of "work" and how the right to control the nature of work might be an act of defiance and therefore a source of stress (James, 1994).[14] Consequently, the mention of work in African American narratives is also a device to indirectly introduce the injustices that occurred while working or having to work and an indication of the character of the person/worker.

1 I was born in 1907, the 16th day of October, on a farm down below Rockcastle,
2 in Shelby County. My daddy was a sharecropper . . . When I was just a little
3 boy, 'bout five or six years old, I guess, we moved from below Rockcastle up
4 here to Wakefield County, to a farm near Cobb's Store. My daddy – I don't
5 know what happened – but he lost everything he had on that farm near Cobb's
6 store, and we stayed there for twelve years, workin' for one half . . .
7 And I said, then, that if I ever get me some more money, I'm gonna save me
8 some money. And then, in different ways, I wanted to be somebody. I wanted
9 to have somethin' – a car, a mule, and all that kinda stuff. Well, all of that
10 come true. How did it come true? Well, when I was 'bout twenty-one years
11 old, I decided that I was tired of workin' and givin' them white folks half my
12 labor. So, I told my daddy 'bout me and him buyin' a farm somewhere. My
13 mamma, Lord, she wouldn't a want us to do that! But I decided that I
14 couldn't, just couldn't keep on workin' and givin' out on my own. For I wanted
15 somethin'. I wanted somethin' for myself.
16 So I went on and hired myself out for wages, for nine months and fifty dollars
17 in money. That wasn't no money back then either! And this old white man
18 who I was workin' for asked me, he said, "Henry, I'll furnish your house off
19 for you and feed you too." I told him "Naw". I knowed he was tryin' to slip
20 me then. I told him, "Naw, I can buy it."
21 So, me and my wife done just that. And we had just a little bit of money left
22 over. And we went scarce with that money. But that fall, we didn't owe that
23 white man nothin but money for our fertilizer.
24 We stayed there four years – workin' for one-half. And this white man, his
25 daughters, sons, wife and all; oh, they was just good to me. They was! They

26 was good to me. For they would leave their house there with me, leave it wide
27 open. But what they was doing, you see, they was feedin' me on sugar! They
28 wanted me to feed the hogs, see to the mules, milk the cow. Well, that was too
29 much work! So my wife's brother, he kept on askin' me 'bout buyin' a farm. I
30 was regular workin', me and my wife. Workin' down at that white man's and
31 workin' for one-half. Well, it wasn't half! See, I had to furnish my clothes, get
32 somethin' to eat, and still he only give a man half. And it ain't even half! So,
33 my wife's brother kept on askin' me 'bout buyin' a place.
34 So, he kept on after me, and I finally went down to Knottsboro to see 'bout
35 gettin' a loan – FHA. I talked to them folks 'bout it, and they told me "Yeah,
36 we'll buy you a farm." That like to scared me to death! But after they said
37 they'd buy me one – furnish me the money – I got interested in it . . .
38 So, the government down there, they kept a writin' me letters and I'd read
39 'em. And the white man I was on halves with – he got a hold to one of 'em.
40 It was 'round bargainin' time, time to bargain to stay on another year. He
41 come out there to my house one day and said, "Henry, you aim to stay on
    with me another year?"
42 I said, "I don't know, suh, Mr. Tucker. I was thinkin' 'bout buyin' me a farm."
43 He said, "Buyin' a farm?!"
44 I said, "Yeah."
45 He said, "Man, you don't need no farm. Them taxes will eat you up!"
46 I said, "Well, you got one, and it ain't eat you up yet, is it?"
47 He said, "Naw, but they're sure high. It's hard times, and it's gonna be
48 harder one of these years."
49 I said, "Well, I don't know." [He said] "You have a home here just as long
50 as you want one." I said, "Yeah, believe I will; but one day I'm gonna get old,
51 and I won't be able to work. And when you get old, well, that home is gone.
52 You don't have no home then."
53 He said, "Oh no, I wouldn't do you like that." I reckon you heard old folks
54 say "white folks put sugar in your coffee?" Yeah, put sugar in your coffee –
55 sweeten you up so they can handle you.

Indexing local knowledge: work, built environment, racism and power

As mentioned earlier, African American stories about social contact
outside the black community often index significant, yet indirect, local
knowledge. Thus John Henry Martin's description of the complex social issues involved in achieving economic independence in the 1920s
is interwoven with local knowledge about "regular workin'," working
your burden, citizenship rights and the assessment of white supremacist
intentions. His revelation in line 5 that his father sharecropped near
Cobb's store includes the local knowledge that his father was under
constant surveillance and scrutiny since local wisdom about shopping
in and living near stores owned and frequented by whites includes an

understanding that a black person could never exhibit his or her dignity in that setting (cf. Gwaltney, 1981; Simonsen, 1986; Whitfield, 1988). In particular, Mr. Martin's narrative reveals that his father's interactions were under constant surveillance and could be assessed and monitored for compliance and display of an attitude that corroborates that the domination is needed (e.g. looping). In spite of these restrictions, Mr. Martin directly and indirectly reveals the cultural and political economy that he desires to outwit, while doggedly analyzing and providing theories about the intentionality of landowners, bankers and relatives. His display of local knowledge occurs through indirection, providing evidence that blacks in the rural South lived under a system of forced labor based on indebtedness, the terror of lynching and the realization that whites felt justified in participation in the system of oppression. At the same time, life as part of agricultural labor often encompassed a middle-class consciousness associated with property ownership. Nonetheless, the longing for property among African Americans was associated with the belief that property rights were equal to citizenship rights.

Mr. Martin also supplies local knowledge about work and the significance of work in his life. His desire for fair compensation for work begins indirectly and becomes increasingly direct as Mr. Martin discusses his desire to own property in the face of possible repercussions. The expression *workin' for one half* first appears in line 6 with the description of his father's working life and is repeated in some form at least five times. This expression refers to a form of peonage where the landlord furnishes everything required to farm except the labor and one half of fertilizers. In return, the tenant gets one half the profit from the crop and the landlord gets the other. Since very few tenants could read, and they were not allowed to contradict whites, they had no access to profit records and most goods had to be purchased at the store owned by the landlord. Unsurprisingly, tenants seldom earned enough to pay all debts and leave the tenant system (Marks, 1989; Woodson, 1930). Of course a landowner was desperate to maintain this system, since he would be bankrupt or have greatly reduced profits if deserted by his tenants. Mr. Martin provides further local knowledge when he considers what appears to be a simple offer of assistance from his landlord, in line 18, to be a ruse to keep him entrapped. This is especially revealed in line 25 where he describes the landowner's demonstration of trust as in the following passage:

oh, they was just good to me. They was! They was good to me. For they would leave their house there with me, leave it wide open. But what they was doing, you see, they was feedin' me on sugar!

The expression *feeding me on sugar* conveys the notion that Mr. Martin thought he was being treated in a special yet patronizing way as an attempt to lure him into believing he had rights and a good life – when he didn't. In the process of telling his story, Mr. Martin deconstructs his expressions of local knowledge for the listener who might not understand what life was like under Jim Crow.

In contrast, Mr. West's story (below) about a lynching provides little direct interpretation of the local knowledge in play. It is a story that requires that we know about lynching and lynchers in order to learn what really happened.

They make it and they break it

When African Americans who have witnessed or been directly affected by lynching tell about what happened, they often provide detailed descriptive accounts of their understanding of what motivated the lynching and how it was carried out. Within the narrative, these details have a dialogic relationship with concepts of citizenship rights, including the right to work, the right to speak and the right to live. At some point in time, while conducting fieldwork between 1979 and 1999, all the generations in all of the Northern and Southern communities I visited mentioned something about lynching. Though people feared it and continued to consider it a possibility, even before the lynching of 1999 in Jasper, Texas, they were mainly disgusted. The nature of this disgust is revealed in the discussion of Emmett Till's lynching.

In 1955, while visiting his family in Mississippi during the summer vacation, Emmett Till was murdered at the age of fourteen because – reportedly – some white men believed he insulted a white woman because he whistled while at a country store![15] The lynchers did not witness Emmett Till's interaction with the woman; rather, it was reported to them after the entire African American community became aware of the incident. When the men arrived to take Emmett Till away, his family begged for his life, explaining that he didn't understand that he should not have addressed the woman in a way some might consider disrespectful because he was not from there and was raised in Chicago! They pleaded that they had already severely punished him and would pay the woman's family restitution. The white men, whom the family knew, assured the family that they would not fatally hurt him, but teach him a lesson. They lied – and Emmett Till was taken, tortured, killed and dumped in a river with weights tied around his body. During the trial the men who lynched the boy said that one of the questions they asked him just before he died was whether he thought he was as good as they were now.

The lynching of Emmett Till challenged many Americans and in 1963 Bob Dylan recorded his understanding of what happened and why.

The death of Emmett Till
'Twas down in Mississippi not so long ago,
When a young boy from Chicago town stepped through a Southern
    door.
This boy's dreadful tragedy I can still remember well,
The color of his skin was black and his name was Emmett Till.

Some men they dragged him to a barn and there they beat him up.
They said they had a reason, but I can't remember what.
They tortured him and did some evil things too evil to repeat.
There was screaming sounds inside the barn,
There was laughing sounds out on the street.

Then they rolled his body down a gulf amidst a bloody red rain
And they threw him in the waters wide to cease his screaming pain.
The reason that they killed him there, and I'm sure it ain't no lie,
Was just for the fun of killin' him and to watch him slowly die.

And then to stop the United States of yelling for a trial,
Two brothers they confessed that they had killed poor Emmett Till.
But on the jury there were men who helped the brothers commit this
    awful crime,
And so this trial was a mockery, but nobody seemed to mind.

I saw the morning papers but I could not bear to see
The smiling brothers walkin' down the courthouse stairs.
For the jury found them innocent and the brothers they went free,
While Emmett's body floats the foam of a Jim Crow southern sea.

If you can't speak out against this kind of thing, a crime that's so
    unjust,
Your eyes are filled with dead men's dirt, your mind is filled with dust.
Your arms and legs they must be in shackles and chains, and your
    blood it must refuse to flow,

For you let this human race fall down so God-awful low!

This song is just a reminder to remind your fellow man
That this kind of thing still lives today in that ghost-robed Ku Klux
    Klan.
But if all of us folks that thinks alike, if we gave all we could give,
We could make this great land of ours a greater place to live.
            (1963/1968 Warner Bros. Inc. Renewed 1991 Special Rider Music)

Though there are many versions of what happened (Dylan's is one of many), it is clear that one reason that the lynching so profoundly affected the entire US African American community was because a Northern boy – who didn't know that he could not have the attitude of a typical teenager – was attacked. Among African Americans who lived during that time, the story of Emmett Till consistently results in the following questions: Did he touch the woman or just whistle? Were the lynchers at the store when he was there? Did they witness the interaction Emmett Till had with the woman? What was said by the lynchers to convince Emmett Till's family to hand him over? Why did his uncle hand him over? Was his mother right to choose to have an open casket funeral in Chicago and to leave his body the way it was found? (cf. Whitfield, 1988)

In my fieldwork in Mississippi and Chicago in 1991, Emmett Till's lynching was still a recurring topic of discussion. However, depending on if or when the teller migrated from the South, there seems to be a significant difference in whether an explanation for the lynching is included with the description of the atrocity. Briefly, those who grew up and were socialized in the South focus on the lack of rights for African Americans and argue that suggesting a reason for the lynching is to imply that a reason was needed for a white person to kill an African American. They argue that "We had No Rights. No one protected us," and they consistently interrogate the notion that Emmett Till did anything in particular because the men didn't *need* justification to do it. As one woman in Mississippi simply explained, "They claimed he whistled (yeah), he whistled at a white woman. Now isn't that something?"

In contrast, those in Chicago tend to speculate on what Emmett Till might have done for the men to viciously attack him. They refer to the need to make "sense" of it. They talk of Emmett Till having the right to be a boy. This type of penetrating contrast between Northern and Southern African Americans focuses on the motivation for lynching. It reflects a different sensibility to urban rights versus Southern repression that was prevalent during the time of the lynching and still exists today.

The black Southerner's understanding of why lynching occurs is further examined through the narrative of Mr. West.[16] It is nearly impossible to understand the meaning of this narrative without the local knowledge about rules of interaction and reference and work provided in Mr. Martin's narrative above. In the case of Mr. West's story though, lynching was a possibility to the point that it "was one thing that we figure."

ROCC to Mr. West: Could you tell us about the person that was lynched?
1 RW: Well this fella killed his daddy. And they ac- looked around – tryin' to
2 find out who done it, and finally some of them got up to him and they got
3 him to admit that he killed him. He wanted to go to a dance – a black dance.
4 This was way young. And I was about twelve years old. But see lynchin' was
5 goin' on before then. And this was one thing that we figure.

6 Anyway, he asked old man Neighbors – he had a gin right down over back
7 behind that church over there. There was a gin over there – a steam gin. He
8 asked for some money to go to a dance that Friday night or Saturday night.
9 He didn't give it to him. And the boy went back and killed him. That was the
10 way we got it – chopped him up.
11 But anyway, they finally got him and they start to lynch 'im. This group,
12 they had him one night and the other people – now who was they? I forgot
13 who they was. But they were fightin' over this one man 'cause they wanted to
14 get him. They'd drag him a while, another would drag him a while.
15 When they got through with him – let me tell you some of the things I'd –
16 you'd never hear. When they made him dig that pit, it's down the hill – I
17 couldn't find it now, I'm all screwed up. But that pit was where he was
18 burned, under the house, after the house was burned. Some of his skin come
19 off in his hand, after he jumped out of that fire. And I never did see it but
20 they said a spot was in his hand because he was an old man.
21 But what happened so long was (?) told us that he had a, a big barrel, like this
22 barrel. And they filled it full of holes and put him up in there. And they'd just
23 boil up water and pour it on him.
24 But when he finally died was after they – got through with him, he just about
25 dead – then they burned him.
26 Now, the truth of the matter is, we don't never know what went on in these
27 places! That woman and Henry and all those people buried out there – see I
28 used to go and – but I don't care how many white people in there, you waited
29 until they got rid of 'em. If they kept comin' in, you kept waitin'. This is some of
30 the Jim Crow we had. Ain't really in your head, whether you use it or not. Now
31 this is what I was brought up through. This is why I'm so glad to be free.

One of the most important things to understand about African American lynch narratives is that they are often dialogic with the "official" narrative about the lynching. These "official" narratives are designed to justify and express the necessity of the act. Because African American lynch narratives could not directly state that someone was murdered, they are laden with details. While lynch narratives focus on graphic details of the atrocity, they use indirection to highlight the depravity of a system that was based on white privilege and the exploitation of blacks.

As discussed in the narrative of Mr. Martin, in the South it was both unusual and dangerous for a black person to assert any say over his or her labor. By using the counterlanguage, Mr. West imparts cultural knowledge regarding this fact. The context or site of resistance, which signals the counterlanguage, is introduced early in the narrative when Mr. West explains in line 2 that *they got him to admit* that he killed his father. As in the case of Mr. Martin above, the exclusive pronoun *they* signals the danger and the omnipresent power of white supremacy. In this context, the meaning of *got* is forced. Thus the lynchers forced him to say that he killed his own father. Throughout this narrative *they* conveys the way in which white supremacy casually immersed everyday life and, periodically, brutally enforced its will. The symbolic capital of the pronoun *they* is intentionally marked in the counterlanguage to the point that in lines 12–14, Mr. West does not provide personal names of the lynchers but explains, *I forgot who they was. But they were fightin' over this one man 'cause they wanted to get him.* Once Mr. West establishes that this is simply something "they wanted," he details both the lynchers' stated reason for the lynching and his view of it.

Though the lynching is horrific, it is Mr. West's use of the counterlanguage that reveals the underlining depravity associated with white supremacy. Mr. West camouflages or embeds information regarding the occupation of both father and son. Lines 6–7 actually provide insight into what Mr. West believes precipitated the lynching: both father and son worked independently in a family business. They ran gin mills and therefore did not rely on white male supremacy to support their livelihood.[17] If the information about the steam gin were extracted from the text, Mr. West's narrative would read:

Anyway, he asked old man Neighbors – He asked for some money to go to a dance that Friday night or Saturday night. He didn't give it to him. And the boy went back and killed him. That was the way we got it – chopped him up.[18]

Considering the nature of white supremacy in Mississippi at the time of the killing, it is unlikely that Mr. Neighbors would be lynched because he killed his father. Moreover, it is farfetched that the boy killed his father because he wasn't allowed to go to a dance. Thus, the act of embedding information on the nature of the men's work questions whether the boy actually killed his father and therefore the motivation of the lynching. Since independent work, as argued above, was a challenge to the repressive system, if a black person indicated that he or she knew a person, like Mr. Neighbors, who worked independently, that knowledge posed a threat to the system. Thus a person's life was in jeopardy if he or she knew that someone worked independently since it meant that it was possible to overcome the system.[19] Because of their economic independence, Mr. Neighbors and his son were lynched. Who did it was inconsequential since it was done under the system of segregation. They did it because they could – without censure of any sort.

Mr. West's narrative also highlights the jeopardy that afflicted every black person who visited the country store in the area in lines 26–31:

26 Now, the truth of the matter is, we don't never know what went on in these
27 places! That woman and Henry and all those people buried out there – see
28 I used to go and – but I don't care how many white people in there, you

29 waited until *they* got rid of 'em. If *they* kept comin' in, you kept waitin'.
30 This is some of the Jim Crow we had. Ain't really in your head, whether
31 you use it or not. Now this is what I was brought up through. This is why
   I'm so glad to be free.[20]

Mr. West's assessment, *Ain't really in your head, whether you use it or not*, bears some mention here. It is a statement regarding the reality of the situation he *was brought up through*. The local knowledge shared by those living under white supremacy included the knowledge that it was regularly experienced with disbelief. But no matter whether a person ignored or refused to believe the situation at the country stores or in the South to be threatening to a black person. It was.

The contact described throughout this chapter is of peoples thrust together and attempting to construct a life under new circumstances that included unbelievable loss, an incredible drive to claim a position in American history and an insistence on the right to tell the story of their experience. Language has been the powerful medium through which to do this since it is – to paraphrase Toni Morrison (1994) – the measure of black life. The language of African Americans does not simply reflect what happened, but through interaction it reconfirms and reconstructs what happened to others and us. Rather than try to erase the first time, the language works to expose it – not to embarrass – but to lay bare the entire range and history of black life in America.

2   Forms of speech: verbal styles, discourse and interaction

When I was a teenager on the South Side of Chicago in the late 1960s, my interests in language and culture were cultivated by the songs and accompanying talk I heard billowing from apartment windows and cascading from the cocktail lounges that populated my neighborhood on 59th and State Street. One song in particular always conjures up "home" and the rich textures and complexities of adult black life. It is by Little Milton, who sings with truth and sincerity:

> If I don't love you baby – Grits ain't grocery.
> Chicken ain't poultry.
> And Mona Lisa was a man.[1]

The men and women in my neighborhood loved this song and applauded its recognition of the struggle between doing what one must do, would do, should do, could do and has to do, and doing what one is "gonna" do. Never believing that the binary revealed enough, the neighborhood employed an inventory of strategies to expose the mind/body/onlooker synergy. They understood these lyrics to be more than mere words, but rather the major unveiling of a truth about black life. How else can one explain the smiles that traveled across normally grimaced adult lips, the nodding of heads and the responses echoing throughout the neighborhood: "You tell it like it is! Talk that stuff!" and "You go on now – fool!" when Little Milton's pleading voice was heard. I understood these statements to be what Goffman (1967, 1997) calls response cries, self-talk that is meant to be overheard and that aligns speakers with events.

Yet, as an adolescent, I didn't understand how these cries work to both corroborate and chronicle facts about life. I remember once attempting to offer my naive theory about the song to my aunt. I suggested: "Yeah, he should have said grits aren't groceries, right?" She said "What?" I said, "He shouldn't say 'ain't' and he didn't put the s on *grocery*. He should have said *groceries*!" My aunt shook her head in disbelief. I didn't know what exactly all the fuss was about.

Of course, the commotion was about how cultures practice love, sincerity and commitment. Not simply the love of another person, but how love for the symbols of home and culture can represent "true love." So "Grits Ain't Groceries" is a song about truth in a philosophical sense: how we know what is real and how we prove what we mean. It illustrates how, as both agent/subject and object, our understanding is directly related to culture and a shared social world. For my community, this social world was local in a particular way.[2] It was a black world that, as a part of cultural practice, interrogated all words spoken but also searched for the "white" lie. After all, many black communities could not assume that even a basic statement like "You can trust me" conveys the true intention of the speaker since they lived with white supremacy for hundreds of years.

Little Milton sang through the love, brutality and irony of black life and sought the symbols that simultaneously embody cultural practice and a bone-chilling social world. After all, grits is only an essential urban grocery item in select neighborhoods. In many black communities, it is not simply a Southern food, but a cultural one. Some argue that no one can prepare, eat and enjoy grits in the same way as black people. Because of its symbol as a "home" food, the refusal of a plate of grits – especially when offered by mothers and grandmothers – is always noticed. Most refusals are considered personal and responded to with indirect jibing about identity and suspicious silences and stares. Moreover, Little Milton pronounces "poultry" as "po'try." Black Chicagoans call this particular style of talk "country," as it connotes further images of Southern "home ways," family and the best fried chicken on the planet. As an old neighbor would say with a broad smile every single time he knew our other neighbor Mary Baker was frying chicken: "Don't trust a man [that] don't likes Mary's fried chicken."

Finally, where I grew up, it was Nat King Cole who interpreted the true meaning of Mona Lisa. According to Nat's crooning of the song, the Mona Lisa is an exquisite painting because it captures the look of women who know their power, and men's weakness and denial. Mrs. Bitts used to say: "Mens cry over her 'cause they can't have her. If they could, they wouldn't want her and she knows it. She [would] be too real! She just might have something to say about they sorry ass!'"

So in my neighborhood, Mona Lisa represented a particular truth about loyalty and commitment because it was thought that she understood her admirer's desires, imagination, dreams, fantasies and wants. The blues song "Grits Ain't Groceries" shows how people use all of their linguistic resources to construct, mediate and instantiate cultural and social beliefs, norms and practices. Little Milton makes himself vulnerable and truthful by proclaiming his version of the essence of blackness and humanness and ultimately the truth that – at least for now – he is hopelessly, helplessly and truly in love.

Language ideology

Whether trying to understand the meaning of a narrative or how a community can turn a song into an emblem and fact of everyday life, one must take into consideration how cultures reflect and express their ideological foundation. In the previous chapter, John Henry Martin and Mr. West laced their narratives with a myriad of symbols and signs including language structures, expressions and discourse practices that indexed the details of Southern life during segregation. The counterlanguage employed in their narratives arose from systems of indirectness common in African interactions. Although legal segregation and punishments were reduced with the civil rights movement, the importance of indirectness remains a central aspect of African American ideologies of language.

As cultural practice, language ideologies are mirrors and tools that probe, reflect, refract, subvert and exalt social and cultural production, reproduction and representation. As Woolard and Schieffelin explain, language ideologies "envision and enact links of language to group and personal identity, to aesthetics, to morality, and to epistemology" (Woolard and Schieffelin, 1994: 56).[3] Moreover it is precisely shared ideologies that link cultural and linguistic phenomena (Silverstein, 1998). In this respect, African American language ideology is not based on an autonomous psychological subject or Cartesian notion of duality of self that is separate from society.[4] Rather, African American language ideology is based on the interaction of the mind/body and social world and language/mind/culture mosaic. In African diaspora settings like the US, this mosaic is constituted through the knowledge that balance and disruption are outcomes of a social order established through a communicative system enmeshed in ambiguity. In spite of this, members insist that speakers produce discourse that is easily understood – by them. It is not surprising that learning to be a proficient cultural actor under this type of language ideology requires extensive and textured language socialization. And it is also predictable that it results in language and discourse norms that highlight social face and the doubt, risk, certainty and the determination necessary to communicate while aware of the meanings and interpretations that may apply.

For the African American speech community, language ideology incorporates the knowledge that the construction and assessment of social face and character are simultaneously performed and grounded within the notion of multiple audiences. Since these audiences include those socialized within the African American experience and outside of it, the knowledge of competing ideologies – and how speakers handle them – are also included in the mediation of social face. Thus the language ideology not only recognizes but relies on the knowledge that language varieties exist and represent different positions of power, politics and history. And any member who doesn't know it, should.

That there exists an African American language ideology should not be surprising, especially since the notion of linguistic homogeneity is itself an ideological construction.[5] In speech communities where there is multiple contact across social class, status and sometimes national origin, local ideologies of language often reflect heteroglossia (Bakhtin, 1981a), the shifting of styles or linguistic codes that exist within and often among communities. Discussion of heteroglossia is especially useful because it questions the claim in US language ideology that linguistic diversity is divisive while linguistic homogeneity unifies society and includes all citizens – irrespective of national origin, economics, education, social status and so on. In a nation as diverse as the US, any claim that language standards are not based on social class, politics or ideology, must be considered perverse. So in many respects, it is alarming yet predictable that black language structure and style have been viewed simultaneously as creative, deviant and deficient.

As with many marginalized peoples, African American language ideology exists within and often in opposition to dominant ideology. It is based on the systemic tension between the subtleties of indirection and the lack of subtlety in directed and confrontational discourse. The tension results in a communicative system that ranges from extreme ambiguity to stark specificity. This system is constructed around an elaborate and ingrained notion of audience that incorporates an array of social classes, generations, contexts and genders. This construction of the audience and hearer is not only based on those physically present, but equally on those who might, can, could, should or will hear or be told the hearer's interpretation of what the speaker said. Thus, it is a system that recognizes the Western concept of the individual as the producer of meaning and actualizes the African and African diaspora concept of the individual as actor, interpreter and intermediary in a world of meanings (Duranti, 1993; Levine, 1977; Mudimbe, 1994). It is an ideology where, to paraphrase Claudia Mitchell-Kernan (1971), if a guest is offered a soul food dinner and refuses it without a clear explanation, that person may have signified that he or she is rejecting the black community in general and the hostess and her family in particular.

Social face and forms of speech: being cool and acting a fool

The system of social face found in African American communities requires speakers and audiences to have nearly equal responsibility, knowledge and power in interactions.[6] Consequently, meaning is co-constructed rather than individually interpreted and a speaker's social face as well as the constant pursuit of corroborated and collaborated truth, intention and meaning is a dynamic process. In fact, discussions of verbal performance and discourse in culture are often explorations into how power and status are expressed and negotiated in society (Brenneis and Myers, 1984; Fabian, 1990; Yankah, 1991a, b). This is especially true in African American culture where social standing and cultural membership are constructed according to how speakers interact in social contexts that include the dominant culture and all social strata of the African American community. The cultural value attached to how one negotiates both interactive domains provides an exegesis of how individuals communicate culture, identity and citizenship rights. In this sense one's social "face" is partially determined by the ability to negotiate a variety of social relationships and deconstruct the power/truth dynamics of interactions that often have different norms of participation and for determining and corroborating status. Thus language must be viewed as a mediated social act and, as argued earlier by Volosinov (1973 [1930]): "what is important for a speaker about a linguistic form is not that it is a stable and always self-equivalent sign, but that it is an always changeable and adaptable sign" (p. 68). Within this particular framework, the words, phrases, grammatical and phonological norms from multiple speech communities are resources that reinforce, highlight, exploit and critique social and cultural roles. This is especially true of African American urban youth, for whom the interminable and relentless invention and reinvention of African American lexicon (e.g. *perpetrate* for pretending an identity, *diss* for being disrespectful, and *readin'* for exposing someone's interactive deception) actually serve to unravel the relation of verbal skill and social and political power (cf. Foucault, 1973, 1980).[7]

While there are many African American terms that are emblematic of the tension between subtlety and non-subtlety and indirect and directed speech, perhaps the most widespread cultural concept of social face that both critiques and symbolizes the tension is the contrast between being "cool" and acting "a fool." The cool/fool contrast is at the core of African American language ideology and has counterparts throughout the African diaspora and Africa (Alleyne, 1980; 1989; Yankah, 1991a, b).[8] Maintaining a cool face is often difficult, especially in interactions, because indirect discourse requires that all participants (including hearers) constantly assess and address potential meanings within and across contexts. In *Drylongso*, Gwaltney (1981) pays tribute to the cultural value of the cool social stance in his description of Nancy White: "She is the exemplar par excellence of the highest status that core black culture can accord – that of the cool, dealing individual" (p. 143). In contrast, Connor highlights the indeterminacy of African American coolness:

Cool is not just a term, it is a lifestyle. It has little to do with the hippest clothes or the latest fad . . . It is the most powerful yet intangible force in Black America. It is to be praised and at the same time it is insidious. (Connor, 1995: 1–2)

Old School rapper Kool Moe Dee, in his 1991 hit "How Kool Can One Black Man Be?," provides more detail on the characteristics of coolness as a lifestyle and identity.

But cool ain't a mood / It's an attitude dude / It's a tone / It's a tempo / A mind set / A rhythm / Lifestyle / Religion / It's just how ya' livin' / I'm righteously cool / While here and hereafter / I'm so cool / That I have to ask ya' / How cool? / How cool? / How cool can one black man be? (Dewese, 1991)

A cool social face is the ability to act on symbolic incidents and subtle varieties of cultural practice with eloquence, skill, wit, patience and precise timing. Those who possess coolness are current and trend setting, calm, detached, yet in control – in any situation (cf. Major, 1994; Smitherman, 1994). Yet coolness as an identity has always been the focus of harsh criticism in African American culture (e.g. Lee, 1969).[9]

Some social scientists and artists have tied African Americans' reverence of a cool social face to racism and/or male coping skills (Abrahams, 1962; George, 1992; Grier and Cobbs, 1968; Horton, 1972; Kunjufu, 1986; Majors and Billson, 1992). In so doing, they have failed to recognize its significance to women and that it contrasts with a fool's lack of social acumen. For example, in *Drylongso*, John Gwaltney provides the story of Mrs. Briar who as a little girl learned how to be cool and the penalty to one's social face resulting from acting a fool.

I was five when I learned not to lose my cool when the trucks backfired. I remember the day it happened. I had asked my father for something and he had said no. But when the trucks came by and backfired, I just sat there like nothing had happened. He said, "Girl, let me shake your hand!" and he gave me money and I felt just as tall as he was. My brother Harry, who is three years older than I am, without even looking at me said, "No cool." Then everybody teased him for running off at the mouth without knowing what he was talking about and he felt bad, I think . . . We don't like to show out, but if you guess wrong, you might be, well, you might be out there all by your lonesome. (Gwaltney, 1981: 192)

Having "no cool" is akin to having a negative social face and being called a fool is to be avoided at all costs.[10] Mabel Lincoln describes this type of outcast: "To black people like me, a fool is funny – you know, people who love to break bad, people you can't tell anything to, folks that will take a shotgun to a roach..." (Gwaltney, 1981: 68–9).

In fact, the black community teaches children early on about the importance of social face and is awash with expressions that expose someone as being a fool. A verbal routine that I remember as a child resulted in my losing face when two of my very "best friends" were talking to each other. I innocently walked up to them, listened for a bit, and then offered my expert advice about their conversation. I knew I was in deep trouble when one of my girlfriends slowly began to turn her head. It was clearly a slow-burn kind of head turn. That's when I noticed that her eyes were also moving in my direction, but slightly (with attitude) slower than her head! Her eyelids cast a shadow over her pupils and they were slowly, coolly – and with just a hint of disgust – headed in my direction. I stood firm. In the midst of her eyes' journey to their target, I noticed that her lips slightly opened and turned up a bit as they said to me: "This is an A and B conversation so C your way out!" Unfortunately, my sister overheard this and reported to everyone that I had no cool and had been made a fool.

Fast forward to the new millennium and what has happened to this kind of verbal death blow? It has becomes even more lethal. The eyes and head still roll, but the lips say something that requires insider youth membership. "Girlfriend" now says something like: "You just AAAAALLL UP in the Kool Aid! – And don't EEEVEN know the flavor!" or "Stop dippin' in my Kool Aid."[11] This may be worse than the "ABC" insult of my youth because outsiders can't interpret it. I once heard an unaware person respond with "I didn't know you were drinking Kool Aid" which leads to laughter and public confirmation that one is – in fact – a fool.

Being accused of acting and being a fool is to lack awareness of symbolic incidents, subtleties, situations, and thus is an insult that both denigrates and dismisses a person as a cultural member. It is precisely the presence of audience input and assessment within social contexts that allow the contrast between *cool* and *fool* or *acting a fool*. Thus it is obvious that cool as a lifestyle, while revered as art, is not admired when it means that a person cannot interpret and act on various social situations. Within this value system, a fool can be described as an adult who ignores social context and the importance of social face, and is therefore separate from and marginal to the sensibilities of a black social world.

Coolness then, is one of the symbolic goods that has exchange value and it can be used to accrue linguistic and pragmatic capital. One can "lose their cool" or positive social face in interactions where participants may be culturally challenged (e.g. not know current lexical terms or meanings), or when the dominant culture (e.g. the police, professors, legal system, school) argues that a particular form of interaction (e.g. baited indirection below) is not understood. But to get caught being a fool – not paying attention to the social and political situation, being afraid to ask questions, acting like you know something and you don't, acting like you have power when you don't – is an insult few endure well. Thus in many profound ways, a speaker's social face, status and standing or "cool" are always at stake (Morgan, 1991; Smitherman, 1977).

Double consciousness and social face

While the previous discussion presents language ideology as constitutive, one of the more troubling outcomes of social science research on African Americans has been the association of African American speech styles and concern with social face with self-loathing and pathology. This negative characterization is often done in relation to W. E. B. DuBois' (DuBois, 1903) theory of double consciousness. In his enduring and influential scholarship on race in America, DuBois wrote:

After the Egyptian and Indian, the Greek and Roman, the Teuton and Mongolian, the Negro is a sort of Seventh son, born with a veil, and gifted with second-sight in this American world, – a world which yields him no true self-consciousness, but only lets him see himself through the revelation of the other world. It is a peculiar sensation, this double consciousness, this sense of always looking at one's self through the eyes of others, of measuring one's soul by the tape of a world that looks on in amused contempt and pity. One ever feels his two-ness, – an American, a Negro; two souls, two thoughts, two unreconciled strivings; two warring ideals in one dark body, whose dogged strength alone keeps it from being torn asunder.

Over the years this quote has been interpreted to mean marginalization within the dominant society, self-hate, isolation, conflicting identities and loyalties, race consciousness and cultural nationalism (e.g. Early, 1993; Isaacs, 1963; Meier, 1963; Myrdal, 1944; Stonequist, 1965; Stuckey, 1987). Whether understood as representing a divided self, the outcome of living in a multicultural society, or a racist one, double consciousness is at the heart of black psychology (e.g. Cross, 1991; Haskins and Butts, 1973; Majors and Billson, 1992; Slaughter, 1983).[12] Indeed, African Americans' persistent appraisal of how they are viewed by the dominant society, and the concomitant exploration into how to address oppression and marginalization, has been described by Gates (1988) as "Afro-American's peculiar psychology of citizenship" (p. 207). Because of its problematic application for much of the social sciences (cf. Reed, 1992), the relation between double consciousness and indirectness, individual

Table 2 *Duality in speech*

Akan	Wet	Dry
	(dull and slurred speech)	(crisp, smooth, concise)
Ewe	Wild	Tame
	(surface speech)	(deep, signifying, local)
Yoruba	Hot	Cold
Wolof	Noble	Griot
	(restrained)	(fluent, hyperbolic)
US	Fool	Cool
	(loose, unmonitored talk)	(controlled, contextually sensitive)

intentionality and co-authorship in languages throughout the African diaspora has been obscured. Yet, as a cultural practice, forms of representation that explicitly reference multiple audiences, ideologies, social practices, cultural differences, histories, agendas and so on, are not problematic.

In many West African societies, metaphors and proverbs mediate local and cultural knowledge and memory for all to hear and evaluate (e.g. Gates, 1988; Hunter, 1982; Irvine, 1990, 1993, 1998; Mudimbe, 1988; Rosenthal, 1995; Saah, 1984; Wiredu, 1992; Yankah, 1995). The hermeneutics involve a duality of speech that aligns the quality of talk and expression of social face with meaning and speaker intent (table 2).[13] Judith Irvine defines Wolof linguistic ideology similarly when she writes, "The Wolof linguistic ideology thus identifies the register system primarily with the speaker..." (Irvine, 1998: 57). In this case, the focus is on the style of speech and speaker as representing social face, and the speech act as representing the social actor or catalyst. Though the focus is on the contrasts and choices available to the speaker, it is the hearer and audience who assess the speaker's social face.

Within the systems listed above, it is often the case that in order to determine what a narrative, statement or proverb means, one first must discern why it occurred in conversation at all. Thus, if a hearer is unaware of local and general cultural knowledge, it may be impossible to understand meaning or intention. This is also evident in Judy Rosenthal's (1995) discussion of the Ewe's "wild crab" proverbs that appear in some narratives. These proverbs penetrate the power relation between the Ewe and their indentured servants and domestic slaves who are from other cultures and obligated to live and work in Ewe households. At times, these domestic slaves marry within the Ewe, become part of families and inherit property. Signifying crab stories include values and contrasts around bought people (wild) and people of the house (tame). To summarize, the Ewe believe that while the slave can use the language, only pure Ewe understand the significance of all that is being said. Rosenthal describes how in Ewe, multiple audiences/hearers and local knowledge work together in constructing what she calls "extreme ambiguity" in the Ewe's strategic inclusion of "the wild crab" proverbs. These proverbs incorporate a language ideology based on multilingual settings where "the uncanny nature of linguistic and cultural difference is both domesticated through a childhood jaded with different tongues and resacralized through ritual" (p. 584). Though the Ewe consider it a practice that cannot be understood and challenged by outsiders, the notion of outsider is entangled with references to African slavery and communal membership. Thus wild crab proverbs often "signify" about one's role in society and the ability to establish and maintain social face. In a similar vein, African American multidirected interaction is constituted via a system of indirectness. This system includes an awareness that cultural norms exist that are not shared by the wider culture that generally does not know that the practice prevails among some of its citizens.[14]

The access to and knowledge of the multiple systems of language and interaction result in a thick ambiguity that allows adults to traverse classes, communities and contexts as they embed their language deep into their conversations and social stances. These interactions are culturally marked so that understanding the signifiers, whether in the form of referents or shifts in language styles, relies on local knowledge.[15] Thus social face can easily be in peril. One instance of how seamlessly the adult stance can be called into question and social face evaluated occurred at an "upscale" cocktail party I attended, where a group of friends enjoyed the following conversation between two men in their early thirties.

MAN 1: You can trust me.
MAN 2: I know I can. (*laughing*)
MAN 1: No, I mean you can really trust me. (*serious tone*)
MAN 2: Yeah man, I told you, I know I can. (*man 2 and overhearers laugh*)

As discussed in chapter 1, some statements are often cultural signs that index and reference situations where those in power are manipulating people or events. If one must speak of trust, it questions the integrity of the speaker. That is why children are often taught that statements like "You can trust me" and "I'll watch out for you," in situations where trust should not be an issue, are indications that a person may not be worthy of trust.[16] It is both the juxtaposition of interactional and broader, often subtle, cultural norms and expectations about statements of sincerity that render the statement insincere. In fact, as discussed earlier, the men who lynched Emmett Till told his uncle that he could trust them not to harm his nephew – and they murdered Emmett Till.

Though an individual has much at stake in these interactions, the issue is not solely about the speaker as an individual but also how others use local knowledge to assess situations. In many cases, one must patiently listen for and interpret indirect references to determine the meaning and significance of a statement. In this regard the song "Never Make My Move Too Soon", by the blues legend B. B. King (King, 1978), demonstrates the wicked irony associated with sincerity when his woman does him wrong and leaves him – with her bills to pay – just before he wins some money in Las Vegas.[17] During the song, B. B. King explains that he's no fool and knows better than to take his girlfriend back after she's treated him so badly. Toward the end of the tune B. B. King also provides details on the complexity of his personal situation.

I take my lovin' everywhere. I come back and they still care. One love ahead – One love behind. One in my arms – One on my mind. But there's one thing baby, I never make my move too soon.

Thus B. B. King demonstrates his sincerity about not making his move too soon – and about monogamous relationships. He signifies that the meaning of trust is essentially his own – that a woman should never betray him but he, on the other hand, takes his loving everywhere – leaving the listener with the notion that perhaps he wasn't treated so badly after all.

In the discussion that follows, discourse genres refer to language and communication styles that commonly occur in socially, culturally and politically defined contexts. In contrast, verbal genres refer to speakers' use of culturally significant varieties and styles that mediate, constitute and construct contexts. Thus, while both discourse and verbal genres may co-construct various contexts, verbal genres can collide with strongly framed discourse norms eroding or disrupting well-defined social contexts. The following analyses locate various speech genres within a system of social face that is partially constructed through directed and indirect discourse. This system includes signifying or sounding, adolescent instigating, adult conversational signifying, reading a person and reading dialect. These styles and practices combine to constitute the African American speech community across generation, gender and class.[18]

Audience and interaction

The system of social face described in chapter 1 includes a notion of audience and participant that is multilayered and multidimensional. In order to participate in African American discourse all participants must be aware at many levels. In the first place, a speaker must know that he or she may be viewed as representing him or herself as well as others

```
                              Overhearers
                              Hearers
        Speaker → Audience →  Immediate target
                              Associated targets
                              Ancestors, family, friends
```

Figure 1 Speaker and audience in African American culture

(e.g. family ancestors and friends) when giving opinions. Secondly, the speaker must know that he or she is not simply addressing a person (or target), but that others may hear and interpret what is said and consider that they might also be targets. These hearers and overhearers seldom speak during the actual interaction, though their presence, whether real or imagined, is integral to it. Within this system, the person addressed may not be the real or only target of the interaction. Figure 1 outlines the role of the audience in interaction. Unsurprisingly, who responds, when someone responds, the nature of the response and whether there is a response at all is governed by a complex series of norms and expectations. This system of indirectness, co-constructed intentionality and speaker responsibility (Kochman, 1981; Morgan, 1991; Smitherman, 1977) demonstrate the coalescence and adaptation of several African language practices, and two practices in particular shape use. One is the tension between indirect and direct speech and the other is the use of intermediaries in conversation.

Indirectness

The array of hearers, overhearers and passersby that are part of the fabric of African American interaction are common throughout Africa and the diaspora. They function in ways similar to the intermediate or instrumental agents that have been reported to be central in interactions and formal talk throughout many African cultures (Fisher, 1976; Hunter, 1982; Irvine, 1974, 1982; Morgan, 1989, 1993; Reisman, 1974; Saah, 1984; Yankah, 1991a, b, 1995). Yankah (1991a, b, 1995) reports that numerous African societies practice social and verbal indirection through intermediaries who protect the public "face" of chiefs. For example, in African societies where audiences must confirm the leader's right to lead, those in power often use a spokesperson to deliver a message and mediate for them in case the audience finds fault in the message. In this instance the sender, who never addresses the audience, has some protection (Hunter, 1982; Irvine, 1974, 1982; Morgan, 1989, 1993; Saah, 1984). As in the Ewe case described above, verbal genres can also serve the function of mediators in interaction. As Yankah explains, these verbal genres, by their very norms of performance, are thus partly conditioned to save face (1991b: 3).

Within the African American community in the US, verbal acts also function to save face as they address multiple audiences, some aware and some unaware, through ambiguity and camouflaging. For example, in the Caribbean as well as the US, musicians often argue that unintended audiences who do not understand that the music has a mediating function cannot hold musical performers responsible for any inappropriate interpretation of the meanings of lyrics.[19] In this respect, intentionality and responsibility are viewed as both socially situated and constituted so that speakers and audience collaborate in determining what is meant by what is said (Duranti, 1993; Irvine, 1993). Thus speakers who use indirectness actually mean to target certain individuals and they mean to do so indirectly.

While African American indirectness can take many forms in discourse, there are essentially two forms that seem to be indicative:

1. pointed indirectness – (a) when a speaker means to say something to a mock receiver that is intended for someone else and is so recognized; and (b) when a speaker refers to local knowledge to target someone else.
2. baited indirectness – when a speaker attributes a feature to a general target and audience that may be true for a segment.[20]

Pointed and baited indirectness are not mutually exclusive and one type of indirectness can quickly lead to another. Pointed indirectness requires local knowledge to understand what a speaker means, and is seldom recognized by non-African Americans when it occurs. In contrast, baited indirectness is often noticed, yet misunderstood by most non-African Americans (see below). This is largely because in baited indirectness attributes and features mediate speakers and targets and are therefore only directed to appropriate targets (cf. Yankah, 1991a, b). That is, for many African Americans, it is not logical that a person would respond to something attributed to him or her unless it was true (cf. Kochman, 1981).

Pointed indirectness

Speakers who employ pointed indirectness assume a shared local knowledge, and focus on the context and plausibility of a surrogate as the intended target of an interaction. This form of discourse focuses on speaker agency and facility at portraying the local knowledge in play in creative and subtle ways. For example, I once heard a woman tell another woman in front of a group of teenage girls "When I was young I wore too much make-up and looked like a fool." Though she later informed me that she was referring to one girl in particular, her statement sent all the girls into a crisis![21] So pointed indirectness gives a speaker room to insult someone in an indirect way because it is based on shared cultural knowledge. This type of indirectness is only successful if recognized by hearers as well as targets who share prior knowledge about events or where the context has been established in such a way that the addressed target and those around can determine the identity of the intended target. It is used by all social classes (compare Fisher, 1976), especially to key signifying (see below) and, in contexts that include non-members, it can function to enact identity, solidarity and/or resistance, among speech community members participating in the interaction. Typically, neither the surrogate or intended targets respond since, for this form of indirection, any response corroborates what the speaker says. This is because the statement is constructed within an act that highlights verbal skill, social face and local knowledge. Thus a direct response should not be within a turn of the particular interaction. In the few cases that I have witnessed where the intended target has responded to the speaker, the target has been aggressive and argumentative (cf. Morgan, 1994b).

This form of indirectness may become precarious if the surrogate responds to the speaker (e.g. does not perform the role of mock receiver) and does not recognize that it is implausible that he or she is the target. In this case the surrogate runs the risk of embarrassment, especially if the comment is complimentary and the speaker and/or hearers believe that what is said is only true for the intended target. For example, at a middle-class social gathering I heard a woman say to a man who was not smiling and did not have dimples: "I like a man with a warm smile and deep dimples." Unfortunately, the man (surrogate) responded with a flattered and beaming dimple-less smile and said "Thank you," which caused everyone, including the intended target to laugh at the surrogate and his loss of cool.

Pointed indirectness can also occur when information is conveyed through cultural/local knowledge that, in turn, becomes the go-between of the message (compare Yankah, 1991b). This occurred with Mary Walker, a folk artist in Los Angeles who was interviewed by a white researcher. Mrs. Walker was eighty-one years old when she told the story about how she met her late husband, whose large portrait dominated her living room. While in her teens, she was a housekeeper and caretaker for a white family who lived in New Orleans along the Mississippi River. Her detailed narrative includes a description of the 1927 Mississippi River flood and how they barely escaped with their lives. She then returned to the story about meeting her future husband.

```
 1 MW:  I was coming to seventeen
 2 Int.: Whew!
 3 MW:  And so here comes Daddy Dickson – the Dickson (.) the
 4       lawn mower man.
 5 Int.: Uh huh
 6 MW:  And he came, and uh, I went and I said, and I paid him. I
 7       was always home with the children. And uh we hadn't got
 8       sent up to Monroe, cause everything was so distressed.
 9       The water was rising just over night. Every time they
10       knock it was higher and higher. But we was sorta on the
11       highest place.
12 Int.: MmmmHmm
13 MW:  And uh, and here comes the yard man. And he come to
14       mow the yard. And it wasn't like old mens today – if he see
15       a young girl he would try to get her for himself. He says,
16       "My wife has a son from (3)St. Louis, Missouri." And says
17       "He's visiting us, and would I like for you to meet him"
18       And oh I was: (3) flip, like most young girls. I was
19       wanting to see what was happening. And I said "Oh sure!
20       Well send him over."
21 Int.: MmmmHmmm
22 MW:  And that's the man up there ((points to a large portrait))
23 →    **He was curly headed in the front. Been like your baby.**
24 Int.: MmmmHmmm
25 MW:  And so when ah, the day he was suppose to come, I was
26       mopping the floor – just making strokes, you know, (2) like
27       that, (2) cleanin' up?
28 Int.: MmmmHmmm
29 MW:  And I said to myself (2) should I tell him the truth?
30 →    I says something close to **"this peckerwood walking"**
31       (laughs)
32 Int.: MmmmHmmm
33 MW:  And when I got there he says are you
34 →    **Miss Mary Cooper?** And then I knew it was him, you
35       know (laughs). And he says yes. And uh, I says, my
36       father in law told me, my step father told me rather, uh,
37       that you were here, that you gonna be here for a while.
```

Mary Walker's story focuses on audience and presumed cultural/social knowledge in a way that is seldom reported for "American Stories" (e.g. Bauman, 1986; Polanyi, 1989) in that she uses pointed indirectness to tell the listener a very important fact. When she first saw her husband, Mary Walker thought he was white. Her confusion about his race is conveyed through culturally significant information and symbols. It is first conveyed in line 23, where Mrs. Walker compares her husband's hair to her friend's (a Euro-American interviewer) daughter's blond curly hair – *He was curly headed in the front. Been like your baby.* It becomes clear that Mrs. Walker intends to say that her husband could pass for white in line 30, when she uses *peckerwood*, a pejorative Southern term for whites, to refer to her husband when she first sees him. The use of a pejorative term in this context suggests both the recognition that her husband could pass for white and an indication that Mrs. Walker did not consider that fact an attribute. That he was not white, but black, is further revealed in line 34, where her future husband uses the respectful address form *Miss Mary Cooper*. In Louisiana in 1927, white men did not refer to young black women as *Miss*. The information in this narrative is culturally constructed and indirect and can be interpreted as follows.

Cultural information	Interpretation
He was curly headed in the front. Been like your baby.	We know that your baby is white.
peckerwood	I thought of a negative term for a white man when I saw him.
Miss Mary Cooper	He showed me respect, so I knew he was black.

Mrs. Walker skillfully uses cultural respect/formal address terms, which reveal that her husband could pass for white. She refers to cultural symbols, e.g. hair, insult term (*peckerwood*), that signify on both her husband and the listener (see signifying below). But once Mr. Walker delivers the respectful and formal greeting, it is clear that he is black (see also Morgan, 1994b).[22]

Baited indirectness

In contrast to pointed indirectness, baited indirectness occurs when a speaker means to talk about someone in general by targeting possible attributes or features. In its most basic form, it is a cultural secret handshake. It is meant to be *audienced*, witnessed and heard by those who have the local knowledge and understand who or what the target is. In contrast to pointed indirectness, it is not always assumed that the target has the local knowledge necessary to know that they are being baited and their social face challenged. That is to say, the speaker may not have anyone in particular in mind and in fact lures potential targets into positions that challenge their social face. If a hearer responds at all, whether protesting or affirming the allegation that he or she possesses these attributes, the audience considers the respondent's recognition of the attributes as an indication that what is said may be true for the protester.

Baited indirectness, which often appears as circumlocution, can employ collective nouns and indefinite personal pronouns, e.g. *something*, *someone*, that highlight that the attribute being discussed is distant from the specific hearers (Morgan, 1994a). Its function is to make unambiguous participant beliefs and attitudes by provoking a response from those who fit the description. An example of baited indirection, which resulted in controversy, occurred when a rapper, Ice T, recorded a rap song entitled "Cop Killer." It seems that the police did not first determine whether they fit Ice T's description of brutal cops before criticizing his rap song. Instead, they seemed to believe that Ice T referred to them. Ice T explains his position:

At the very beginning of "Cop Killer," I dedicate it to the LAPD and to police chief Daryl Gates. The lyrics are blatant and very specific: the chorus explains that the record's about:

COP KILLER, it's better you than me.
COP KILLER, fuck police brutality!
COP KILLER, I know you family's grievin'
Fuck 'em!
COP KILLER, but tonight we get even.

Better you than me. If it's gonna be me, then better you. My anger is clearly aimed at *brutal* police. The song was created to be a protest record – a warning, not a threat – to authority that says, "Yo, police: We're human beings. Treat us accordingly." (Ice T and Siegmund, 1994: 168–9)

In the above quote, Ice T argues that by naming the Los Angeles police department and its chief, Daryl Gates, he had explicitly stated that he is *only* talking about corrupt and brutal police – not all police. However, if the aggressive and relentless attack on "Cop Killer" by many police departments in the US is any indication, dominant American culture is not prepared to accept the rules of baited indirection, especially when they are presented by Ice T. That is, either there are only a few police officers for whom the statements did not apply and were willing or able to distinguish that they were not the target of Ice T's comments or there is no such person as a cop who is not brutal.[23] In the end, Ice T successfully exploited their ignorance of baited indirectness as they collaborated with him in his depiction of the culpability of the police.

Direct and directed speech

The system of indirection outlined above reveals that African American audiences are co-authors (Duranti, 1993) who, along with speakers, contribute to and determine the intent of what is said. In this sense, speaker intent is constituted through collaboration and is not considered complete without it. In contrast, direct discourse is marked by the absence of collaboration and the sense that speakers and audiences rely on each other for meaning. It involves the speaker acting as an individual independent of collaborators and with nothing to lose. Either the speaker has no control or refuses to exercise control over what he or she says, or the speaker is in a powerful position so that audience collaboration is not necessary.

There are two types of direct discourse. The first type occurs in institutional settings where the event or context prescribes speaker intent (e.g. school, work). The other type I call directed discourse (Morgan, 1989) and is marked by the absence of indirection, audience collaboration and a disregard for social context. Directed discourse is often used to make what is implicit *explicit* and determine truth, etc.

African American attitudes toward direct discourse have been discussed in educational, work and legal contexts where formal communication is defined in relation to tasks and individual activities, and where power relationships are extreme. Some researchers have called this communication style work or school language (e.g. Dandy, 1991; Kochman, 1981) because how a person speaks is often considered part of a job rather than a reflection of the attributes or attitudes of the speaker. Consequently, this form of discourse is considered to be functional, rather than truthful or dishonest. Because direct discourse is void of co-constructed intent, it is often viewed suspiciously outside institutional contexts. This is especially true for direct questions, which many African Americans view as "confrontational, intrusive, and presumptuous" (Kochman, 1981: 99) and potentially harmful (Jones, 1988).

Within the framework outlined above, direct questions are institutional ways of knowing which are not based on the truth (intentionality) of the questioner or respondent. The black expression "Talking like a man with a paper in his hand" (Gwaltney, 1981: xxiv) refers to those who ask questions without recognizing or understanding that both listening and hearing are culturally constituted and socially situated. Thus from a black perspective, questions should appear in social contexts which incorporate or reflect their reasoning, rather than simply satisfy institutional or intellectual curiosity and need.

While direct discourse is considered formulaic and does not focus on the participants' role or intentions, directed discourse focuses on a clear target and is unpredictable regarding language variety and discourse style. Although they both share an absence of audience collaboration, directed discourse evolves from the notion that speakers are advocates and there is no such thing as an impersonal position (cf. Kochman, 1981). Thus during conversation, directed discourse can occur in response to direct discourse when hearers believe that speakers should possess or demonstrate their own beliefs and intentions. It can also occur within indirect discourse when hearers believe that speakers are misrepresenting themselves in some way (e.g. John Henry Martin above).

Reading

One cultural enactment of directed discourse is called "reading."[24] This form of interaction occurs whenever a speaker denigrates another to his or her face (Goffman, 1967) in an unsubtle and unambiguous manner. Though there may be self-reporting of reading having taken place without witnesses (e.g. in a story, the narrator may simply report "I *read* her!"), reading is legitimate only when it is accomplished in the presence of other witnesses who collaborate that it, in fact, occurred.[25] It is directed speech to the point that it is often accusatory. When a target gets read, he or she is verbally attacked for inappropriate or offensive statements or what is perceived, by the reader, as the speaker's false representation of his or her beliefs, personal values, etc. It is not unusual to get read for acting out class privileges, failing to greet friends, pretending to have beliefs that are not actually held, etc. (Morgan, 1996). The point here is not that a reader is correct or incorrect, but that the reader is willing to jeopardize his or her own face (as well as that of the target) by disclosing what the reader believes is the target's attempt to camouflage his or her beliefs, attitudes, etc. regardless of setting or context.

A modern example of public reading is the use of "the diss" in rap and hip hop culture. The style of dissin' or criticizing another artist was once a hip hop trope. It essentially involves scathing personalized critiques of rap lyrics, images, the ability to represent the essence of urban life, physical appearance, reputation, authenticity and so on. Artists diss each other when one believes that someone did not "come correct" either in terms of representing hip hop's sense of fairness and truth or not being supportive to another group member. One aggressive dissing sequence occurred between 1989 and 1995 around the break up of the rap group NWA (Dr. Dre vs. Ice Cube; Ice Cube vs. Dr. Dre; Ice Cube vs. Eazy E; Dre and Eazy E). Apart from the dissing war that erupted in recordings and in interviews, an East Coast rapper launched an additional attack on Dr. Dre. The diss occurred when Tim Dog, a rapper from the Bronx, criticized Dr. Dre for physically attacking the female video jockey (Dee Barnes) of a popular hip hop television program "Pump Up the Volume."[26]

> I crush Ice Cube, I'm cool with Ice T
> But N.W.A ain't shit to me

Dre beatin' on Dee from Pump It Up
Step to the dog and get fucked up
I'm simplistic, imperialistic, idealistic
And I'm kickin' the ballistics
Havin' that gang war
We want to know what you're fighting for
Fighting over colors?
All that gang shit is for dumb motherfuckers
Come to New York and we'll see who gets robbed
Take your jeri curls, take your black hats
Take your wack lyrics and your bullshit tracks
Now you're mad and you're thinking about stompin'
Well I'm from the South Bronx

Fuck Compton!   (Tim Dog, 1991: Fuck Compton)

In his rhymes, Tim Dog refers to ex-NWA member Ice Cube, rapper Ice T and Dee Barnes. He signifies (discussed below) on both NWA and the entire West Coast urban youth culture by referring to their dress and hairstyles as reactionary and lame. The word *colors*, refers to street gang colors that are often the source of conflict in the Los Angeles area. Some members of NWA wore a Jheri Curl. It is an African American hairstyle that is often ridiculed because it – literally – drips and is considered outdated and unfashionable. Men who have long hair in this hairstyle are often thought to be a-political, have self-hate and are referred to as *wannabes* (literally: want to be).[27] Finally, the word *wack* means unbelievably stupid.

Another significant aspect of reading involves a prosodic system that prescribes specific responses from speakers, targets and hearers. This prosodic system includes *loud-talking, marking, high pitch* and *timing/rhythm. Loud-talking* occurs in the presence of an audience or overhearers when someone talks about someone else at a volume which is either louder than necessary for the addressed target to hear or markedly different in volume (louder or quieter) from utterances which precede or follow. It can occur on a word or an entire segment. According to Mitchell-Kernan (1972b),

Loud-talking often has the effect of unequivocally signalling the intent of the speaker from the perspective of the addressee. That is to say, it assures that intent will be imputed beyond the surface function of the utterance, which might be to seek information, make a request, make an observation, or furnish a reply to any of these. (p. 329)

The target of loud-talking is always directly addressed and hearers generally make an effort to pretend that they are not aware of the speech event underway. In contrast to loud-talking, *marking* is a mode of characterization where mannerisms are mimicked. When marking, a speaker "copies" a language variety out of context. This is done in such a way that the marking is attributable to a "type" of person who is different from the speaker and/or intended hearers. As Mitchell-Kernan explains: "Rather than introducing personality or character traits in some summary form, such information is conveyed by producing or sometimes inserting aspects of speech ranging from phonological features to particular content which carry expressive value" (Mitchell-Kernan, 1972b: 333). Thus, marking is a side remark about a person and the speech style serves as a commentary about the person.

Pitch and timing are also important resources in interaction. High pitch is associated with dishonest, authoritative discourse and low pitch with honest or true discourse and AAE. Pitch contrast can occur across words or expressions and often co-occurs with other linguistic features involved in dialect opposition. Its appearance often reflects the attitude of the speaker toward the interlocutor or topic.

Timing also signals speaker attitude in that rhythm is viewed as an important aspect of what is said. As in other communities (Levinson, 1983; Pomerantz, 1984; Sacks, Schegloff and Jefferson, 1974), skipping a beat (or two) suggests that a speaker has a view or attitude which does not align with the other interlocutors. In contrast, speaking rhythmically (often with regularized intervals between talks and pauses) signals that the interaction is highly marked as African American and likely to lead to conversational signifying.

Finally, laughter and other vocalic expressions like sucking teeth (Rickford and Rickford, 1976) often signify disapproval and the opposite meaning of what is being said. Laughter, when used by women is often the "fool's laugh," and indexes and signals that what is occurring or being talked about is considered foolish. Women also use laughter when they believe someone thinks that they are the fool, and are mistaken in their assumption.

As the preceding section suggests, perhaps the most outstanding quality of African American interaction is the way in which speaker agency and audience instantiation combine to shape and evaluate both the choice of styles across interactions and the choice of varieties within each style. While African American discourse is based on a system of indirectness, the uses of directed and direct discourse styles are viewed as choices. The use of indirect discourse requires knowledge of AAE and, in most cases American English norms. The pervasiveness of indirectness and the function of direct and directed discourse are learned from adults and as younger children are socialized through play with older children (cf. Ochs and Schieffelin, 1984).

Language play and play language

Children and young adults explore the complexities, intricacies and haz-ards of an interaction system based on directed and indirect discourse through games, which often implode on speakers and explode on targets and hearers. Children's play language, which includes teasing, bossing friends etc., can quickly move to language play, where verbal prowess can be honed, old scores can be settled and the play day can be brought to a proper close. Both males and females participate in most forms of verbal play (Goodwin, 1990), though depending on context and ado-lescent social standing, each gender tends to favor some activities more than others.[28] Two widely known forms of language play are signifying and instigating.

Signifying

Signifying is a verbal game of indirection also known by the regional names of sounding, the dozens, joning, snapping, busting, capping, bagging and ranking (Abrahams, 1962; Garner, 1983; Gates, 1988; Kochman, 1972b; Labov, 1972a; Mitchell-Kernan, 1972b, 1973; Percelay, Monteria and Dweck, 1994; Smitherman, 1977). Mitchell-Kernan describes signifying as "the recognition and attribution of some implicit content or function which is obscured by the surface content or function" (1972: 317–18). Signifying is a form of play for adolescents that can serve indirect functions in verbal interactions among adults (e.g. conversational signifying). Many (e.g. Abrahams and Troike, 1972; Dollard, 1939/1973; Kochman, 1972b; Percelay et al., 1994) have suggested that signifying started as an outlet for racial oppression. But it is more likely that its function as a means to address racism is an added bonus for youth that must learn both the verbal and social face rules of being black in America. Unfortunately, many examples of signifying are produced in popular culture and lack local knowledge, audience and timing rules. The result is often a minstrel display of stereotypes rather than a play at verbal skill.

The notion of "play" involved in signifying differentiates the real from the serious (Abrahams, 1970, 1976; Goffman, 1974; Kochman, 1983, 1986) by focusing on that which is socially and/or culturally signifi-cant (e.g. relatives, sexuality, physical appearance, political figures, class and economic status) and placing it in implausible contexts. Whether a context is plausible or implausible is culturally determined. For example, a signifying episode that includes a police officer who "serves and protects" the black community would be considered an implausible context. Once the implausible or unreal state is established, these cultural signs interact with the context through irony, sarcasm, wit and humor in order to "play" with the serious signifier. For example, one commonly heard signifying turn regarding appearance is: "You're so ugly, you went into a haunted house and came out with a job application." If it is plausible that the sign fits the context (e.g. you *are* ugly), the interaction is considered to be an insult rather than play.[29]

Gates (1988: 48) has referred to signifying as the "the trope of tropes" of African American discourse and believes that it functions as a stylish critique of African American rhetorical and cultural styles. Gates' definition is a far cry from earlier (Dollard, 1939/1973) and recurring (Dandy, 1991; Kunjufu, 1986; Majors and Billson, 1992) assessments that signifying functions as a way for adolescent males to cope with overbearing black women. As Percelay et al. (1994) clarify: "Ironically, the focus on 'your mother' in so many snaps points to a reverence most contestants share for their mothers. In the dozens, this reverence is used as an emotional weapon" (p. 22).

While some folklorists and anthropologists (especially Abrahams, 1976; Kochman, 1972b) successfully placed signifying within verbal performance genres, they focused on the place where they saw these performances – the street – as the locus of men's cultural and social activity. Generally, everyday-life stories are not the focus of discussion in the street where fantastic, fantasized and improbable tales of heroism, strength, wit and virility function as semiotic or symbolic capital (Bourdieu, 1977/1991; Rossi-Landi, 1983). This is especially evident today when signifying is a standard part of televised American comedy routines, advertising for sporting events, clothing and fast food, and public service announcements oriented toward friends and family.[30]

In its form as verbal play, signifying or snapping is mainly performed by adolescent males, though it also occurs among adult males and females involved in competitive activities (e.g. sports, stock trading). Percelay et al. introduce seventeen adjectival categories of snaps, including: fat, stupid, sex and ugly.[31] "Playing the dozens" is the term often used for signifying sequences which include the noun phrase *your mother* or *yo mama*. While playing the dozens may be an important part of adolescent male activity, members also recognize it as a language socialization activity (cf. Goodwin, 1988, 1990; Schieffelin and Ochs, 1986), especially for conversational signifying (discussed below).

Playing the dozens: deconstructing *yo' mamma*

As Percelay et al. (1994) suggest, *your mother* (or *yo mama*) statements both highlight and subvert the notion that mothers are sacred
(Smitherman, 1977). These statements should not be misunderstood to
relate specifically to someone's particular mother since that is not a requirement to participate. *Your mother* statements are a device to practice
and perform verbal skill and this practice often occurs in the presence of
family members, including mothers, who help judge their effectiveness
and comment on the wit or irony in the statements, often offering other
examples which they deem more impressive.

Along with being constituted through African American cultural contexts, *your mother* statements are also grammatically constituted. They are
usually marked by both AAE and GE prescriptive grammatical practices
which are juxtaposed in terms of both the linguistic level and the system
of indirection being employed. That is, there is a tendency to use AAE
and GE categorically within linguistic levels but not across levels. This
tendency is apparent in what Hutcherson (1993), a stand-up comic and
comedy writer, argues is the anatomy of a mother joke. He describes it
as beginning with *Your mother so* followed by an adjective that will be the
straight line of the joke. He argues that it is also acceptable to begin with
That's why, your mother, even if what follows is not an explanation (p. 52).
Derrick Fox (1992) provides two examples.

That's why your mother is so dumb: she was filling out a job application and it
said, "Sign here." And she put "Aquarius." That's why your mother's so bald
headed: every time she gets in the shower, she gets brainwashed. (Fox, 1992: 20)

Hutcherson (1993) suggests that one can never use *This is why* or *this
is the reason your mother*. There may be restrictions on this form because
deictic constructions using *this* make the referent specific, immediate, and
possible in the future while *that* suggests that the descriptive adjective and
following clause (usually describing a physical deformity) which follows is
in the distant past, and possibly not a real depiction (not near) of the past.
In this sense, *that* serves an existential function (cf. Quirk, Greenbaum
and Svartvik, 1972). The cases of "the dozens" under discussion will be
those coded with the structure:

Your mother (is) so *adjectival*... (that)...

where the adjectival phrase is followed by a clause. In these cases, the
full-form copula *is* appears with the same frequency as the phonologically
assimilated (preceding *so*) or contracted *s*. While plural and verbal *s* are

variable, both are seldom variable within the same clause. The comparative correlative subordinator (*so . . . that*) adds emotive emphasis and *that* is often omitted.[32]

Thus it is possible to hear:

1. Your mother is so fat that when she sits on a quarter she gets two dimes and a nickel.
2. Your mother is so old that when she read(s) the Bible she reminisces.

As well as:

1a. Your mother so fat (that) (when) she sit(s) on a quarter she get(s) two dimes and a nickel.
2b. Your mother so old (that) (when) she reads the Bible she reminisce(s).

In the first case of signification, *so fat* and *quarter* are combined to reveal that the act of "sitting" results in the squeezing out of the component parts of the quarter coin (two 10 cent coins and one 5 cent coin). In the second example, the age of the mother is related to when the Bible was written so that the mother is as old as the Bible and some of the events reported there might be childhood memories.

When one considers the above examples, it seems clear that with "the dozens," prescriptive or regularized grammatical norms may actually allow the audience to pay attention to the level(s) of indirection present What makes the above cases signifying with the dozens, and not simply indirection, is the combination of grammatical structure and form and the level of deconstruction of the characteristics and attributes of the adjectival – the logic. Cases of signifying like "playing the dozens" or *your mother* statements are constructed through the interaction of both grammar and speech event. Moreover, this verbal genre is but one aspect of a multilevel grammatical system that is constructed through AAE and GE linguistic and pragmatic systems.

Once a *your mother* sequence is launched, it is usually acknowledged as "in play" within an interactive episode when another person responds with a statement and is therefore in competition with the initiator (Abrahams, 1962; Kochman, 1983; Labov, 1972a, b). The episode continues until someone delivers enough witty, acerbic and indirect statements that the audience or participants determine the winner. As Hutcherson (1993) explains, the true essence of the dozens is the relationship between choice of signs and the "logic" of the implausibility. For Warren Hutcherson, this "logic" is culturally loaded and refers to African American local theories (cf. Geertz, 1983; Lindstrom, 1992) that include knowledge of cultural celebrations as well as US racism, bigotry, injustice, etc. One of the logical examples that Hutcherson cites is as follows:

Your mother is so fat they won't let her have an X jacket because helicopters keep trying to land on her back. (1993: 52)

The local information necessary to understand the irony in the signification is that the X jacket is in reference to an emblem associated with Malcolm X, an African American leader and activist known for his criticism of US racism and his anticapitalist leanings. Malcolm X was assassinated in 1965 and a movie depicting his life was released in 1991. The X appeared on clothing of urban youth in the early 1990s. It was a part of the massive commodification of Malcolm X after the release of a movie based on his life. The helicopter is in reference to both knowledge of landing markings and first-hand experience of how helicopters (called ghetto birds) patrol, constantly scan, descend and land in urban communities.

He-said-she-said

Unlike their male peers who play signifying games that are fast paced and considered outside of conversation, girls' language socialization often involves interactions which include several verbal styles. Goodwin's (1990, 1992) analysis of he-said-she-said disputes among African American girls illustrates the elaborate lengths to which they are willing to go in order to determine who said what behind someone's back. Girls focus on the content of previous and future interactions – what someone actually said, could say, or would say if given the opportunity. Consequently, the language style is not formulaic, but focuses on pragmatics and the re-establishment of the social order.

In children's he-said-she-said disputes, the offended party does not generally investigate the role or motive of the person instigating (see chapter 4). Rather, the offended party works to maintain and or re-establish her social face through future stories in response to instigating stories, retold stories, hypothetical stories, parallel stories, harvested parallel stories retelling stories, building audiences, harvesting stories and building future hypothetical stories (Goodwin, 1992). As Goodwin explains, "The goal of the instigator's storytelling is to elicit a statement from the offended party which leads to her confronting the offending party" (1992: 187).

As girls get older, however, they shift their focus to include language variety, the intention of the instigator and all participants in the process. Moreover, talking about someone behind her back takes on a new seriousness, so that the activity is not simply gossip, but rumor. In the African American speech community, when a rumor achieves widespread audience discussion and assessment, it is often treated as truth, even when it is not believed to be factual (cf. Turner, 1993). That is, collective talk about someone is treated as an important fact in and of itself. Because it also signals a loss of social face, the target of a rumor must defend her honor.

The childhood practices of signifying, the dozens, he-said-she-said and instigating are not discarded in adulthood. Instead they socialize youth into a language ideology that requires long-term observation, participation, criticism, analysis, punishments and awards. They are reconstructed in adult conversations and narratives that increase in complexity and subtlety and take into consideration possible hearers, and the speaker's intentionality and social face. These practices also incorporate knowledge of grammar and attitudes toward speakers of AAE.

3 Language norms and practices

While working as a linguistic consultant for a job-training program in Philadelphia in 1987, I was asked to settle a dispute between a supervisor and a trainee. The job program was designed to train urban youth so that they could compete for positions in the cable industry. One of the supervisors, Lou Murray, was from a white ethnic community in northeast Philadelphia and one of the trainees was a young black man from north Philadelphia named Jesse Monroe.

For some reason, Lou Murray did not like Jesse Monroe and monitored him constantly. So one afternoon, it was not surprising to find Lou clearly agitated about something – and looking for Jesse. He confronted Calvin, a young man from Jesse's neighborhood who was also being trained, and asked whether he had seen Jesse. Calvin said: "No I ain't seen him." The supervisor said: "I only said he could take a bathroom break. How long has it been since you saw him?" Calvin, visibly concerned with Lou's anger said "I don't know how long. But I had seen him." Lou then flew into a rage and attempted to find Jesse with the intention of firing him for leaving the job training without permission.[1]

Fortunately my partner, Deborah White, intervened and we attempted to mediate the misunderstanding. As we compared notes we realized what had happened. Jesse was actually at work in another part of the building. Lou had forgotten that he had sent him there. In spite of this, Lou still insisted that Jesse be fired since Calvin confirmed that Jesse had been gone for an extended period of time. I asked Lou what Calvin said and he replied, "He said he had seen Jesse." So Lou reasoned that Jesse must have been gone a long time!

Then, in the presence of Lou, we interrogated poor Calvin. I asked him to repeat his part of the story and he said, "I told him I had saw Jesse!" I asked, "When did you see him?" He replied, "I had saw him!" Then I asked "How long was it, in terms of time, when you saw Jesse and then Lou asked you?" He replied "About a minute or two because I was with him just before Lou come looking for him." Lou then yelled at Calvin, "Well why didn't you tell me then!" Calvin replied, "I told you I had seen him in the bathroom just before you came!" At this point Lou was incredulous. I explained to Lou that in this particular case *had* did not refer to the distant past but to the recent present. I told him that Calvin wasn't lying and trying to cover for Jesse.

The whole incident was exasperatingly surreal. I presented various forms of documentation to Lou in order to get him to concede that it was possible that Calvin had recently seen Jesse. Once I provided research on tense and aspect in AAE, Deborah and I were able to convince Lou that Jesse had only taken three minutes to use the bathroom, and the incident was resolved. Afterwards, Deborah and I decided to include classes for the trainees on the subtle interpretations of time reference in AAE. We also agreed that we needed to watch out for Jesse – and find a way to get rid of Lou.

Background

The rich discourse and interaction practices typical in African American communities and described in the previous chapters extend beyond issues of speech and discourse style to include linguistic and grammatical structure. Though speakers are not always aware of the grammatical relationships and systems in their repertoire, by the time they're adults they know that there is something unique about African American speech. In fact, as with discourse styles, the African American speech community operates according to an elaborate and intricate integration of language norms and values associated with the symbolic and practical functions of African American English (AAE) and General English (GE).[2]

Indeed, as discussed earlier (see introduction), many studies provide extensive evidence of the systemic nature of AAE.[3] These publications were considered somewhat controversial when they first appeared because they opposed widely accepted stereotypical theories about African Americans' cognitive and linguistic abilities (see chapter 6). Instead of describing AAE as a deficient variety, researchers such as William Labov, Walt Wolfram, Joey Dillard and Geneva Smitherman demonstrated its systematicity, function and importance in African American culture. Still, in view of the historical facts described in chapter 1, it is appropriate that discussion about the constitutive phonological, morphological, syntactic, semantic and pragmatic features of AAE also have social and political implications beyond linguistics.

The study of AAE is a part of the study of African American culture in general and incorporates many of the same arguments described in the preceding chapters. Unsurprisingly, debates concerning AAE often involve the examination of two questions that focus on its origin and subsequent relation to GE. The first question is whether the underlying linguistic system of AAE is shared with others who speak English as a first language and natively – without significant linguistic influences from other languages that may be in their repertoire. The second concerns the source of AAE's underlying linguistic system. It asks whether AAE is the linguistic consequence of a culture that underwent violent and repressive contact that resulted in African Americans speaking English and retaining some influences from African languages as well. In other words, these linguistic debates focus on whether it is best to describe AAE's historical ancestry primarily in terms of: (1) general American English varieties, (2) other languages and varieties in the African diaspora, (3) African languages or (4) a combination of the three (cf. Morgan, 1994; Mufwene, 1992b).

The first view is considered to be the dialectologist and early socio-linguistic position (Bailey and Maynor, 1987; Fasold, 1972; Krapp, 1924; Kurath, 1928; Labor, 1972a, b; McDavid, 1963; Schneider, 1989; Williamson, 1970; Wolfram, 1969). Though many of the early settlers in the US spoke other European languages (cf. Mufwene, 1999), dialectologists generally assumed that their English was not greatly influenced by other languages. The second and third approaches represent the creolist or substratist position (Bailey, 1965; Dalby, 1969; DeBose and Faraclas, 1993; Dillard, 1972; Stewart, 1967; Tolliver-Weddington, 1979; Winford, 1992). Linguists who argue this view are interested in the relationship between AAE and African languages and Caribbean varieties.

The fourth view, the multiple influence position, has been held at various times by both sociolinguists and creolists, depending on the linguistic level of analysis and whether the research was a synchronic or diachronic study (Alleyne, 1980; Baugh, 1980; Mufwene, 1992a, 1994; Rickford, 1977, 1997b). This view assumes that the language contact situation was diverse and linguistic influences varied.

Although many linguists analyze and collect data using more than one of the above perspectives, today each approach is based on specific notions of representative speaker and linguistic features and suggests different ideologies concerning the conditions and contexts under which AAE emerged. Yet the question remains, is the language of a sixteen-year-old boy representative of the African American speech community? Is he representative if we include his friends and social network? If he graduates from high school or even gets a GED, is he still representative? Is he representative if we include his extended family in the analysis? Is he representative if we discover that he's middle class? Is he representative if we make him a she? Is he more aligned with the African American community if he goes to prison rather than college? Is everyone representative if we just get enough examples to analyze? These questions concerning methodology, sample choice and age, class, gender and identity are imbedded in all linguistic arguments on AAE. They have in turn led to complex disputes in education, public policy, sociology, cultural studies and literary criticism.

The above questions suggest that it is not enough to consider whether AAE can be described outside of political contexts – it can. Rather it is necessary to explore its function within this context – as both a stigmatized sign and an authenticating one – especially in relation to linguistic findings and descriptions. In this regard, this chapter explores data from tape-recorded interviews of thirty-one people (five women and twenty-six men) between the ages of eighteen and twenty-six living in Philadelphia in 1989. They were all enrolled in entry-level job-training programs and all were high school graduates or had high school equivalency. As part of the study they read from a word list of 130 words, read a story out loud and told a story about their work experience, family, friends or any event they chose (e.g. frightening, celebratory, etc.).

What is African American English?

African American English is the language, discourse and interactional styles and usage of those socialized in the speech community. Still, it is impossible to provide a simple definition of the African American speech community, or any urban speech community. This is true not only because of its complex political and social history, but also because the community expands and contracts across social class and geographic lines. Considering its complexity, it is not surprising that one source of criticism of linguistic plans and proposals regarding AAE can be traced to early descriptions of the African American speech community and what constitutes membership. Controversy regarding who speaks AAE began in the late 1960s with the pronouncement from creolists and dialectologists that "80 percent of all Black people speak Black English" (Baratz, 1973).

How we know who speaks AAE remains a significant question since many theories were based on racial and economic classifications where being African American and having non-middle-class status were synonymous with being an AAE speaker. Considering the diverse perspectives on language style described in chapter 2, it was predictable that the African American community would resist linguists' attempts to identify speakers based on race and class. Theories about AAE and GE linguistic structure and usage are part of everyday philosophizing in the speech community and these "philosophies of language" are radically different from those of linguists in many ways.

In the first place, among members of the speech community, disputes regarding language choice tend to revolve around how those living under slavery and later social and economic discrimination viewed their reality. Since social reality is constructed via language, two perspectives emerge.[4] The first concerns whether AAE signifies the resistance to an imposed definition of self and identity that constructs African Americans as dependent "Others" who rely on those of European ancestry for recognition and existence. The second focuses on whether AAE represents acquiescence and participation in the imposed definition. These perspectives, which are the outcome of the restrictions and forms of talk described in previous chapters, are essential to understand attitudes toward both AAE and GE. They underlay many modern arguments concerning what beliefs and practices best represent African American culture.

The first question refutes the definition of US slavery as a language contact situation that "stripped Africans clean" (e.g. Phillips, 1918) of culture, language, memory and history. It focuses on the ways in which Africans sought to forge an identity within slavery by employing generalized African norms of communication to establish an antisociety with AAE as counterlanguage (see chapter 2). The second question implies that language is neither constituted through culture nor is it a social construct, but that all individuals have control over the language variety of their group. It evaluates AAE speakers exclusively in terms of GE ideals, suggesting that GE is the vehicle with which one can transcend a marginalized status and become the model of good and humanity and, therefore, citizenship. Within this framework, monolingual GE in intragroup interaction symbolizes self-hate regarding an African American identity and an exaltation of European values that marginalize those of African descent.

Irrespective of the position one takes, an environment exists where both varieties symbolize ideologies regarding African American cultural practices. Consequently, in terms of language choice, GE is the only variety that one can *choose* to speak, while AAE is a variety that one may choose *not* to speak. That is, in the African American speech community, both AAE and GE function as the language of home, community, history and culture. For families that use both varieties, one is not necessarily valued over the other though one may be considered more contextually appropriate. Within this system AAE is not only what one may hear and speak at home and in the community, but it is also the variety that delivers formal and informal knowledge as well as local knowledge and wisdom. It is the language of both the profound and the profane.

On the other hand GE, rather than AAE, has a context-free exchange value outside of the speech community.[5] Within the dominant cultural system, GE is under-scrutinized and indexes intelligence, compliance and so on. Indeed, today's populace seems to believe that people who speak languages other than English and dialects other than middle-class ones simply shouldn't, or at the very least, they should hurry up and speak middle-class English! And if they don't speak middle-class varieties, it is their fault and they should suffer the consequences. As Dell Hymes notes in his preface to Charles Ferguson and Shirley Heath's 1981 text, *Language in the USA*:

To be sure, it may sometimes seem that there are only two kinds of language in the United States, good English and bad. Only one kind, if some people are to be taken literally: English surrounded by something else that cannot be called "English," or even perhaps "language." (Hymes, 1981: v)

Because the social and political context outside of the African American community stigmatizes AAE, how members of all social classes exercise their language choices is interpreted in terms of cultural and class values, advantages and educational privilege. While the middle class may be socialized with both GE and AAE, the working class and poor have less chance of opting out of AAE since GE may be more productive in specific environments like church, school and the media and so on. It is because of the uneven language socialization of GE within the working class, coupled with dominant society's reification of it, that GE usage becomes a symbol that indexes a speaker's desire to distance him or herself from African American culture.

Good grammar and bad attitude

In light of society's reverent attitude toward GE and condescending attitude toward AAE, it is important to explore how the speech community addresses and reframes these attitudes within its own ecology. Questions concerning the language "legitimacy" of African Americans who seek citizenship rights have been a recurring issue in all segments of American society (Frazier, 1968; Mitchell-Kernan, 1972a; Winfrey, 1987). Yet, as Mitchell-Kernan (1972a) demonstrates in her classic study of African American attitudes toward AAE and GE, the interplay between "good" English and AAE is extremely complex because both are considered crucial to improve life chances. Those who choose to accommodate the demands of non-African American society and use GE exclusively risk losing community membership and, as Mitchell-Kernan (1972a) warns, earning a pariah status that can lead to abuse (Fordham, 1996; Fordham and Ogbu, 1986). Indeed, there is a pejorative variety of English referred to as "talking white" that was widely discussed during the 1970s Ann Arbor Black English case.[6]

> It is not foreign for blacks to have suffered condescension from other blacks for not being able to master the "King's English." By the same token, it is in the experiences of the "good (white) English user" to have received "compliments" from whites like, "you don't talk like the rest of them," insinuating that you are different and "better" because you speak more like whites. The inability to master the language becomes equated with being "uneducated," "deprived," "disadvantaged." In other words, black is defined from its racist perspective. (Burgest, 1973: 41)

Though exclusive use of GE is disparaged, it is considered odd if one cannot speak it as a young adult. And those who are suspected of having little or no facility in GE are routinely teased. Yet it is also odd if one cannot speak AAE to some extent and without error too. Whether a person has access to the code-switching skills expected depends on the relationship between education, social class and community of language socialization. Thus, William Labov's description of linguistic insecurity (Labov 1966, 1972a) is only partially shared with members of the African American speech community: "linguistic insecurity is shown by the very wide range of stylistic variation used by lower-middle-class speakers; by their great fluctuation within a given stylistic context; by their conscious striving for correctness; and by their strong negative attitudes towards their native speech patterns" (Labov, 1972a: 117).

Since linguistic ambiguity is always an aspect of AAE, and AAE and GE systems include the expectation of choice, everyone experiences some insecurity irrespective of social class. Mono-AAE or GE speakers – those who do not have a range of stylistic variation – routinely experience linguistic insecurity because they cannot shift their variety according to the appropriate social context or topic. Those who have knowledge of both must not only consider two related and separate systems, but whether the use of one over the other signifies a negative value toward either. So in many respects, choosing dialects or being aware of dialect choice is more difficult than, yet as significant as, recognizing discourse styles. In spite of the complexity inherent in both situations, the African American community treats those who opt for one system and the comforts of linguistic respectability as an anathema.

This problematic is played out on many levels. Table 3 lists some of the folk expressions in reference to those who cannot exercise both varieties in appropriate contexts. The taxonomy in table 3 is dialectic and indexes the contextual, functional and ideological significance of what is perceived to be language choice. It suggests that linguistic insecurity

Table 3 *Contrast between GE and AAE single-dialect speakers*

General American English	African American English
devil's language	bad talk
talking white	street talk
talking like a man with paper in his hand	pimp talk
feeding sugar	country
educated fool	talking smack
no common sense	smooth talk
smart mouth	

develops around when to consider questions of loyalty versus social context. It suggests that to use GE exclusively is to have no involvement in the black community. The inability to use GE is also stigmatized and exclusive AAE usage suggests that a person has no involvement with education, employment and so on. That is why arguments regarding either variety are often fraught with misunderstanding.

Because GE is a political sign that can imply rejection of African American culture, defending the variety is problematic if one's support of African American culture is questionable. Many African American scholars and community activists have participated in the public debate regarding AAE and GE usage. They often appear on local and national radio and television and publish in newspapers and popular, theoretical and research journals, especially where the subject of education is concerned.[7] Yet, only those who celebrate African heritage and identity escape stinging criticism and have the "authority" to talk about the politics of its use without being castigated for "trading" identities. And those without a proven track record carefully, openly, meticulously and unambiguously state their position on AAE. For example, in *The African American Guide to Better English*, Garrard O. McClendon (1993) directly discusses his view of both AAE and GE usage: "This book was in no way created to try to insult or diminish the speech patterns of African-Americans. This book's purpose is to inform the Black community of the devices used against it to perpetuate the misuse and disuse of language" (p. v).

McClendon's chapter titles include "A Time and Place for Black English," which explains the importance of middle-class English for job opportunities. "The Glossary" focuses on words that the author believes should not be used outside of a black context.[8] In the chapter, "The Origin of Black English," McClendon describes AAE as resulting from slave masters' attempts to restrict communication between slaves. He calls this the language restriction construction (LRC). There are also chapters titled: "The Good and Evil in Rap Music's Language" and "Black Leaders' Use of Standard English." The book's conclusion includes the following statement: "The average African American child wants success. What we as adults have to do is to identify what success is and to show children what steps and measures have to be taken to achieve this goal" (p. 57).

Language, race and social class

As the above discussion of the cultural and political significance of AAE and GE suggests, both social class and racial discrimination affect the larger society's attitude toward AAE. Unfortunately, many sociolinguistic studies of the 1970s described speech community membership and style in ways that incorporated the dominant culture's indexing of AAE as a sign of poverty and – at times – ignorance. By doing so they suggested that there is no cultural significance in AAE and considered the middle-class usage they did discover to be marginal. In only a few cases were generational differences, social context, group, individual variation and African American systems of class and status distinctions considered within the overall analysis. AAE usage became synonymous with hip, male, adolescent, street and gang-related speech. The alternative – non-vernacular speech – was described as weak, lame or white (Labov, 1972a).[9] According to the sociolinguistic paradigm, those who did not fit the ideal of the vernacular speaker were not African American enough to belong to the speech community or – to put it in modern terms – not the "authentic Other."[10]

The problem that arose cannot be overstated.[11] Many sociologists and policymakers like Massey and Denton (1993) have used the vernacular description to rationalize what amounts to racist practices in hiring and education. They reason that continued reliance on and use of AAE is due to racial isolation and segregation. Their logic is that since whites believe that AAE usage reflects ignorance, criminality and immorality, African Americans should not use it.

Employers make frequent use of language as a screening device for blue-collar jobs, even those that involve little or no interaction with the public. They assume that people who speak Black English carry a street culture that devalues behaviors and attitudes consistent with a "good worker," such as regularity, punctuality, dependability, and respect for authority. (Massey and Denton, 1993: 165)

Massey and Denton as well as Wilson (1987) suggest that the use of GE would remove one more barrier to employment discrimination. But this is an extremely simplistic argument about the function of language in society. Somehow, it is disingenuous to suggest that the problem of blue-collar discrimination and its social and economic origins and elements is related to the use of AAE rather than employers' bigotry. This is especially true since employers routinely address their own regional and ethnic linguistic biases in hiring. That blacks, in particular, should be required to speak a prestige dialect in order to work in a factory should cause great alarm! In fact, these formulations of the relationship between language and employment opportunity often reflect sociological debates over the relationship between class and racial consciousness in the African American community.

Because the African American community has historically been denied access to traditional indicators of the middle and upper class – e.g. housing, employment, occupation – how the community assigns class and status remains open to question. An analytical problem emerges because in order for class differences to exist, "a population must differentiate to a minimum extent with respect to an attribute before that attribute can serve as a basis for invidious distinction" (Glenn, 1963: 665).[12] Prior to the 1980s, the majority of African Americans who earned sizeable incomes did so outside of typical middle-class occupations (Drake and Cayton, 1945). This inequity, based on a lack of access to life chances, meant that earned income did not play a significant role as a class indicator since it was secured through non-traditional means. Instead, other status indicators came into play (e.g. education). This also holds true today where affluent African Americans are often entertainers and sports figures. Thus in 1999 one of the richest African Americans on record was a hip hop performer/producer who aspired to play professional basketball (Master P).

Yet in 1978 and later in 1987, William Julius Wilson argued that in spite of the presence of race consciousness in the African American community, class consciousness is becoming more important than race in determining life chances. He argues that one consequence of the change in life chances is that the African American middle and working classes are becoming more stratified. If Wilson is correct, it would explain Labov's (1985) contention that racial integration leads to access to GE since, following Wilson's theory, middle-class African Americans lose their racial identity and take on the characteristics of middle-class whites. However, there is considerable and provocative evidence that "race matters" for the middle class too.

Dillingham (1981) argues that in an ethnically stratified society it is more feasible that subjective feelings of ethnic group or racial identification become a more powerful determinant of behavior than objective assessments of socioeconomic status. In a study of three hundred African

Americans, Dillingham (1981) found that contrary to Wilson's (1978) analysis, the higher the class of the respondent, the higher the racial consciousness. Other studies (Ginsberg, 1967; Kronus, 1970; Sampson, 1975) also report that middle-class African Americans have a positive attitude toward the lower class and continue to feel an obligation to their race due to their more "privileged" position.

In fact, the dissatisfaction of the black middle class remains a growing concern in the social sciences and popular media. Thus while Melvin Oliver and Thomas Shapiro (1997) concede the rise of the black middle class, they insist that their plight still reflects "two paychecks away from poverty" syndrome. They write: "an accurate and realistic appraisal of the economic footing of the black middle class reveals its precariousness, marginality, and fragility" (pp. 92–3). Moreover, Lawrence Bobo (1997, 1998) finds that the sense of alienation among middle-class blacks is so great that many have a detailed critique of American institutions and culture as well as various narratives and "proofs" that race remains an integral part of all black life. This is supported by political scientists including Jennifer Hochschild (1995), who writes that middle-class blacks "recognize their own mobility, they are pleased by it, but their commitment to the American dream is declining, not rising. That is an unprecedented risk to an ideology that depends so heavily on faith in its ultimate fairness and benevolence" (pp. 86–7).[13] As Cornel West attests, the black middle class respond to this racism in many ways. "The accumulative effects of the black wounds and scars suffered in a white-dominated society is a deep-seated anger, a boiling sense of rage, and a passionate pessimism regarding Americans' will to justice" (1993:18).

It is clear that many middle-class African Americans recognize the paradox of their own situation and that it is shared with urban working-class communities. In some cases, the use of AAE is one way to represent solidarity with the larger African American community and their racial consciousness. This is borne out by informal research conducted by J. Lorand Matory at Harvard University (personal communication) and John Baugh's (1992, 1999) research on African American college students' use of AAE at Stanford University. In both cases we find African American students at elite universities desperate to incorporate vernacular features of AAE in order to show solidarity and maintain social face through code switching when among the African American speech community. Baugh's analysis of hypocorrection or overgeneralization errors in AAE usage among African Americans who have learned GE natively reveals the political importance of AAE irrespective of social class. Charles DeBose (personal communication) and Arthur Spears (1988) report that in their research on language use among working- and middle-class African American adults, both AAE and GE are used in informal mixed-class conversations irrespective of the class of the speaker.

In fact, many participants in African American speech communities celebrate the lexical and linguistic creativity that often marks each generation of youth. The recognition of loyalty to AAE for diverse members of the African American community has led some to argue for the importance of both AAE and GE in relevant social contexts. But advocating code switching is only a "band aid" solution if the social and cultural implications of language use are not considered.

Code switching, style shifting and identity

Within a system of meaning where language variety indexes status and cultural loyalty, shifting between the two varieties may reflect social context, ideology, social class loyalty and disloyalty. For the purpose of this discussion, code switching can be defined as the use of linguistic and discourse systems associated with more than one language, dialect and ideology within the same speech exchange and social context.[14] Within this definition, cases of situational code switching (Blom and Gumperz, 1972) can be viewed as symbolic and indexical (Silverstein, 1985), even when one code associated with the context is employed exclusively. What is important is that the speaker has knowledge of the choice or possibility of switching, whether a switch occurs or not.

Code switching incorporates linguistic and cultural knowledge and must be learned throughout language socialization within African American cultural practices (c.f. Zentella, 1998). This socialization can occur during adulthood when those who were raised in non-African American communities and those who were socialized in extremely marginalized circumstances acquire the skills from their fluent peers (e.g. Baugh, 1992, 1999). Thus, as Heller (1993), Woolard (1998) and Zentella (1998) argue, symbolic domination (Bourdieu, 1977, 1982) does not tell the whole picture. "Code-switching becomes available as a resource for the exercise of, or resistance to, power by virtue of its place in the repertoires of individual speakers, on the one hand, and of its position with respect to other forms of language practices in circulation, on the other" (Heller, 1995:159).

Code switching in the African American speech community indexes and thus accentuates the possibility that linguistic, cultural and ideological knowledge will be targeted. It is not related to romanticized depictions of hybridity and choosing between two conflicting and often colliding worlds. Rather it is about recognizing and exercising discourses of power and representation within these worlds. Its value is linked to the extent to which it facilitates access to situations where other kinds of symbolic and material resources are distributed, and where resources have value based on the prevailing modes of organization of social life in the community and those who might exercise control (e.g. Heller, 1995: 160). In this respect, the tensions between power and solidarity alignments are bound up in identifying, constructing and dismantling borders. There are many forms of code switching within African American linguistic style. One that involves grammar I refer to as reading dialect.

Reading dialect

Reading is the name given to an African American interpretive practice discussed in detail in chapter 2. Reading dialect occurs when members of the African American community contrast or otherwise highlight what they consider to be obvious contrasting features of AAE and GE in an unsubtle and unambiguous manner to make a point. The point itself may or may not be a negative one. These lexical and grammatical structures are very well known in the community and are often the focus of verbal play, humor and irony. Reading dialect often leads to new grammatical and lexical forms and is the source of many recent innovations that have emerged within urban communities involved in hip hop culture. For example, to stress a point members might say, *It's not simply that I am cool. I be cool. In fact, I been cool (a very long time)*. In the African American community, interlocutors not only consistently read the two dialects of AAE and GE but also varieties within those dialects.[15]

Reading dialect involves dialect opposition: highlighting and exploiting GE and AAE forms which members consider to be different (Morgan, 1994). When speakers employ dialect reading in interactions, they immediately signal to members that some indirect form of communication where the varieties are contrasted is in play. Since the many features of GE and AAE are shared or structurally similar, it isn't always clear to members of the African American community when one or the other is in operation. What reading dialect accomplishes is to transform the status of a lexical, prosodic, syntactic or discourse structure that could be either AAE or GE into a framework that exploits the congruities and incongruities of each system and how they impact on each other. This is achieved through the use of features or rules of AAE that are generally known and culturally marked.

Similar cases can be found for dialect opposition in syntax, prosody and discourse. For example, one can accomplish dialect opposition by responding to the greeting *what's up* with AAE *whazzup!* and *whadup!*.

Among members who use these contrasts, *whazzup* and *whadup* serve as a put-down mainly because it contrasts a hip urban African American identity with an unmarked one. Similarly, on a black TV situation comedy,[16] an editor returned a writer's article and explained: "It needs work." He responded, "How much?" She responded with "A lot!" When he asked, "How much is a lot?" The editor responded with "How about beaucoup?" (pronounced / bu:ku / and / bo:ku /), a term adapted from French and used throughout the African American community as a quantifier to mean a tremendous amount as in *There were beaucoup people at the party!* These examples reveal that many performances of dialect opposition index AAE and GE as socially constructed. Speakers often use dialect opposition to key conversational signifying episodes.

Reading dialect indicates that members of the African American community have knowledge of AAE and GE dialect systems as well as a sense that the two systems are distinct. While the two dialects certainly overlap in grammar and lexicon and while members of the AAE community play on that overlap to create ambiguity, they also are constantly keying into what distinguishes the two dialects in order to interpret what is going on at any one interactional moment and thereby act on it. Members search for distinct forms and functions and contrast them with their possible linguistic counterparts in the other dialect and constantly make use of the possible meanings implied by the particular forms and functions chosen.

It is clear that mono-GE speakers do not share this awareness of dual dialect forms, meanings and functions. For example Rickford (1975), Spears (1982) and Baugh (1984, 1999) report that GE speakers overwhelmingly misinterpret utterances containing AAE forms such as stressed *been*, the modal semi-auxiliary *come* and the predicate adverb *steady* as in

1. Hey, I *bin* know his name! (Rickford, 1975: 172)
2. He come walking in here like he owned the damn place. (Spears, 1982: 852)
3. He steady be tellin 'em how to run they lives.

In the first example, stressed *been* (*bin*) refers to the remote past and can be written as:

1a. I have known his name for a long time, and still do.

In the second case, Spears argues that *come* is not a motion verb but functions as a modal semi-auxiliary to signal the indignation of the speaker. In fact, according to Baugh (1988, 1999), *come* functions to convey personal observation and opinion. Thus sentence 2 can be written as:

2a. I don't like him walking in here like he owned the damn place.

Spears uses the notion of camouflage to explain why GE speakers and researchers alike misread these forms:

It is the form itself which provides the camouflage, and the meaning which is being camouflaged...Word camouflage, then, has to do with meaning and function: they are camouflaged by the form that bears them. In the case of syntactic camouflage, meanings are camouflaged not only by the form that bears them, but also by their syntactic environment. (1982: 869)

John Baugh (1984, 1999) considers *steady* as a predicate adverb to show intensity, consistency and continuity. Thus the third example can be written as:

3a. He's always telling them how to run their lives.

What makes these forms camouflaged is, first, they may not be detectable without previous socialization in AAE. Second, speakers of AAE may not realize that GE speakers don't share this usage. In many respects these camouflaged forms represent the structural adhesive of the counter-language. They may also represent instances of AAE grammaticalization.

Grammaticalization

Grammaticalization is central to understanding AAE because it relies on the examination of the boundaries between grammatical categories, and the interdependence of structure and use (Hopper and Traugott, 1993). The process of grammaticalization, where new meanings are linked to grammatical structure, can result from vernacular varieties that affect other varieties as word meanings and/or grammatical categories are rearranged (Wolfram and Schilling-Estes, 1998). That is, as Salikoko Mufwene (1991) argues, grammars are not monolithic. In situations where there are prominent dialect and language differences, systems overlap and language norms (as rules) are based on the notion that they are not identical. Needless to say, not all instances of language innovation lead to grammaticalization. Many interesting changes occur that have nothing to do with it. Rather, grammaticalization should be seen as where innovation can lead – as both a new end and new beginning for a form which has undergone (or is undergoing) structural change, and stabilized.

Features of African American English

There are numerous linguistic features attributed to African American English and there are many excellent reviews of the characteristics of AAE (e.g. Baugh, 1983a, 1999; Butters, 1989; Labov, 1972a; Mufwene et al., 1998; Rickford, 1999; Schneider, 1989). Many of the phonological and

Table 4 *AAE reductions, deletions and alternatives*

Word-initial position:
1. *thr-* as *th-*: *through/thew*
   Word-final position:
2. final consonant clusters: *grasp/gras*; *risk/ris*
3. final *-ng* as *-n*: *walking/walkin*
4. voiced *-th* as *-d* or *-v*: *mouth /mouf*
5. voiceless *-th* as *-t* or *-f*: *birth/birf*
6. deletion or vocalization of *l* after a vowel: *told/ tol*; *roll/ro*
7. deletion or vocalization of *r* after a vowel: *more/mo*
8. realization of syllable-initial *str-* as *skr-*: *strength -> skrength*
9. realization of *-ing* as *-ang*: *king -> kang*
   Tense, mood and aspect:
10. absence of copula *is/are*: *She is the president/She the president.*
11. use of invariant *be* for habitual action: *He is clowning all the time/He be clowning*
12. use of invariant *be* for future: *She will be a super star/She be a super star.*
13. use of *done* to emphasize the completive nature of a task: *He done did it now!*
14. use of *had* to mark the simple past: *They had went to the store.*
15. absence of third-person verbal *-s*. *She work hard.*
    Nouns and pronouns:
16. absence of plural: *That cost five dollar.*
17. absence of possessive *-s*: *They took Terry money.*
18. use of *y'all* and *they* to mark second-person plural and third person possessive: *It's they money.*
19. multiple negation: *She don't know nothing.*
20. appositive or pleonastic pronouns: *My principal, he crazy.*
21. negative inversion: *Ain't nobody ever give me nothing.*
22. direct questions without inversions: *Why I can't have none?*

---

syntactic features and lexical principles associated with AAE have been reported from as early as 1865 (DeFrantz, 1979). While these features are seldom discussed in relation to each other, they do represent a system of variation within and across grammatical phrases. Some features generally attributed to AAE pronunciation, phonology and grammar, and that appeared in the Philadelphia data, are listed in table 4.

Data from the thirty-one young adults involved in the Philadelphia program were analyzed to answer three questions.[17] First, what is a general description of AAE for these speakers? Secondly, what are the most consistent features of AAE usage – especially regarding the vernacular? Finally, are there any extra-linguistic factors that may influence the use of AAE or GE?

Although all of the features listed in table 4 appeared in interviews, interactions and oral reading data from Philadelphia, some features occurred categorically, others appeared to be governed by structural constraints while still others were contextually constrained. The Philadelphia group also varied across speakers in terms of what features were more variable or categorical. For example, it was common to find *ng* as *n* (no. 3), and *r*-less (Baratz, 1973; Burling, 1973; Labov, 1972a; Luelsdorff, 1975) or non-rhotic (Mufwene, 1994) pronunciation in word-final position producing [*mo*] for *more* or before a consonant producing [hʌd] for *hard* (no. 7).[18] Many other phonological features attributed to AAE were also found throughout the data. The overall usage and variation of the speakers reflect the current literature on AAE and will not be discussed in detail. Instead, two examples of participants' usage of AAE and GE will be reviewed.

Philadelphia's Precious Jones and Maceo Brown

Maceo Brown was twenty-nine and Precious Jones was twenty-five years old at the time of the interview. Their pattern of usage is representative of the Philadelphia group. That is, most speakers used some features of AAE though the frequency of usage as well as particular features varied widely. AAE methods of pluralization, possessive marking and verbal agreement are variable for Precious Jones, Maceo Brown and all the Philadelphia participants.[19] Ms. Jones uses some of the linguistic features in both highly monitored and less monitored interactions. When reading a word list she deleted final consonants on seven out of thirteen occasions (54 percent).[20] Overall, when reading the list and text she represented every word reduction, deletion and alternative reported in the literature except one. Ms. Jones was the only participant who did not employ the *-ing/-ang* alternative (no. 9). In all other speakers, it was nearly categorical (99 percent) for single-syllable nouns (*king/kang*) and none of the speakers pronounced *bring* as *brang* when reading the word list.[21]

When reading an excerpt from "To Hell With Dying," a short story by Alice Walker about a feisty older man adored by children and too alive to die, Ms. Jones omitted the past tense *-ed* nine times (31 percent), out of twenty-nine possible occurrences. Surprisingly – and in contrast to the formal reading of the word list – Ms. Jones didn't delete final consonants when telling the following story about her sister-in-law and used past-tense verbs 100 percent of the time in her interaction.[22] That is, if she monitored her pronunciation during the formal exercises (oral reading and word list), she did not during her narrative. She enjoyed the story she read and her theory about appropriate usage of GE and AAE may have been more sensitive to the content than the particular literacy or research activity.

Precious Jones uses both AAE and GE in her interview. She had two occurrences of third-person verbal -*s* absence (lines 7 and 27).[23] She did not use the invariant form of *be* though she deleted the copula on three occasions. She also used simple past *had* three times (lines 37 and 39). Her use of past *had* with the irregular verbs *came* and *got* aligns her usage with that in other studies and also provides some insight into the grammaticalization of *got* discussed in chapter 5. Line 24 – *I mean she been there before* – includes a case of unstressed *been*. Finally, Ms. Jones used the appositive at least five times in her interview (e.g. line 6: *grandmother, she sick.*).

Precious Jones

1 PJ: What was the story about? It was about – about, ((*comments on story*))
2   um Jesus – I mean a preacher oh, oh oh oh oh oh – tell you a story?
3 Int.: Yes
4 PJ: Oh! Tell YOU a story about my job, my kids, family. My family – We
5   have grandmother, my grandfather that I live with. And I, they um – they
6   old now. My grandmother, she sick. We think she has cancer ya know –
7   'cause she know – and uh my grandfather – I don't know what to tell you
8   about him [except] that they wonderful people ma'am.
9 Int.: Do you have any sisters?
10 PJ: No I don't have any sisters. I have two brothers. My olderest brother, he's
11   married to a blind girl – yeah. They met in college – Craterville College.
12   and uh she – she was in her first year there – no her second year when he
13   met her. Then after they finished they went four years. Then she grad-
14   uated before he did and then they got married after he finished college.
15   Now she's a wonderful person. I love her. She's my only sister
16   now cause I didn't have any sister. She – well she doesn't get around really
17   now cause my brother, he takes her around but in college she walked
18   around by herself. No cane or nothing! When she comes to my house when
19   just walks around. She knows where the foods at. She go up the step –
20   everything. She just – she's a gem! She took care of my son when I went
21   back to work. He was eight weeks old til he was three and she did a
22   wonderful job. She cook and clean. She does everything. I think she kind
23   of senses – because while we was at ah – my brother's father we went to
24   their house. And she had never been there before. I mean she been there
25   before yu know but she didn't go there regularly. And ya know she just
26   walked around. She can – like sense things that is in her way – you know –
27   she just walk around it. 'Cause ya know I would like take her hand, and
28   ya know guide her, but she seems like she doesn't want that – ya know. She
29   wants to do things on her own,
30 Int.: Was she born blind?
31 PJ: No since when she turned thirteen, she had the eye disease, glaucoma.
32   My mother has that too now but my mother is being treated for it. My
33   sister-in-law was younger. They never had ya know – yeah – and my
34   mother she just got it as she got older.
35 Int.: Did you say thirteen?
36 PJ: Yeah thirteen yeah and then she went to college though. That's the thing

37   she did good. And she was supposed to work. She had came to college.
38   She went to Drake University and she was supposed to work ya know
39   after that. But she didn't go cause my brother, he had got, he had got a
40   good job and she didn't really have to work. um hum Ain't she lucky>? I
41   wish it happen to me like that. huh? yeah He's a good person. I love him.
42   He's really good. He had you know – changes but now he's doing good
43   now

Mr. Brown's usage of AAE and GE is similar to that of Ms. Jones in that the nature of variation within formal and informal contexts does not represent a move toward GE norms. In contrast to Ms. Jones, Mr. Brown uses nearly categorical AAE reductions, deletions and alternatives in word-final position (85 percent). When reading the Langston Hughes passage "Salvation" he pronounced final -ng as -n 42 percent of the time (table 4, no. 3). He pronounced all other word-final consonants and clusters without exception. Thus, though Mr. Brown's AAE usage includes a slightly different set of variables, he too uses nearly all of the pronunciation features listed in table 4.

However, the beginning of Mr. Brown's interview contrasts greatly with his narration. Maceo Brown does not use AAE features until he begins the extended narrative about his children. In line 43, he uses *got* instead of *have* or *have got*. He uses singular rather than plural agreement, *the two girls is very . . .*, but then corrects himself and uses plural *are*. He also uses *f* for voiceless *th* (line 46). He uses appositives three times, and marks the possessive with both *they* and *their* (lines 69 and 71). Like Ms. Jones, he uses nearly a third of the grammatical features of AAE listed in table 4.

Maceo Brown

 1 R: O.K. now tell me a story different from the last time. Give me a life
 2   experience.
 3 MB: A life experience? – man
 4 R: Let me see your ring. It's very interesting. What is it?
 5 MB: It's um
 6 R: Is it a mood ring?
 7 MB: It's more of a mood ring but it's a bio- it's a biofeedback ring
 8 R: Oh, what is it supposed to do?
 9 MB: It tells my temperature and my blood pressure and when it gets high it
10   goes to a certain color
11 R: What color is it when it's high?
12 MB: Well right – it's got to be red. It turns red orange, yellow.
13 R: Has it ever turned red before?
14 MB: Once.
15 R: Really?
16 MB: Uh-huh.

17 R: So is that accurate?
18 MB: It is accurate.
19 R: Really?
20 MB: Right now, I'm ya know – I'm real into
21 R: laid back
22 MB: yeah, comfortable
23 R: Let's see. Wow! That's interesting!.
24 MB: The blue and the purple and the green
25 R: Yeah
26 MB: It'll change
27 R: It's like an olive.
28 MB: Yeah
29 R: What does that one mean?
30 MB: Well it says I'm comfortable. You know, I'm not into a state of uh ya
31   know anger – anything like that. But um
32 R: I guess if it's all the way blue that means you're dead doesn't it?
33 MB: No, no. If it turns all the way blue around here that means your pressure is
34   up.
35 R: Oh. What's the red?
36 MB: The red means that you're in danger sign
37 R: That you're getting ready to die?
38 MB: That's what is says. It tells it by the heat and the temperature of your body.
39 R: That's interesting. So tell me something. It could be about anything you
40   want it to be.
41 MB: O.K. Let me see. Um
42 R: Tell me about your kids.
43 MB: My children? Humph. Well I got three. It's three boys and one girl, two
44   girls really. And uh – they're um – the two girls is very – they're more
45   intelligent than the boys I think. 'Cause they – they do better work in
46   school. I don't have no problem outta the girls in school bof of them uh
47   go to Montgomery School. And uh they come home, do they homework
48   and they pass they test and stuff you know. They – I think they grasp
49   things more faster than the boys do. Uh – I seen it that the boys do a lot of
50   playin and the girls – they more interested in their work. You know – they
51   uh follow and see whatever
52 R: How old are they?
53 MB: Bof of um girls are twelve
54 R.   They're twins?
55 MB: No they're not twins. But they're like a year apart
56 R: Oh so one will be thirteen
57 MB: Yeah one'll be thirteen, one just turned twelve. But the boys uh one is
58   nine and he'll be ten in June and the other one is eight and he'll be nine in
59   September of next year and the baby he's now six
60 R: So from six to almost thirteen!
61 MB: Yeah. So they uh the boys – one of them are very playful. The oldest one
62   is playful. He's constantly – he likes to be playful. But I think it's a stage
63   that adolescence is going through. And uh – he does his work. But then

64   he'll play first before he does it and it takes a longer time. The baby is the
65   one that stays up with the work cause he follows his sisters. He sees his
66   sisters, they doing the work. He does the same thing. But the two in
67   between – they uh – they rather play first before they do the work and
68   sometime they uh they really don't get they work done at all and they have
69   to wait for they mother to come in to uh help them. But they really don't
70   need the help you know. And they use the psychology to uh try to get
71   their mother to think they need help. But they don't need the help once
72   she gets down to start helping them. Then they go ahead and do it
73   themselves. But um – I think children um – if you bring em up right in
74   this society to respect people and you know – go to school and learn uh –
75   you don't have any problem of em playing hooky from school and stuff
76   like that then. Uh like when I was comin' up it was different. My father,
77   he stayed on top of us. But he didn't stay on top of us for the right things
78   and uh school wasn't more – as important as it is stressed today you know.
79   Uh – I think if my father had stayed on top of me the way I stay on top of
80   them as far as the homework and thing – I might have made me a different
81   person. But then again you know my life is different from their life and
82   I'm gonna make sure that their life is better than mine.
83 R: Thank you

At first glance, these two excerpts may suggest that neither Precious Jones nor Maceo Brown code switch or read dialect. What these excerpts show is actually normal usage for lower-middle-class and working-class African Americans for whom both varieties are resources. That is, whether we consider research on vernacular AAE as age graded or representative of language socialization in progress, once adolescence is passed, adults make use of both AAE and GE. In these cases, as with much of the Philadelphia data, language use was not indexical. In fact, as is shown in the following chapters, switching and reading dialect occur frequently in conversations with friends and speech community members. The Philadelphia data suggest that theories of AAE and GE usage may be heavily weighted toward what is being said, who is participating in the interaction and lastly, the type of speech activity (see also Rickford, 1999). That is, Precious Jones and Maceo Brown use GE in their interactions when they have something to describe.

Ms. Jones uses minimal AAE features as she explains the life of her blind sister-in-law and Mr. Brown uses GE to explain how his mood ring functions to register his blood pressure. In contrast, both Ms. Jones and Mr. Brown seem to read the passage and word list because they have been asked to do so. In fact, Ms. Jones once confided that she thought that I had them read to see whether they could read – and I asked them to provide a narrative to see if they could talk! This suggests that Precious Jones and Maceo Brown may employ different symbols to represent a range of social and linguistic formality and informality. In fact, Baugh

(1999: 19) supports this argument in his depiction of formality registers among all social classes of GE and AAE speakers.

Although speakers may not be aware of all grammatical relationships and systems in their repertoire, by the time they're adults they know that there are different contexts for usage and forms of AAE. They also know the politics of language use and attempt to adjust accordingly. As the following chapters illustrate, urban youth and adult women employ their understanding of how language mediates race, culture, class and gender among themselves and under the glaring spotlight and scrutiny of cultural critics.

4   When women speak: how and why we enter[1]

I have always marveled at the "black woman laugh." This is not a hysterical or deep laugh that ripples through your body. I mean the laughter that sits ready at the surface to comment on the irony and hypocrisy witnessed daily in black life. In black women, this laugh is an audible breath that escapes as what Irving Goffman has called a response cry – a ritualized act and dramatization that displays alignment with events and others (1981: 100). It occurs as a surprise even to the speaker, as though she didn't know that opening her mouth would reveal what lay beneath the layers of her memory and longing. I have heard it many times. It was there after a researcher asked Rebecca, a young, pregnant black woman in Los Angeles, how she felt about her health care. Before her car broke down, it took only twenty minutes for Rebecca to get to the doctor's office. Now she has to wait for two buses and it takes two hours to get there. Then, after sitting in the waiting room for another two hours, she spends five minutes with the doctor. To the question do you like to visit the doctor Rebecca responded, "Yes, I like my doctor (*laugh*). He's good (*laugh*)."

What is this laugh about? I also heard it in a conversation when two women in Chicago talked about their trip to New Orleans and marveled at what they referred to as "the beautiful, wonderful and courteous black men." When they returned five years later, they found that the black community was literally gone with no remaining trace – no monument to those who had lived there – nothing. In its place was a new gated community and fashionable stores.

ARTHEL: When I went back um this year Judy to the world's fair, I didn't see NONE of those men. (*laughter*)
JUDY: You mean, so they're gone from there now?
ARTHEL: They're GONE honey.
JUDY: We don't have ANYthing on the FACE of the earth?
ARTHEL: That's right.

I've also heard it when, without warning in the middle of a conversation, women use the voice of slave masters as commentary to describe feelings

84

of loss, betrayal and frustration. Judy and Arthel use it when they talk about how black women are expected to be grateful to get a job and not complain when they are not compensated:

JUDY: You know, well the – "You know my slave drank the milk. She's dead."
  (*laughter*)
JUDY: "No sense in you taking her to the hospital! She's dead!"
ARTHEL: (*laughs*) Right

It appeared again in Mississippi when a retired schoolteacher talked about life during the civil rights movement. Her school was located near the home of slain civil rights leader, James Meredith. Mrs. Snowden laughed as she recalled that her principal regularly yelled over the intercom "Hit the floor!" to warn of home-made bombs being thrown into the school by the Ku Klux Klan. Others have heard it too. This laugh also appears in countless novels of great writers of black women's lives. Sometimes it locates a fool – but mostly it locates the truth, even if for one quick second. When you hear "the black woman laugh," it's never about anything funny.

Language and gender: "no crystal stair"

During the 1970s, research on African American language and discourse seldom included women's voices. Most of the data gathered were from boys and men involved in street life and included the philosophy that accompanies the world of gangs, pimps and men hanging around on corners and in bars.[2] Scholarly references to the African American women involved in these men's lives, as well as the men's reported philosophies about women, set the stage for a one-dimensional and scathing generalization of black women that persists today. Even more troubling was the linguistic description of black women as surly and flagrant that actually mirrored sociology's relentless attack on black women's role in the black family (Glazer and Moynihan, 1963). For example, in his Philadelphia folklore project *Deep Down in the Jungle*, Roger Abrahams (1970) described black women as the dominant and dominating force in the black home. Yet, he did not include them in his folklore collection, remarking that they refused to participate. He then attributed the rise of the male gang world to black men's rejection of what he believed to be female dominance in the home (1970: 31).[3]

Other reports of African American women's language use include comments about their roles and motives in encounters. They are often described as linguistically conservative; the "real" target or foil and often the audience, observer and supporter of male signifying games;

and willing collaborators in street encounters (e.g. Abrahams, 1962; Kochman, 1972b; Labov, 1972a). Many of the women mentioned in Thomas Kochman's (1981) influential and insightful work on black discourse styles, *Black and White Styles in Conflict*, are described as sexual predators and the accepting object of lascivious talk. Alarmingly, some Black Nationalist theorists (e.g. Kunjufu, 1986; Dandy, 1991; Majors and Billson, 1992) seem to concur when they suggest that signifying and snapping (described in chapter 2) function as a way for adolescent males to cope with overbearing black women. These theories of the emasculating, loud and sullen black woman were routinely introduced as fact and are even more damning when contrasted with those emerging in the social sciences and white feminist scholarship. In contrast to stereotypes of the dominant, submissive and subversive, emasculating, uncaring black woman, feminist psychology and linguistic theory have stereotyped middle-class white women as indiscriminate "people pleasers," concerned with harmony, being accepted and so on in life and in conversation.

The consistently negative characterization of black women in relation to black men and white women has always been perplexing. After all, black women endured slavery and racism along with black men and emerged as workers with progressive views on families and women's role at home and in society. It stands to reason that language scholars would be interested in all aspects of their use of language. Unfortunately they weren't. It wasn't until 1971 that Claudia Mitchell-Kernan produced one of the first works that did not describe urban African American women mainly in relation to men and as aggressive, domineering and emasculating. Her rich ethnography demonstrated that women participate in conversational signifying (1971: 65–106) and employ linguistic practices similar to those of men. Moreover, her detailed analysis of African American language and culture in Oakland did not give exclusive attention to adolescents. Yet Mitchell-Kernan's work received unprecedented criticism, not because of its scholarship, but because of her own gender, race and presumed class background. Sadly, many of the progressive men involved in resolving some of the bigotry and racism associated with African American culture and language were not willing to have women represented in the scholarly discussion. In an influential review of her study, she was reprovingly described as a young, attractive, middle-class black woman whom black men were willing to talk to because they desired her (Kochman, 1973: 969, 970)! In a vindication of Mitchell-Kernan's research, Henry Louis Gates Jr.'s highly acclaimed work *Signifying Monkey* (1988) relied on Mitchell-Kernan's description of signifying as a foundation for his theory of African American discourse.[4]

The marginalization of African American women in language research has not been about gender exclusively. Since language is a social act, research on language constitutes social and cultural production influenced by issues of race, sexuality, class and power. What seems to bias scholarly research on African Americans is how black women are viewed in relation to others, especially black men and white women – how their identities are assigned as part of a system of dichotomies rather than discovered as something much more complex. In this respect, the exclusion and marginalization of black women is not limited to linguistic research. In the legal system too, according to Kimberlé Crenshaw (1992), race, class and gender consistently intertwine in African American women's lives (see also Giddings, 1984; Hull Scott and Smith, 1982). Crenshaw refers to this tripartite identity as intersectionality. In reviewing legal cases involving race, class and gender, Crenshaw found that black women were either excluded from participation or forced to choose one aspect of discrimination. That is, black women who sue employers for sexual harassment can seldom include white female workers in their suits. Similarly, they cannot include black men in racial-discrimination cases.

It is even unclear whether black women can lay claim to their literate voices among white feminists. Though Sojourner Truth's 1851 Akron, Ohio, speech ("Ain't [Ar'n't] I a Woman") is considered one of the first reflecting black feminist thought, the authenticity of its most popular version has been called into question (Painter, 1994; Harris, 1996). This is because there is substantial evidence that Truth was semi-literate and heavily edited by suffragists, and that her own words may not have been considered her own property. Thus African American women's issues are hyper-marginalized and considered typical neither of all women's issues (because the women who face them are black) nor of black issues (because the blacks who face them are women). It is not surprising, then, that all linguists whether they include, marginalize, or fetishize black women always, at some level, take a position on this situation.

The position taken here is that African American women participate in culture at all levels including the development of language norms, the introduction of innovations, and the use of all varieties of AAE. Black men and women are not segregated and influence each other throughout their lifetime. Moreover, women's contributions are most apparent in cultural settings where they are social actors – in places, that is, where their identity as women and as black women is neither questioned nor marginalized.

The issue of African American women's identity, and women's identity in general, is shrouded in postmodernist discussions that are seldom based on the choices and challenges of everyday life. In fact, ethnographic and linguistic descriptions are often summarily dismissed as essential-ist if they do not apply to all cultures and to all issues of globalization. Stuart Hall critiques this practice when he applauds feminists' rejection of the Cartesian and the sociological subject: "feminism challenged the notion that men and women were part of the same identity – 'Mankind' – replacing it with the question of sexual difference" (1995: 611). While this description may suit Western academic feminism, it only begins to address the complex ways women throughout the world (and in the West itself) experience and theorize their identity as women.

The majority of black women, after all, are workers who also have authority at home – a reality still unrecognized in white feminist politi-cal agenda. Thus Judith Butler's admonition that "reading identities as they're situated and formed in relation to one another means moving beyond the heuristic requirement of identity itself" (1995: 446) is appro-priate. This is especially true given American feminists' defining moments of gender and race in the black community during the mid 1990s: the Clarence Thomas Senate hearing and O. J. Simpson's murder trial. Both cases heightened awareness that race and gender are not interchangeable concepts for black women but rather fused and simultaneous. Still, it was painful to see the contortions black women were willing to engage in to find a reasonable position as white feminists hissed that these issues had nothing to do with race and black men scowled that they had nothing to do with patriarchy. Yet these events are significant not because they illustrate a racial split within feminism and a feminist split over fight-ing racism, but because they forced everyone to juggle issues of racial and sexual discrimination in reality rather than theory. Notwithstand-ing the resulting acrimony, white feminists and feminists of color have a great deal in common. As bell hooks (1990, 1992), Kamala Visweswaran (1994), Dorinne Kondo (1997) and others challenge, feminist theory must be situated at home, and a place we have been before but never really experienced. To explore this place is crucial, for the intersections of these factors greatly affect linguistic analysis in general and descrip-tions of language use among African Americans, women, and African American women in particular.

The misrepresentation of African American women in sociolinguistics resulted from a narrow interpretation of vernacular language. The study of the vernacular, the ordinary language of a people, implies analytic fo-cus on language use in everyday activities and among social actors living in the speech community. Yet as discussed in chapter 3 and above, many descriptions of African American speech have been based on data from adolescent boys (cf. Morgan, 1994a; Mufwene, 1992a). The focus on boys is problematic at several levels. It does not take into consideration that language socialization is underway. It does not acknowledge and study others in the community. It simultaneously characterizes young, urban male speech as virulent and outside of "normal" speech. The result is that AAE is stigmatized by dominant society, while in linguistic study it is equal to all dialects – including standard ones. This characterization renders it as a male variety and leads to generalizations and stereotypes across academic disciplines. The following critical discussion and analysis of African American women's language and cultural practice across generations is not an attempt to address previous omissions. Rather, it is seen as an effort to consider African American women's language within their daily lives and practices with each other as they deal with their race, gender, class and sexuality.[5]

Girls' language play

As discussed in chapter 2, at an early age, girls learn that they must traverse through ambiguous conversations and listen through and between adult indirection in order to get all of the message(s). They socialize each other and learn that a girl who talks about another girl behind her back risks being labeled an instigator. Unlike her male peer who plays mainly signifying games, a girl cannot redeem herself during the next day's play. Instead, she must undergo an elaborate waiting game and reconciliation session before reestablishing herself among her peers. Goodwin's (1980, 1990, 1992) analysis of he-said-she-said disputes among African American girls illustrates the elaborate lengths to which participants are willing to go in order to determine who said what behind someone's back. During these disputes the role or motive of the instigator is not generally investigated by the offended party (Goodwin, 1992), who works to maintain or reestablish her social face by telling narratives projecting her own future action in response to instigating stories.

Goodwin outlines three principal stages plus initializing event in the he-said-she-said accusation sequence: confrontation, reporting and offense as shown in figure 2.

Barbara to Bea:	They say y'all say I wrote *every*things over there.	
Bar→Bea	Barbara speaks to Bea	4 Confrontation
Ker→Bar	about what Kerry told Barb	3 Reporting
Bea→Ker	that Bea told Kerry	2 Offense
Bar→Bea	about Barbara's writing in Bea's presence	1
Ker	about Kerry	

Figure 2 Goodwin's four-stage accusation pattern (Goodwin, 1990: 204)

Younger girls maintain social face by demonstrating that if someone is suspected of talking about another girl behind her back, the offended party will investigate the action and then confront the offending party. This response is expected; as Goodwin (1992: 187) explains, "The goal of the instigator's storytelling is to elicit a statement from the offended party which leads to her confronting the offending party."

Instigating

As girls get older, however, they shift their focus to include the intentions of the instigator and other participants as "trouble stirrers." As young adults, girls have learned how to listen and maintain their social face when accusing or being accused of talking about someone. What they must accomplish as young women is to determine not only who said what, but the motives of the presumed intermediary and messenger. That is, they learn how to deconstruct the ambiguity around interaction that includes speaker and audience, co-authorship and participants. They engage in a series of intentionality checks and balances and elaborate and extended talk and negotiation. Moreover, talking about someone behind her back takes on a new seriousness: the activity is not simply gossip but rumor. In the African American speech community, when a rumor achieves widespread audience discussion and assessment, it is often treated as fact, even when it is not believed to be truthful (cf. Turner, 1993).[6] That is, it becomes a fact of discourse within the social fabric. And because a rumor also signals a loss of social face, its target must defend her honor.

So by the time girls have become teenagers, they have a significantly different focus on the instigator in he-said-she-said events. Young African American women treat talking behind another's back with the same seriousness as a capital offense. Before the alleged offending party is confronted, the accused party must prove that the intermediary who reported the offense is not simply an instigator. Moreover, friends should not be co-authors of the rumor or participate as hearers or overhearers. When the offending party is ultimately confronted, she may avoid physical confrontation if she admits to starting the rumor and apologizes or if she convinces the offended party that her intentions were misunderstood. Often the offending party admits to making the incriminating remark but does not apologize, or she refuses to admit that she said anything, although others report that she did.

Because teenage instigating episodes focus on social face, they often occur with audiences or overhearers present. Thus it is a co-constructed event with the offended party attempting to determine both intentionality and guilt. Instigating events are therefore about participants and occurrences of talk as intermediary, as well as about what was allegedly said by whom. It is about the truth. It is about lies and insults and loss of social face. These events are initialized through the telling of the rumor and naming of the offender. They are resolved through some sort of social face defense. The majority of the effort is spent confronting and investigating friends. The interaction can take weeks and appears as follows.[7]

1. Initialization: a. Telling of rumor offensive about her b. Naming of offending party	C tells A that B said something
2. investigating instigator as main source	A believes C that B said something offensive about her
3. investigating instigator as co-author	A determines if C is an offender too
4. resolving that instigator is not a co-author	A believes C is not an offender
5. confronting hearers (friends) as source	A determines if her friends are co-offenders
6. investigating hearers (friends) as co-authors	A believes her friends are not co-offenders
7. confronting offending party	A confronts B in front of friends
8. offending party statement	B confirms and defends offensive statement true
9. Resolution: Social face defense	A saves face

The procedure involves determining who is telling the truth at each stage and can be halted (moved to stage 9) at any time it is determined that others have performed the offense. The offender and potential backstabber is not contacted unless everyone along the way is proven innocent of starting the rumor.

For teenagers, the event exposes and either acquits or convicts the instigator and the back stabber. Days or weeks may elapse as statements are denied or confirmed and analyzed by witnesses. The offended party's aim is to determine who started the rumor and whether the instigator is indirectly supporting the offensive statement. In the process, friendships are tested, conversational roles are assessed, and all parties become invested in proving that they were not co-authors of the offending speech event. These events can spill into classrooms and school-related activities. If it is interrupted by well-meaning teachers and counselors, the results can be disastrous. That is because the offended party is prevented from learning the truth and does not get to redeem her social face. The messenger may appear to be the true offender and unable to defend her honor through the elaborate process. To make matters worse, the offended party will not know whether she has supportive friends if she cannot resolve the rumor. Finally, the purported back-stabber has been talked about in a negative manner without the opportunity to defend herself.

The following story told by Zinzi, a twenty-year-old college student, describes an instigating episode initiated by Tyrone telling Zinzi that Sheila spread a rumor about her sleeping with a boy when both girls were in high school. This rumor was especially insulting because Zinzi was a born-again Christian. Zinzi told this story in an undergraduate class after reading Goodwin's (1990) book detailing he-said-she-said interactions. She introduced the episode amid joking from classmates (who had similar stories) that the instigator had told the truth; Zinzi then adopted a defensive posture, her head and eyes slowly rolling, and began.

```
 1  Zinzi:  And then so she thought that she was close enough to
 2          Tyrone and so Tyrone wouldn't tell me. BUT↑Tyrone
 3          being the BEST friend that he is, he's just like, "You
 4          know? Sheila is spreading ru↑mors about you. I don't know
 5          if anybody else↑ told↑ you, but you know, she saying that
 6          you and Barry been DOing things and
 7          duh↑duhduh.dahdah.dah↑" And I was just like (2) "Oh?
 8          she di:d↑ huh?" And then so I decided (2) just instead of
 9          going up in her face! cause I didn't like her anyway! instead
10          of going up in her face, that I'd go and ask my OTHer
11          friends and things like that. So I went and asked them, and
12          they were like, "Yeah, yeah, ((high-pitched, soft voice)) she
13          did tell me about that but I didn't believe her" And I'm like
14          – Uh huh, yeah, right! That's how come you didn't TELL
15          me, because you didn't BELIEVE her. Yeah (2) okay And
16          so an↑yway, when I went and confro:nted↑ her. And then I
17          just got the satisfac↑tion out of it (2) because all it took was
18          like a little↑ confrontation and
19  MM:     What did you say?
20  Zinzi:  Well I, I asked her↑ – well not ACTually ASked her – but I
21          accused↑ her↑ and I was like "Oh, so I heard that you been
22          telling ru↑mors about Barry and I."↑ And then she↑ (2) didn't
23          deny↑ it. And she was just like "It DID↑ happen." And I'm like
24          "How do you know it happened then?" So, at first↑ we were
25          talking↑ lo:w↑ and then got kind↑ of lou::d and the:n↑ since
26          this was like in front of the church↑ house. And then it was
27          like, okay (2) let's just take this ELSEwhere. And you KNOW
28          how when HIGH school kids get – just like (2) when you
29          TAKE stuff elsewhere and then EVERYBODY! FOLLOWS.
30          And then it's like (2) ALRIGHT (2) now I'm going to have to
31          fight her 'cause EVERYbody else is over here too. And then so
```

```
32              she was still talking her little SMACK LIP↑ (2) and things like
33              that. And you know (2) everybody was like "Yes you DI::D say
34              that (2) and I HEARD IT" and she was like "Yeah I DI::D say
35              it because it IS TRUE↑" And I'm just like "You DON'T know
36              NOTHING about NOTHING and dah↑dahdahdahdah↑ And
37              then soo ((sucks teeth)) that was it (2) when she just got up in
38              my face. And I could just (2) SMELL her breath↑ and FEEL
39              her spit↑ and it was just like ((claps)) tat! And it was ON
40              ((laughs)).
41 MM:          Wait a minute. No! You fought?
42 Zinzi:       Of course. ((laughs)) Like, what did you WANT me to DO?:
43              "Well that's okay you can↑ go ahead and tell rumors about me?
44              Go right ahead" ((in a soft, hypercorrect, high-pitched voice)).
45              No!
```

Girls' instigating often leads to physical confrontations, which are not viewed as a loss of face or coolness but as a logical last resort. Zinzi confirms this in lines 8 and 9, where she reports deciding to ask her friends what Sheila said instead of *going up in her face*.[8] Zinzi's story shows the development of the he-said-she-said process. It differs from Goodwin's four-stage accusation pattern (1990, 1992) and includes investigating and clearing the messenger (instigator), investigating, interrogating and clearing "so-called" friends, the offending parties, voice and resolution.[9] The sequence is as follows.

(You know? Sheila is spreading ru↑mors about you. I don't know if anybody else↑ told↑ you, but you know, she saying that you and Barry been DOing things and duh↑duhduh.dahdah.dah↑)

Ty → Zinzi	Tyrone tells the rumor	1. Initialization:
Zinzi → Ty	Zinzi asks other friends	2. Investigating Instigator/ offender/messenger
Zinzi → Ty	Zinzi confirms allegiance	3. Investigating Instigator (as co-author/audience)
Zinzi → friends	Zinzi asks other friends	4. Confronting hearers
Zinzi → friends	Zinzi finds out what friends said during offense	5. Confronting hearers (as co-author/ audience)
Zinzi → friends	Zinzi confirms friends allegiance	6. Confronting hearers (as co-author/ audience)
Zinzi → Sheila	Zinzi asks Sheila why she is lying about her	7. Confronting offending party
Sheila→ Zinzi	Sheila says it is true	8. Offending party defense
Zinzi → Sheila	Zinzi hits Sheila	9. Resolution

(And I could just (2) SMELL her breath↑ and FEEL her spit↑ and it was just like ((claps)) tat! And it was ON)

The social order is clearly in jeopardy as Zinzi canvasses her friends for their role in Sheila's conversations in lines 11 through 14. She determines who her "real" friends are and whether Tyrone's report is true by interrogating friends and bystanders. Zinzi then finds out exactly how her friends responded to Sheila. During this time, all parties focus on past, present and possible conversations with and about Sheila. Once she has established the truth, Zinzi searches for, finds and confronts the instigator. Sheila accepts responsibility for what she says (lines 22–23 and 34–35), Zinzi denies that it is true, and eventually she strikes Sheila. She explains her physical attack on Sheila by defending her right to protect herself against unfounded rumors.

While all of the above language activity is fraught with confrontations and accusations, it also illustrates the construction of social role and relationship through indirectness, cultural symbols, and audience co-construction and collaboration. Participants desperately maintain a social face and the respect that it entails. As African American girls grow into women, their expression and defense of social face appears in everyday conversations rather than ritualized routines. In fact, active participation in discourse is often based on the extent of personal involvement in the events being discussed. Signifying and instigating also occur in adult conversations, though in slightly different forms.

African American women in (inter)action

Adults maintain and often expand the level of complexity common in childhood. But they have a very different attitude about how to play with available language styles and varieties.[10] Within women's interactions instigating all but disappears and is replaced with baited and pointed indirection in conversation. Interactions are laced with conversational signifying and take into consideration the speaker's intentionality, social face and the importance of co-authorship. Thus, instead of focusing on who said something negative about another, as pre-adolescent girls do, or on who intended to start a confrontation, as teenagers do, women support a speaker's right to be present to represent her own experience. This right is fiercely protected, for it provides the conditions for the more fundamental right that women and men should be allowed to interpret their own experiences. Yet adult women's social face is even more delicately constructed because it is continually challenged and tested by the audience.

Women operate with two dialogic styles, "behind your back," and "to your face," as represented by the statement "I wouldn't say anything behind your back that I wouldn't say to your face." These statements are regularly heard in the black community. They automatically challenge someone's social face and can halt he-said-she-said or instigating attempts.[11] A woman who makes such a statement is viewed as standing up for what she believes in and says. Not surprisingly then, interactions about people who are not present are considered tactless and divisive. In this case talking about someone behind her back does not mean that the speaker says something derogatory, but that the teller's intentionality or actual words do not have the benefit of co-authorship, and as a result the interaction may be misunderstood. The "behind your back/in your face" dichotomy stipulates that intentionality is socially constructed and anyone who subverts this construction intends to deprive others of their discourse rights.

In fact, women are less likely to participate in any elaborate ritual to determine if someone said something about them. Instead, their inter-actions and narratives are laden with a baited and pointed indirectness and complex and non-ritualized versions of signifying more common to males (see chapter 2). Thus one must be aware of local cultural signi-fiers in order to determine that she has been targeted. One must also be aware of reading dialect (chapter 3) and the beliefs and attitudes indexed through AAE and GE contrasts. In fact, participants must be aware of all cultural signifiers as well as detailed references that are often exophoric and discovered – if at all – well into the conversation.

Conversational signifying

The following conversational segment is illustrative. Participants include three related women who grew up together: Ruby (a jazz musician, age seventy-eight), who does not speak in this segment; Baby Ruby (a retired prison guard, age sixty-three); and Judy (a retired data-entry worker, age sixty-three). Ruby and Judy are sisters and Baby Ruby is their niece. Baby Ruby is not happy that she is still called by her childhood name, and she is not happy that Ruby and Judy are her aunts, a fact she laments to anyone who will listen. Also present are Judy's six daughters (including me). Other than my attempts at questioning, no daughters participate in the conversation, because for African American women and girls, mere presence during a conversation does not authorize participation.

```
1 MM:  NUMBER ONE uh – the First! question is:
2      (.)
3      now: in terms of growing up: right. you two were born
4      (.)
5      same year? right
6      (.)
7 BR:  =Six months apart and I'm in [I'm
```

```
 8 Judy:                              [And she NEVER let me forget
 9                                    it.=
10 MM:  = ((laughs))
11       (.)
12 BR:   Right
13       (.)
14 BR:   [But I
15 Judy: [She's SIX months older than I am
16       (.)
17 BR:   But that's the aunt.
18       (.)
19 Judy: And I AM her aunt.
20       (.)
21 BR:   And I:: don't like it.
22       (.)
23 Judy: And I:: don't care =
24 MM:  =((laughs))
25       (.)
26 Judy: I am STILL the aunt
27       (.)
28 MM:  NOW: you have to understand we never knew::
29       (.)
30       that – you were her – she's your aunt
31       (.)
32 BR:   [YOU – you's
33 MM:  [WE WERE AL:WAYS:! confused?
34       (.)
35       Yeah we – we were like what's the reLA:tionship
36       (.)
37 BR:   ((gazes at MM)) You're KIDDIN?
38       (.)
39 BR:   That's my DAD'S si:ster ((nods head toward Judy))
40       (.) Ain't THAT disGUSTin?
41 Judy: Your bad what?
42       (.)
43 BR:   [My DA::D'S sister
44 MM:  [My DA::D'S sister
45       (.)
46 Judy: Right.
47       (.)
48 Judy: I AM her fa:ther's sister ((winks at granddaughter/camera))
49       (.)
50 Judy: My dad- father- And uh:: she- I don't know why: you all didn't
51       know it because she AL:ways sa::id: that I'm
52       [six months ol:der than you
53 BR:   [I SURE DID!
54       (.)
```

55 MM: Well YEAH- But you- Yeah- I'm six months older than you::
56   than you doesn't mean:: [that –
57 BR: [AH – DO – AND YOUR AUNTISM
58   DOESN'T GO ANYWHERE
59 Judy: [And she'd always call me (?)
60   (.)
61 Judy: She [A:Lways said it
62 BR: [CAUSE I'M THE OLDEST (.) So your auntism: is: like
63   nothing?

In "auntism," Judy and Baby Ruby offer competing perspectives on their relationship. In the process, they talk about each other, using hearers (Judy's daughters) to mimic talking about someone behind her back. Lines 1 through 14 initiate an interactional sequence in which Baby Ruby and Judy respond to my question about their being the same age, which for them is also a kinship question. This interaction quickly becomes a competition over who will tell the story: Judy overlaps Baby Ruby (line 8) and completes Baby Ruby's point while overlapping with Baby Ruby again in line 15. Beginning in line 17, Baby Ruby and Judy argue about their kinship, addressing each other and their daughters and granddaughters, who function as mock receivers and overhearers. Judy and Baby Ruby do not use direct eye contact with each other, although they do manage a few sideways glances.

Baby Ruby and Judy signify on each other by reading dialect and using mock receivers. In particular, Baby Ruby signifies through reading dialect in line 17 when she invokes the unambiguous AAE usage of the demonstrative pronoun *that* to refer to an animate entity, namely Judy, in order to convey a negative reading. In AAE *that* is frequently used to emphasize that a person is the target of signifying. In these contexts *that* is marked negatively because many members of the African American community, especially older members, interpret use of an inanimate term in reference to a black person as insulting, regardless of the speaker's race. *That* bears additional significance because many older African Americans were raised in the South where white supremacists referred to black adults as children or objects.

Baby Ruby directs her statement about Judy, *But that's the aunt*, to me (the mock receiver). Judy signifies back by also directing her comment to me and by reading dialect with the first-person GE non-contracted copula *AM* spoken loudly in line 19. *AM* is spoken as part of loud-talking, since it is noticeably louder than preceding and following utterances (cf. Mitchell-Kernan, 1972b). It thus marks the claim made in GE as authoritative: Judy *is* the aunt.

This turn also begins a series of contrasting parallel statements that are conjoined by *and* (lines 19–23), which are part of signifying because their rhythmic similarity highlights their contrasting lexical and grammatical relations. Line 17 begins the assessment dispute over the nature of the technical definition of *aunt* and the term's associated social norms. In line 21 Baby Ruby offers her subjective negative assessment of Judy's being her aunt. Judy responds with a parallel structure in line 23, a negative comment regarding Baby Ruby's statement, and in line 26 she mirrors line 19, with the adverb *still* highlighting the fact that although Baby Ruby doesn't like it, Judy will always be the aunt. However, the dispute over who has the right to define their relationship has not ended.

Although Judy's topic change interrupts the signifying episode (line 50), Baby Ruby has not finished asserting her right to define the relationship. In line 57, she further diminishes Judy's status by recasting Judy's repeated assertion *I AM her aunt*; *I am STILL the aunt* as YOUR AUNTISM. She changes the quality of the noun *aunt* by adding the suffix *-ism*, which denotes the attitude, role and responsibilities of being an aunt (cf. Quirk et al., 1972). Thus Baby Ruby replaces Judy's formal definition of their relationship with her notion that Judy never had the duties, responsibilities, role and therefore status of an aunt. Baby Ruby successfully closes the signifying sequence with the statement in lines 62–3: *So your auntism: is: like nothing?*.

Judy and Baby Ruby signify by using the lexical, grammatical, prosodic and interactional resources available to members of the African American community. Signifying in this interaction concerns how speakers assert and contest the unequal aunt/niece relationship and simultaneously negotiate the solidarity of age-based friendship. Judy and Baby Ruby recognize when they are the intended targets and verbally collaborate in signifying through a turn-for-turn matching of comparable resources. The skills they developed as children are used both to tease and to confirm, mediate and constitute familial and personal relationships. Judy signifies that she is the aunt, but Baby Ruby signifies that Judy is much more her friend and peer and the "auntism is like nothing."

Conversational signifying: she *is* Regina

Another occurrence of conversational signifying occurred when Judy was with her friend Arthel. This episode is remarkable mainly because the local knowledge required to know that signifying is occurring is so textured. Conversational signifying begins when Judy mentions her participation in a pilot study I conducted three years prior to the interview. The study included a fictitious short story about a woman named Regina who brought a friend to a party who insulted other people at the party (Morgan, 1989, 1993). Those participating in the pilot heard a taped account of the story. Though Regina did not insult the people at the party, she was held responsible for bringing a friend that insulted everyone else.

In the following excerpt, Judy uses Regina's character to refer to a friend of mine in a negative manner.[12] Judy successfully gets me to co-author her negative assessment of my friend and, through association, her criticism of me. She uses indirection – that I have to deconstruct – to successfully critique me – and my choice of friends.

1	Judy:	What's that woman's name in that – on that thing?
2	MM:	[Regina
3	Arthel:	[ReGIna.
4	Judy:	ReGIna.
5		((*all laugh*))
6	Judy:	Tell Hazel I said she::: IS Regi::na
7	Arthel:	Is – is that the one? and the same person?=
8	Judy:	YES (2) [Hazel IS ReGIna
9	MM:	[NO-NO-NO:::! I wrote that – I wrote that thing – I
10		wrote that
11		t script – I WROTE it. -But I A::Sked her to READ it.
12	Arthel:	[Uh huh ((*sarcastically*))
13	Judy:	[But she::: IS ReGIna. ((*to Arthel*)) You know where she li::ves?
14		In that second brick building down there on ah North Lake Shore Drive?
15	MM:	710 North Lake Shore Drive
16	Arthel:	710 North Lake Shore Drive
17		((*describes, discusses and draws building*))
18	Arthel:	Oh that's ugly
19	MM:	Well, it [doesn't look quite like that ((*laughs*))
20	Judy:	[ri:ght
21	Arthel:	Well that's ugly. [I ain't never seen a building like that.
22	MM:	[It doesn't really look like that
23	Judy:	[But that's the way it LOOKS.
24	MM:	It doesn't really look like that. Its SI::des come out like [this.
25	Arthel:	[Uhum
26	MM:	And then the
27	Judy:	And where did she live before that? On North Michigan? uh Ontario?
28	MM:	*Ah no she lived on*=
29	Judy:	DAMN near close to it=
30	MM:	*No she lived on*=

31 Judy: She's ((*inaudible*))
32 MM: on Calumet
33 Judy: NO she didn't MarcylieNA! Before THAT then – Where'd she live?
34 MM: Sixty-Eight Eleven Calumet
35 Judy: Okay then before THAT where'd she live?
36 MM: *She was living with her sister.*
37 Judy: She didn't live on the north side?
38 MM: *She never lived on the north side. She has never lived on the north*
39   *side.*
40 Judy: Who was you going over there to see ?
41 MM: *I – I used to live on the north side*
42 Judy: Nah
43 Arthel: Now she's trying to get in your business right?=
44 MM: Right ((*all laugh*))

In line 1, Judy successfully elicits a response from me so that I begin in unison with her and Arthel in their discussion of Regina's character in the story. As in the previous "auntism" episode, the demonstrative pronoun *that* suggests that conversational signifying is in play. But in the initial context, its negative reading is camouflaged by Judy's suggestion that she had forgotten the details of the story. After everyone laughs Judy links the character of Regina with Hazel in line 6. Arthel mischievously asks a question about the identities of Hazel and Regina and mirrors Judy's use of *that* in reference to the women. Lines 8 and 9 overlap and are non-corroborative as I attempt to clarify what I at first believe is a misunderstanding. Line 12 includes Arthel's uptake of Judy's statement and is followed by Judy repeating her statement in lines 6 and 8.

In line 13, Judy makes it clear that she is not confused and believes that Hazel is a negative person = like Regina. She accomplishes this when she tells Arthel that Hazel once lived in an affluent neighborhood on the north side of Chicago. This residential reference is actually a critique of Hazel's race consciousness rather than social class. It includes the local knowledge that due to segregation in Chicago, those on the north side routinely receive city services and privileges not provided to black residents on the south side. Consequently, middle-class blacks who move to middle-class sections of the north side are routinely accused of rejecting the black community.[13]

Once it is clear that Judy is signifying on Hazel and me, I have no choice but to complete the episode and save as much social face as possible. Though I still present some defense of Hazel, it is a soft tone (italics) and remains so throughout the conversation, even when I confess that I am guilty since, in fact, I use to live on the north side! Arthel ends the signifying episode in line 43 with the acknowledgment that the (negative) focus is now on me, and probably always was.

Signifying laughter: "he had start preaching now"

In conversations and narratives, African American women's laughter often functions as a critique on situations where injustice and the exercise of power define their role in the event at hand.[14] What I call "the black woman's laugh," resembles what Irving Goffman (1978/1981) calls response cries. These are instances of what appears to be self-talk that appear in conventional conversations that actually function in reference to beliefs outside of the talk. This laugh can seem out of context because it often occurs in reference to bigotry, patriarchy, paternalism and other situations that may be responded to with outrage and indignation. What's more, it is never accompanied by a direct explanation. It seems to occur as a reflex within discourse that is tragic or may have dire consequences for the speaker – who never provides an explanation for why she's laughing. As a response cry, it is talk meant to be overheard and that aligns speakers with events. Yet this form of self-talk also aligns the speaker with a competing or contradictory assessment of the discourse and is

...situational in character, not merely situated. Its occurrence strikes directly at our sense of the orientation of the speaker to the situation as a whole. Self-talk is taken to involve the talker in a situationally inappropriate way. It is a threat to intersubjectivity; it warns others that they might be wrong in assuming a jointly maintained base of ready mutual intelligibility among all persons present. (Goffman, 1981: 85)

Though it often seems inappropriate when it appears, it functions to signal the strong social face of the speaker since it is an indictment of the person/statement to which the laugh refers. It is an acknowledgement of the local knowledge in play and the options available to the speaker and participants.

The following story told by Mrs. Banks was part of a three-hour session with a group of women in Mississippi. Mrs. Banks is a retired schoolteacher who, along with ten of her friends and neighbors, talked about the importance of the Black Church and life in Mississippi during the civil rights era. She uses the laugh as she tells of Fred, who conspired with white supremacists to perform cowardly and violent acts against those participating in voter registration of blacks in Mississippi. The following discussion began with talk about school desegregation efforts in the South and then focused on civil rights organizing efforts in the early 1960s.

```
 1 Mrs. Banks: But the N double ACP used to march on things like that you
 2              know. They would go to Washington DC and MARCH in
 3              Washington.
 4 MM:          Were they active around here at all?
 5 All:         Ye:::s, y:::es, su:::re. Rea:::lly.
 6 Mrs. Banks: SU::::RE! (3) One of the boys – he had start preaching now, was
 7              called Fred Barnes at the time. He beat down one of the
 8              NAACP member one time (.) cause the WHITE folks told him.
 9 MM:          Uhuhm
10 Mrs. Banks: Now he had start preaching and every time you know he's
11              preaching. When – whenever he comes around this way. I said,
12              you know Miss Thomp↑son? ((smiling and nudging the person
13              next to her)). Who is that?
14 All:         ((laughter))
15              She say "Oh its FRE:::D you know (.) He's PREACHing now (.)
16              you know" ((laughter from the group)) H' use to do EVerything
17              (when) he was young (he) didn't have no BUSiness. ((laughter))
```

Mrs. Banks' story of the civil rights movement is a story about traitors who now seek redemption by participating in the church. In line 5, the group confirms that there was NAACP activity in the area as Mrs. Banks said. Information on the social, political and cultural context is provided in line 6 – when Mrs. Banks reveals that a current evangelical preacher was once a person named Fred Barnes. She ties NAACP activity in line 2 to line 6 so that the presence of spies becomes part of the overall activity (see chapter 1). In lines 7–8 she reveals that in his youth, Fred Barnes informed on and then beat members of the NAACP for white supremacists in the area. Fred Barnes' identity as black is apparent in line 8 when Mrs. Banks reports that *white folks told him* to beat the NAACP members. We learn that Fred Barnes is back as a preacher using another name in lines 10–12.

Mrs. Banks laughs and then acts out her story by nudging a woman sitting next to her and who also knows that it is Fred Barnes – and is saying nothing. This laugh suggests that the woman is involved in supporting the traitor's return, but will not publicly admit it. It also suggests that Mrs. Banks, who previously identified herself as a Christian, does not intend to forgive or forget Mr. Barnes' earlier actions. She reports forcing the woman to admit who it is when she asks directly in line 13. Mrs. Banks reports the woman's reply in line 15 in a soft voice that implies that she is caught. She ends with a description of Fred Barnes punctuated with laughter that serves many functions. It shows that she is no fool, it identifies the tragedy of betrayal, the deception to bring him back into the community as a preacher, the trapping of the woman who was protecting his identity and the realization that though they could not prevent it, they did not intend to forget it.

The women's narrative: "I don't think that's a good idea"

The significance of indirectness and signifying in interaction is magnified in African American women's narrative practices. There are several narrative styles identified in African American folklore, writing and art. Those unique to the African American experience and identity are slave and migration narratives (e.g. Adero, 1993; Griffin, 1995; Hine, 1991; Marks, 1989; Painter, 1977; Smith, 1987; Starling, 1981; Stepto 1979). As demonstrated in the anecdote at the beginning of this chapter and others, slavery references and symbols of injustice can appear as local knowledge in conversation without forewarning. While similar to slave narratives, migration narratives also play an important role in depicting life under segregation in both urban and rural areas. Farah Griffin (1995) identifies four pivotal moments in artistic depictions of African American migration narratives. These include: (1) events that propel action northward, (2) detailed representation of the initial confrontation with the urban landscape, (3) an illustration of the migrant's attempt to negotiate that landscape and the negative effects of urbanization, and (4) a vision of the possibilities and limitations of the urban landscape (1995: 3). Each of these events is part of the social and cultural life of the migrant so it is not surprising that many life narratives that take place during the time of the great migration are often about the migration itself. Moreover, while slave narratives focus on the conditions of slavery and ascent from plantations and later Jim Crow, women's migration narratives wrestle with the self-reliance of urban life as well as the racial and sexual liberties and conflicts surrounding a new and alluring empowerment.

When describing women's narratives, it is necessary to consider how these stories are situated in other narratives and how they are constructed on their own. For example, Gwendolyn Etter-Lewis (1993) finds that African American women routinely use three narrative styles – unified, segmented and conversational – within interactions and narratives (1993: 178). These styles appear in a non-contiguous yet complementary fashion as they shift according to topic, imagined audience, local knowledge and so on. Since these narratives are co-authored, incorporating the experiences and values of a generation, they include issues of changing values and culture, especially regarding what it means to be a "full-grown woman," morality, personal responsibility and sophistication. Consequently, while the narrator's point of view includes gender, race and class, she must also cope with the new realities of urbanization and increased citizenship rights. Thus the form and structure of women's narratives must be evaluated along with the content since it can serve as the intermediary of attitude toward local norms. With this is mind, the narrative of Mrs. Doris Jones at first seems like an extraordinary childbirth narrative. It is, somehow, much more than that and provides insight into the special constraints women face in constructing migration narratives and how they simultaneously deal with their intersectionality.

I recorded Doris Jones in 1981, as part of a long-term study on language use among women in the African diaspora (Morgan, 1989). Mrs. Jones was an effective community activist and organizer in Chicago. Because I knew of her reputation as an organizer before I met her, I was quite surprised with the story she told me about the birth of her child. Early in our discussion Mrs. Jones revealed that she moved from Mississippi to Chicago because of a strong desire to work for herself and her family and to escape an abusive husband. Though she worked while in the South, she believed that most of the families for whom she worked "in service" exploited her. Never afraid of hard work, Doris Jones assumed she would have to struggle for everything she got and was proud of that fact that she had come so far. While sharing the same attitudes and values toward work as the male narrators, Doris Jones also mediated her intersectionality. First, she lived in a system of special oppression for black women who were stereotyped within white patriarchy as breeders and workers. Secondly, she had to negotiate the new northern urban landscape that offered both choice and responsibility.

In earlier episodes of her narrative, Mrs. Jones discusses the importance of work as a symbol of economic independence and provides numerous and detailed examples that demonstrate that she is and was a trustworthy and reliable worker. She begins this segment with a description of her job and boss, who did not want to lose a conscientious worker and therefore tries to convince her that she could and should work longer – for her own benefit. She then provides the details of what the delivery of her child was really like.

1 When I went to my boss and told him that I was stopping – I wanted maternity
2 leave – he suggested I should work a little while longer, you know. So he spoke
3 very funny and said, *"Oh Doris if I was you:: I would work a little while longer and*
4 *PUT the money in the bank, you know↑"*
5 So when he said that I just laughed, because I carried my children in the
6 HIPS. I wasn't NEAR 'bout as large as I am NOW. Once that happened,
7 I was on the switchboard. I could always just change clothes – you know –
8 and get a size bigger, and bigger, and bigger↑ – you know. But I – I HAD
9 NO WAIST! I sti::ll really don't have that much waist. I have LOT of hips,

10 you know ((*laughs*)). So my HIPS was getting BIGger, and BIGger and
11 BIGger. I was the youngest person on the job. And, uh, people didn't know
12 I was pregnant. Maybe some of the older ones may have, but they was just
13 feeding me A::LL of the pastry that I could eat and everything – you know.
14 So when Mr. Jennings told me that I should work on↑ – put my money in
15 the bank↑ I told him I said, "I don't think that's a good idea." TWO
16 WEEKS to the date that I reSIGNED – you know, stop my job – my baby
17 was born – which is Zonella. She was named after my baby sitter that was
18 watching over my children, you know. And actually, I only know those two
19 people name Zonella. Well, we made the Courier paper. *You may be able to go*
20 *back in 57 and see that. Yes, ah, it wasn't no pictures or nothing. It wasn't no*
21 *headline or nothing. It was a small article.*
22   The reason that we made the paper↑ WAS, because -uh – Mulberry
23 Center, which was the center here where you can have your children at
24 home, you know – like the doctor come into your home↑ – I had made
25 arRANGEments already for them to come out to my home. This is the
26 clinic that I went to. I made arrangements for that because except for my
27 cousin, I really didn't know nobody that I wanted to leave my CHILdren
28 with. So, then they didn't have the sterilized material to bring with them. So
29 you had to put your water on, you know, and have the water boiling. I didn't
30 have a phone. My landlord had discovered that I was pregnant – had given
31 me a, like a Hollywood basement instead of the fifth floor where I originally
   was living.
32   So I went into labor and I knew it was time for my baby to be born. ((*in a*
33 *sing-song voice*)) And then I called my oldest daughter, Miche:::lle – who was
34 just born in 54 herself, so you KNOW she wasn't nothing but a baby. And I
35 told her to go down the hall and tell the lady down the hall to call the doctor.
36 I gave her the number. But she wasn't there. Her husband was there. You
37 know how MENS get upset anyway. So I told him – well – I said, "*That's*
38 O.K. If you call the doctor they'll come. *Just let them in the door at the front for*
39 *me.*" So the reason we made the paper – *because when the doctor got there I*
40 *couldn't cut* the NAvel cord. But I had cleaned my *baby's mouth. She was*
41 *already born. I had washed me –PERIOD. And was in bed. I had my baby*
42 *covered up.*

In many respects, Mrs. Jones' construction of her situation and the injustices of black life are identical to those of Mr. Martin and Mr. West in chapter 1. Yet, though she addresses racial oppression in much the same way as the other narrators, she does not present subjugation by men or society as intentionally devious. Instead, she portrays men as essentially non-supportive or clueless. In so doing, she constructs events beyond her control as agent-less – so black women like her are completely responsible, and without expectations. Thus after she makes her request for maternity leave, she characterizes her boss's voice as soft, concerned and patronizing in line 3 but does not report a direct response to him until line 15 when she tells him *I don't think that's a good idea*. Similarly, in lines 36–37 when she discovered the landlady's husband was the only person home when her labor accelerated, she reasons

You know how mens get upset anyway. So I told him – well – I said, *"That's O.K. If you call the doctor they'll come. Just let them in the door at the front for me."*

Before she tells what she said to her boss, Doris Jones reports that her first response was to laugh. This laugh functions to suggest that her boss is a fool and it constructs her as knowledgeable. It signals that she is aware that he did not respect her right to request leave or her ability to determine the extent of her pregnancy. This point is further substantiated with the accompanying description of her pregnancy. This description, with voice contrasts that highlight her hip and waist size, supports that the laugh is ironic (lines 5–10). It is only after she has provided extensive explanation for her needing to quit that she provides the statement she gave her boss. This is immediately followed by the information in line 16 that she had her baby two weeks after she resigned. Doris Jones successfully establishes that she is aware of her surroundings and exercises control over her situation by leaving work when necessary. That is, she recognizes and copes with the gender, race and class issues on her job. However, she is less successful in the negotiation of health and city services and her rights and responsibilities during her delivery.

Mrs. Jones begins her description of the delivery by reporting that there was a newspaper article about it. As in the segment on giving notice to quit her job, she introduces the information about the newspaper article (line 19) and then provides details that seem peripheral to her story before telling what happened (line 22). Yet it is in the details (lines 22–37) that we understand that she is attempting to present a positive social face within a migration narrative. While recognizing that her delivery was special, the site where she concentrates her story is one that situates her as part of the experience of African American woman recently from the South.

As mentioned above, Doris Jones endures both racial and gendered oppression and her identity is fashioned according to her ability to negotiate her life within these realities. Unfortunately for Doris Jones, there is yet another stereotype with which she had to contend. It is the stereotype of the newly arrived black Southern migrant whose ignorance of resources and services is often interpreted, by African Americans, as a fear to exercise citizenship rights. She could have had a hospital delivery at little cost. She could have used an ambulance at little cost. Mrs. Jones could have contacted a number of city agencies for assistance. Thus the pressures that Doris Jones coped with included not only her particular social, historical and personal circumstance, but also the cultural knowledge that her difficulty could not be expressed within the community of African American women who suffer similar catastrophic hardships. Her narrative focuses on her skills at survival within a system of direct racial and often indirect gender oppression. The cultural knowledge that is central to her narrative includes Northern or urban black attitudes toward new migrants from the South who are "country." Doris Jones attempts to explain that her preparation for delivery was logical, reasonable and responsible because she... *really didn't know nobody.* Thus, without the extensive explanation of how she tried to get help and be prepared, Mrs. Jones' unassisted delivery would appear irresponsible to Michelle, Zonella and Doris Jones herself.

The details about the preparation for the baby – a planned home delivery with the Mulberry Center – includes information that she intended to take care of her family immediately after delivery since there was no one else to take care of the children. Her preparation for the birth (lines 24–37) further demonstrates her knowledge about her responsibility as a pregnant woman and mother. Her knowledge is simply stated in that she knew it was time (line 32). In this light, her assessment of why she made the paper – *I couldn't cut the navel cord* – strongly suggests that her triumph in delivering her own baby might have fed the stereotype of the black woman as breeder.

In 1990, I played an edited recording of Mrs. Jones' narrative for separate groups of white and black women who were in their mid to late fifties. The white women focused on Mrs. Jones' delivery and considered her a heroine. In contrast, the black women did not even discuss Zonella's birth. Nor did they mention that Doris Jones performs a heroic act. Instead, they focused on whether Doris Jones understood the resources available to all pregnant women in Chicago, including black women.

The black women argued that to ignore services and resources in the North was to embody the injustices of the South and one's "place" within the system of white male privilege. One woman stated "To me a woman like that is just stupid! – and country! It's ridiculous!" They then discussed every possible resource and questioned whether she should have asked other women for help. They never considered that the landlord would be helpful. Within this social context and considering her generational audience, rather than a story of overcoming insurmountable odds, by working, taking care of her children and delivering her own baby, Doris Jones' story is perfectly cast. It is one where she must explain herself. She negotiates her urban existence, but within the norms of the South. She is able to successfully deliver her baby and clean up afterward, but she is unsuccessful at exercising her rights as a black woman in Chicago.

Indirectness: explaining racist acts

As in all of the previous interactions and narratives, the following discussion about the 1919 race riot in Chicago[15] is dialogical and incorporates all those present as well as referring to prior interactions and social relationships. Like Doris Jones, Rose and Nora must convey their knowledge of urban life and racism in Chicago during the migration of African Americans from the South. Unless discussing civil rights atrocities directly (e.g. lynching, specific acts of discrimination, Ku Klux Klan), none of the twenty-seven African American women over the age of fifty who participated over a five-year period ever directly described racism or complained about racist practices in society.[16] Instead, as in other interactions and narratives, they introduce situations that reflect local knowledge and thus reveal and signify the extent of white supremacist influence in systemic oppression. As they tell their stories of life in Chicago during the early 1920s, they constantly deal with how they represent their own and their generation's confrontation with the urban landscape and how they negotiated the negative aspects of the experience. In the following story of life during Chicago's 1919 race riot, Rose and Nora refer to street names and neighborhoods to signal the boundaries of the black community and the knowledge that they also served as "whites only" signs for new black immigrants to Chicago.

```
1   MM:   Do you remember the race riot Rose?
2   Rose: Yeah. [Yeah I REmember
3   Nora: [Ye::ah! – must' served corn bread a week – we slept on the
4         floor. We shou::ld? Oh yeah, we knew.
5   Nora: Yeah.
6   MM:   What happened – I mean tell me about it. How did it start?
7   Nora: Well it star::ted on the beach (.) with the white and the blacks. So
8         THEY got to fighting. I think the first starting of it – a white boy
9         drowned a black boy. And then they – then they drowned a WHITE
10        boy. And then the whites started fighting the blacks. And they were
11        shooting too and KILLing (.) because one fellow stayed with
12        us – they killed him – poLICE killed him↑ though didn't they?
13  Rose: =Yeah
14  Nora: =Yeah police killed him. Right THERE on 50th and State. Police
15        killed him. And they fought for a lo:::ng time. To me it's like
16        who::le month↑ we couldn't go to school. We couldn't go OUT. you
17        couldn't do NOTHING but stay in the HOUSE and sleep on the floor.
18  Rose: And then they called out the (.) ReSERVES (.) and this is what calmed
19        people down.
20  Nora: Plus these Italians was staying across the railroad tracks – they was
21        over by Federal
22  Rose: Yeah
```

23 Nora: Cause we were on Dearborn. They was on Federal or Wentworth
24 MM: When you say plus the Italians what do you mean?
25 Nora: Ah the Italians – they help the coloreds because it was more BLACKS
26   in that area than it was Italians. [So they was with the BLA::cks
27 Rose: [Yeah, they he::lped us↑
28 Nora: Yeah, they were with the BLA::cks (.) I really don't know what year
29   that was in – it had to be – It was because I didn't COME here until
30   1919 so it had to be, so
31 MM: Yeah, yeah – Which beach was that at? The 57th Street beach?
32 Rose: It had to be 31st
33 Nora: It was that or either the – in Jackson Park beach – one of them where
34   they – unless the other one was on the north side where they drowned
35   the white one. Because the whites and the blacks didn't go to the same
36   beach↑ back then. They didn't go to the same beach.
37 MM: Mhm
38 Nora: So it had to be on the north side for the whites – I know
39 Rose: Blacks weren't allowed at Jackson Park
40 Nora: That's right cause that's all white neighborhood
41 Rose: Ahah yeah. Oh ye::a::h. It HAD↑ to be around 31st↑ Street
42 Nora: Yeah oh yeah
43 MM: Why – why do you think the uh tensions were so bad that all that
44   happened?
45 Rose: Just – to me::: the tensions were here today↑ and gone tomorrow
46   and I (.) STILL haven't figured this out↑ – unless it was the type of
47   MATTRESses that we were sleeping on (.) that must have BRED these
48   things. But I'm telling you it was really – re- HOrrible. It was really
49   HORrible.

Rose and Nora slowly build a racial description of their Chicago neighborhood as they outline the location and boundaries of segregation. They
begin by overlapping their talk to confirm that they remember the riot
that occurred over sixty years ago. In lines 3 and 4 Nora confirms that it
was so frightening that they should remember it. Nora's response to the
question *How did it start?* is the location – the beach (line 7). The location is in fact the reason for the riot. The 31st Street beach[17] included
an imaginary line in the water separating black and white swimmers. A
young white man accused a young black man of swimming across that
border.

Nora describes the ensuing fight, including the police killing of a tenant.
It is important to note that neither the police nor the community mainly
involved in the attacks is described as Irish though that was the main
white ethnic group involved in the riot (Drake and Cayton, 1945). That
the police and the attackers were one and the same is corroborated by
Nora's use of *the whites* in line 10 to refer to those who were fighting the

blacks. She then uses *they* in line 10 and 12 to refer to those who were shooting and killing. The use of *they* is then tied to the police in line 12 and is repeated in line 14 twice. In contrast, in line 20 the Italians are identified directly and tied to lines 18–19 in reference to *what calmed people down*. In line 20 Nora explains that the Italians lived among blacks, though I didn't understand that she had named streets that were part of residential segregation and considered traversable on Chicago's black, south side.

The importance of location, and the identification of the beach as representing "whites only" policies, is highlighted beginning in line 29 when Nora says *it had to be* to refer to the time of the riot. Rose uses the same expression to answer my question about which beach the riot started on. Nora identifies another possible beach where white swimmers might have been killed because it was an all-white beach. In fact, the black reprisals for the killings seemed to happen mainly on the south side in surrounding neighborhoods (Drake and Cayton, 1945). Rose reminds Nora that blacks were not allowed in Jackson Park and Nora describes it as a whites-only area. Rose then repeats in line 41 that *It HAD to be around 31st Street*. The interaction concludes with a response to the question of why it happened. Rose's response is much like Mr. West's in chapter 1 when he was asked to explain lynching. It includes a folk expression (Jacobs-Huey, 1999) that signifies that there is no explanation for racist acts; it had to be the mattress. The riot happened because white supremacy exists. If one does not want the truth, the mattress is as good an explanation as any.

When women speak, how they mean and therefore how they say something is what they are talking about. In order to accomplish this, they must learn, as girls, that talk is always meaningful and much more is at stake than just words. For girls it is social face and friendship and being truly understood. For women, the stakes include stamping their identity as African American into the social moment as they read, introduce ambiguity and disambiguate conversations and intentions. And for urban youth in general, the stamping of identity is even more important. They do not just want their existence to be an imprint. They want to ram their identity into the social order so that they are not only a part of it, but so that it is forever changed.

5 Urban youth language: black by popular demand

When I first arrived in Los Angeles in 1990, I was constantly asked whether I intended to study hip hop's influence on black youth. Women who participated in my research asked why I wasn't studying "what the kids are doing?" And students would offer, without any urging from me, "What you *need* to be doing is studying hip hop." But since I already had a research agenda, and thought urban youth language had been over-emphasized, I tried to ignore their advice. In frustration, I contacted Ben Caldwell, an established filmmaker who owned a studio – Video 3333/KAOS Network – in the Leimert Park section of Los Angeles. I thought he would direct me to a youth program that dealt with language and art. Instead, he matter-of-factly said, "Why don't you checkout freestyle hip hop at Project Blowed on Thursday nights here at KAOS Network."

I canvassed many youth and hip hop devotees before I finally ventured into underground hip hop at Project Blowed – and I had both expectations and anxieties. I knew that the Thursday night crowd was usually filled with hip hop aficionados and regulars who were intolerant of weak, unimaginative rhymers, along with neophyte onlookers and hangers-on who knew little about hip hop culture. And I had already received the word on the distinctive rap style used by Project Blowed. One young woman from New York who used to rap there described her departure from performing at Blowed because "They didn't like my style and I had to be true to the East." A young man explained, "You have to be careful when you go there if you're a rapper. The style is catchy and before you know it, you're using it. I call it a virus 'cause it just takes you over!" The style itself was rapid-fire language; I finally understood the expression "insert the power chord." This was power discourse in its rawest form.

In a dimly lit room with video cameras running in the back and a deejay mixing beats, African American, Latino, White, Asian and Pacific Islander youth formed a line along a small stage. Standing on the stage was the MC from Project Blowed who held one mike and the previous freestyler who had failed to "Get in where you fit in!" The audience, which mirrored the racial, gender and age mix of the group on the stage, was not pleased as they yelled and motioned to him to pass the mike to the next in line. When the next rapper took the mike, he pulled down his cap so it fit firmly on his head, listened to the beat provided by the deejay, crouched, raised his hands and began his rap. The crowd bobbed their heads to the beat as he demonstrated creativity, linguistic finesse, and knowledge of popular cultural symbols. Suddenly, someone yelled, "That's not freestyle!" The rapper quickened his delivery and the crowd, now on alert, remained riveted, bobbing their heads with serious expressions as they critiqued every word, symbol, reference and index. Slowly, they began chanting their rejection, "Pass the mike! Pass the mike!" But the "no-skill" rapper refused to leave and pass the mike to the next in line.

Suddenly the Project Blowed rapper Terra (Pterodactyl) jumped on the stage, clearly agitated that the neophyte contender didn't want to play by the rules. At the sight of Terra the audience threw up their hands and formed a W with their fingers and began screaming "Westsiiide! Westsiiide!" Terra grabbed the mike from the contender and paced back and forth, all the while looking frenetically at the crowd. Then, within the 4/4 time of the music mix provided by the deejay, Terra demonstrated his skill by rapidly firing off his syllabic retort in sixteenth time!

> What happened to your apology?
> It's time for a little sermontology
> That's hypocrisy
> You jump to the microphone
> But you ain't knocking me
> You stepping up to poetry
> Yeah, you know it's me
> Yeah it's Terra
> Terror – whatever you want to call me
> In any section
> I'm not battling you
> I'm looking for something bigger
> You need to be trudging
> In some other corner of the globe
> Some other corner of this episode

The crowd went wild! People were yelling Word! Word! As Terra's head jutted back and forth and he looked menacingly at the crowd – all the while pacing and challenging "You want some of this?!! You want some of this?!!" Finally, the "contender" shamefully exited the stage, left the room, and went out into the night. I couldn't imagine that anyone would dare come forward now, and try to match the linguistic skills of Terra.

The wait was frenzied as Terra continued to pace with his head darting back and forth on top of his long neck – in honor of the reptile for which he is named. The crowd kept screaming "Westsiiide!" with hands waving and fingers in the form of the letter W. Finally, after continuous yelling and chanting from the crowd, the rest of the Project Blowed crew rushed forward in victory and jumped on the stage. The place erupted in an uproar and Project Blowed began their power discourse.

The "real" black community: regenerating generations

Hip hop was conceived on the streets of New York's brown and black boroughs according to African American counterlanguage practices. In many respects, it has done more to crystallize a young, urban African American identity than any other historic and political change since the late 1960s. While the civil rights movement and black power struggles of the 1950s, 1960s and 1970s may have introduced the promise of a united, culturally, politically and linguistically homogeneous African American community, hip hop members boldly and brazenly argue for a "real" that incorporates individual, regional and local identities. They celebrate the African American system of counterlanguage and community by pub-licly displaying cultural practices of indirection and directed discourse, reading and so on as though all of America shares – or should share – the same norms. Thus instead of using adults as models or references, youth have targeted the stage of cultural and social knowledge acquisition – before the compromises of adulthood – as what is real. However, unlike traditional AAE practices where symbols and references are based on shared local knowledge, hip hop has introduced contention and contrast by creating ambiguity and a constant shift between knowledge of prac-tices and symbols. Thus, while the hip hop nation is constructed around an ideology that representations and references (signs and symbols) are indexical and create institutional practices, what the signs and symbols index remains fluid and prismatic rather than fixed.

In many respects, this ideology addresses Frege's (1977) and Austin's (1962) attempts to resolve how individuals interpret utterances, refer-ents and meanings while simultaneously recognizing that there are differ-ent senses and therefore possible interpretations of referents (see below). But it goes even further. Urban youth recognize that their voices are routinely marginalized and their language ideology assumes that agency and power reside in the form of language use itself. That is, reference to public individuals, events, objects, etc. is indexical and can stand for, point to, connect and target particular groups and contexts (Peirce, 1960; Silverstein, 1979, 1993, 1998). Thus for youth, indexicality is the focus on contextualized existence and points to the sociocultural context or their "real world" and reality. It refers to the secret handshake, knowing look and coded message. It signals the existence of an alter-entity – black youth as thinkers, critics and creators of language, culture, art and ideas.

In this respect, referring to hip hop as the foundation of a black urban cultural institution is not an overstatement. Its role in addressing modern notions of community, kinship, relationship, morality, injustice, representation and responsibility cannot be denied. In urban areas throughout the US arts groups, community organizations and even some churches now rely on hip hop to involve youth in educational and political efforts.[1] In fact there is a variety of hip hop styles including old school, hard core, gangster, gospel, social and political consciousness and others. The choice of style is associated with how the artist constructs him or herself or the type of message in the rap. Both men and women use a variety of styles, though some artists are strongly associated with one type of rap.

The core of the Hip Hop Nation consists of adolescent males and females between twelve and seventeen years old who exclusively listen to, memorize and write raps (Wheeler, 1992), dress in the current hip hop style, keep up with the current dances, and often tag or at least practice graffiti writing.[2] This younger group also practices freestyle (spontaneous, improvised and/or re-stylized) rapping and members compete with each other over the best rap, delivery, style, etc. This group is mainly imitators who, through constant memorization, indirectly study the system of AAE and contrasts with GE.

While the core purchases the most recordings and is essential to hip hop's stability as an artistic form, the most influential segment of the Hip Hop Nation is urban youth in their late teens to middle twenties. These long-term (LT) members may also practice freestyle, participate in local and underground open mike performances and competitions, and identify with particular rap genres or crews. This segment of hip hop often writes letters of praise or complaint to various hip hop publications or rap sheets to give "props" (respect) to artists. Long-term members also serve as nation builders and often offer political and historical commentary and context to current hip hop styles and artists. They highlight grammatical contrasts between AAE and GE and introduce, replace and circulate lexicon.

Clearly, youth outside of urban areas are attracted to hip hop for the same reason as its primary audience. Suburbia's uncritical acceptance might signify that the artist is a "perpetrator," a term that is the equivalent of a spy and the antithesis of what hip hop symbolizes. If LTs reject an artist because the words, referents, experiences and symbols evoked do not reflect the reality of the streets, the core audience will fade away – along with suburbia. In this regard, Adler's famous quotation that hip hop "is adored by millions in the streets and reviled by hundreds in the suites" (Adler, 1991) is at best a limited view of the real relationship between the streets and suites. If LTs designate that an artist has sold out, that artist generally cannot perform without reprisals anywhere that hip hop members congregate in the African American community. LTs have the power to influence artists and monitor whether they actually "represent" when they claim a region and neighborhood as theirs. And language is one of the most important tools that LTs have at their disposal to identify who is part of the African American youth experience and who are the wannabes and perpetrators.

The rebirth of urban language

The language of African American youth residing in urban areas has been a subject of interest to linguistics and sociology since the 1970s when work of William Labov (1972a) focused on the importance of urban youth as dialect innovators. Labov investigated many layers of the African American speech community including "the language, culture, the social organization, and the political situation of black youth in the inner cities of the United States" (Labov 1972a: xiii). Alarmingly, sociolinguistic descriptions that proved AAE to have a logical and predictable system were used to monitor and punish AAE language use (see chapters 3 and 6). While Labov's writings helped launch a new era of study on urban youth language and culture in general and AAE youth language in particular, it also suggested (perhaps unintentionally) that youth operate with a highly structured language ideology and counterlanguage. However, this version of counterlanguage was not concerned with sustaining a system hidden from dominant culture (chapters 1 and 2), but was a strategic, in-your-face anti-language. Vernacular theories demonstrated that African American youth both ignored and responded to society's attempt to stigmatize and marginalize AAE usage by their continued innovations within the norms of both dialects. Moreover, discourse styles, verbal genres and reading dialect became tools to represent not only African American culture, but also youth alienation and injustice in general.

By the 1990s, AAE language and discourse had become a symbol of both truth/realism and disaffection among youth throughout the country. Urban youth have recognized, co-opted and capitalized on directness and indirectness, reading dialect and signifying, and have incorporated them in dress, body and art. It is in this respect that hip hop represents the integration of the African American experience within American culture.

Black urban youth have taken counterlanguage and in turn exploited it by focusing on the following tenets: (1) sounds, objects and concepts embody and index memory, community and social world, (2) choices of language and dialect can signify status, beliefs, values and specific speakers, (3) all meaning is co-constructed (co-authored).

The first tenet refers to the importance of signifiers or indices and emblems of black urban life, much like those mentioned in the previous chapters. These may include use of and references to AAE, GE, proverbs, popular and children's television, kung fu movies, neighborhoods, streets, public transportation systems, police stations and prisons that youth must deal with. However, these items' value may change quickly. Thus it is not only the popular items that have exchange value for youth culture but also how they function within a system of markedness where the notion of normal, expected and stable are disrupted by forms, references, expressions and so on that question what is considered normal and accepted. Moreover, a system of markedness functions within popular and local trademarks (cf. Coombe, 1996) and youth may use the system to mark the same symbol as positive and negative in any given moment.

An example of the tension between trademarks and signs with pliant indexicality occurred when the Project Blowed rapper Terra (see above) confronted a young man who was exiting KAOS Network. He was wearing a tee shirt with the name of the California rap group Pharcyde (pronounced far side) and a cap with a B on it representing Boston. Under normal circumstances, affiliation with Pharcyde would be considered support of Project Blowed since some Project Blowed members have been affiliated with the group. Yet, Terra said:

> Rap in California?
> You be down with the Pharcyde?
> Over there on the far side?
> Down with the West Side.

Terra's willingness to mark his uncertainty about the West Side (California) loyalties of the wearer of the Pharcyde tee shirt is astonishing since his question could be without warrant and considered an insult. Terra avoids direct confrontation through the use of an uninverted question: *You be down . . . ?* He then targets the obvious ambiguity by clearly marking the semantic relationship according to whether the word is a noun (*Pharcyde*) or the object of a prepositional phrase (*far side*). He then closes with his identification and declaration of the West Side. Thus, while he did not demand that the young man "represent" his regional affiliation, Terra successfully represented his – the *Westsiiide*!

The second position is related to identity, ideology, power and attitudes toward language use. It refers directly to the possibility of altering symbols and trademarks as a means to exploit and subvert them. As Stuart Hall says, "Identities are . . . constituted within, not outside of representation . . . within, not outside, discourse, and constructed through, not outside, difference" (Hall et al., 1996:4). It seems that Hall may have had youth in mind when he described identity as the changing same (see Gilroy, 1994), and "not the return to roots, but the coming-to-terms-with our 'routes'" (Hall et al., 1996:4). Youth expose and "flash" their routes all the time, on their way to asserting their difference as well as their sameness and recognizing the power in the expression of their identity. Adolescent social identity is one that experiments and thus fuses crucial identity issues into play and back again. What's more, identity is viewed through referential and indexical language use where the discourse evokes times, places, experiences and ideologies that underpin not only the terminology itself, but also the power of the discourse ideology.

The third and final point illustrates that neither youth nor the artists stand alone as independent individuals. Rather, it is a person's ties to the audience/generation and urban youth that bring him or her into existence. An artist is a composite of his or her audience – representing his and her own experiences that are shared – and the audience determines whether the artist can assume that role. In this respect, the notion of peer group is constructed around the sharing of values of social face alignment as well as age, region and so on.

As described earlier, since 1997 I have conducted an ethnographic study of an organization in Los Angeles that supports the creative arts and various youth initiatives. Among the activities is a freestyle hip hop venue called Project Blowed that performed at Ben Caldwell's KAOS Network in the Leimert Park neighborhood of Los Angeles. Project Blowed refers to itself as a performance workshop and it attracted MCs and about 200 LTs every Thursday night. Along with data from Project Blowed this analysis incorporates norms of hip hop language use.

In 1998, I asked fifty urban African American LTs between the ages of sixteen and twenty-five to identify their top five favorite hip hop artists and crew. Comments and opinions of youth from Los Angeles, Boston, Alabama and Chicago were recorded, transcribed and analyzed. Eight male and two female artists were selected who released recordings during 1997–8 and represented a range of hip hop style and region. Draft transcripts were taken from website lyrics like www.Ohhla.com and from lyrics available on album jackets.[3] They were then compared to the actual recordings and amended accordingly. Recordings of all artists in conversations were transcribed.

Their African American English and Ours

I'm outspoken, my language is broken into a slang
But it's just a dialect I select when I hang.
(Special Ed, "I Got It Made")

I'll damage ya, I'm not an amateur
But a professional, unquestionable, without a doubt superb
So full of action, my name should be a verb
(Big Daddy Kane, "Cold Chillin'")

Yo! I'm the anti-circle
On the mad train like a rain
That's verbal I storm
Never comin' twice in one form
(The Roots, "Organix: The Anti-Circle")

Of course, not all of the linguistic features of AAE are targeted by urban youth. Nor are contrasts between AAE and GE always a major component (see chapter 3). The concern of hip hop is not merely in reading dialect and contrasting the two varieties but in the demonstration of linguistic and delivery skill and therefore the performance of language and discourse knowledge. Accordingly, this section is concerned with how, when and what forms and categories are the focus of attention. Thus it looks both at situations where language style may not be at issue and those where it may be as important as the speech act itself. In that way we may determine both the way the system functions in different contexts and which aspects of the system are thought to be representative of culture, region, neighborhood and all aspects of identity.

The following analysis includes Project Blowed and artists in other cities in the US. Table 5 lists all of the artists and albums included in the analyses. Aceyalone (pronounced AC alone) is a well-known freestyle artist in the Los Angeles area and one of the leaders of Project Blowed. He has been rapping professionally since the late 1980s and is a member of Freestyle Fellowship. Common (formerly Common Sense) is a socially conscious artist from Chicago and represents the Midwest. Ice Cube is from Los Angeles and was originally with NWA. Wu Tang, Jay-Z and KRS-One are from the New York area. KRS-One is considered a significant figure in hip hop and East Coast hip hop in particular. Jay-Z's 1998 recordings are actually two related versions of one recording. MC Lyte and Salt 'N Pepa are the women artists included in the analysis. Though both represent the East Coast and though they may be considered "old school" by some, they are among the most regionally stable of women hip hop artists.[4] The Goodie Mob and Outkast are groups from the South. Though many of the albums listed generated remixes, they were not included in the overall discussion.

Table 5 *Artists and recordings*

Artist	Album	Region	Year
Aceyalone	A Book of Human Language	West	1998
	All Balls Don't Bounce		1995
Common	One Day It'll All Make Sense	Midwest	1997
	Resurrection		1994
	Can I Borrow a Dollar?		1992
Goodie Mob	Still Standing	South	1998
	Soul Food		1995
Ice Cube	Lethal Injection	West	1993
	The Predator		1992
	Death Certificate		1991
	Amerikkka's Most Wanted		1990
Jay-Z	Streets Is Watching	East	1998
	Vol. 2 Hard Knock Life		1998
	Reasonable Doubt		1996
	In My Lifetime Vol. 1		1997
KRS-One	I Got Next	East	1997
	KRS-One		1995
	Return of the Boom Bap		1993
MC Lyte	Eyes On This	East	1989
	Act Like You Know		1991
	Bad As I Wanna Be		1996
	Lyte as a Rock		
Outkast	Aquemini	South	1998
	Atliens		1996
	Southernplaylisticadillacmuzik		1994
Salt 'N Pepa	Hot, Cool and Vicious	East	1987
	A Salt With A Deadly Pepa		1988
	Blacks' Magic		1990
	Very Necessary		1993
Wu Tang	Enter the Wu	East	1993
	Wu Tang Forever		1997
	Killa Bees: The Swarm		

Pronunciation

All of the artist recordings included the nine items listed in table 4 (chapter 3) for phonology and morphophonemics. In fact, items were categorical with the exception of 8 – realization of syllable initial: *str-* as *skr-: strength -> skrength* – and 9 – realization of *-ing* as *-ang*: *king -> kang*.

For example, no artist pronounced *str-* as *skr-* in syllable-initial position. But this may largely be due to the stigma the form has received because it is targeted as a point of ridicule among black comics who lump it with *shr-* as *skr-* (the favored joke is a request for *shrimp* pronounced *skrimp*).[5] They refer to it variously as stupid, country, simple-minded and so on.

In contrast, the realization of *-ing* as *-ang* is not stigmatized and its use varies according to region. The artist Jay-Z uses it frequently as does MC Lyte, Salt 'N Pepa and Wu Tang. Common (Midwest), Ice Cube and Aceyalone (West Coast) use *thing* categorically. The exception is when *thang* is used in order to rhyme with another word. Thus on "Color Blind" Ice Cube says, *Cuz I slang these thangs like a G*. The word *slang* is in reference to both the noun *slang* and the verb *sling* pronounced with *-ang*. Goodie Mob and Outkast (the South) use both *-ing* and *-ang*. Goodie Mob uses *thang* in all cases except when *thing* is used to rhyme with another word and when *thing* is a part of an established expression. Thus in the song "Live at the O.M.N.I." they say *Worried about the wrong thang this paper aint' gon' set you far*. While on "Blood" they say: *Don't make a decision in haste. Your blood is a terrible thing to waste.*

The above examples highlight the value of both *skr-* and *-ang* in urban youth discourse. While both forms are recognized as AAE, one may be stigmatized (*skr-*), and is thus marked within AAE, while the other (*-ang*) is recognized as an alternative to *-ing* in appropriate contexts. Thus the presence or absence of *-ing*/*-ang* does not signify reading dialect and the counterlanguage unless it is contrasted with another word in the text. On the other hand, *skr-* indexes ignorance irrespective of the context.

Grammar

All artists employ all of the tense, mood, aspect, noun and pronoun characteristics listed in table 4. In addition to the items listed in table 4, all participants in hip hop incorporate American regional urban Spanish styles in their pronunciation of vowels and in some aspects of their syllable stress.[6] Thus the West (West Coast) is more likely to show pronunciation influence from Chicano English and Spanish phonology, while the East (East Coast) has a strong Caribbean Spanish language influence (see below).

Expanding the semantic realm[7]

The shifting of word classes and meanings found today has been reported throughout the literature (e.g. Smitherman, 1994; Major, 1970, 1994).

As part of reading dialect, this is often accomplished through semantic inversion, extension and the reclamation of GE and AAE forms.
Perhaps the most basic form of lexical expansion is inversion (Holt, 1972;
Smitherman, 1994). In this case, an AAE word means the opposite of at
least one definition of the word in dominant culture. For example, the
word *down* can have a positive meaning of support in the sentence *I want
to be down with you*. It can also be used as part of a locative with *low* to
mean secretive as in *Keep it on the down low*. In the early nineties, first-
syllable stressed *STUPID* meant good, though its usage is archaic in hip
hop today.

Extension emphasizes one aspect of an English word definition and
extends or changes the focus of the word's meaning and it may or may
not include a grammatical change. One common AAE form of word art
is an aspect of lexical expansion. In this case a word's meaning(s) and/or
part(s) of speech reveal a particular aspect of the word and/or the context
for which it is often associated. For example, the verb *wack* – whose definition includes smacking and hitting – is combined with the adjective *wacky*
which means absurd or irrational. This combination of meaning has lead
to the new adjective *wack* as in *That idea is wack* to mean unbelievably
inept, inadequate and deficient (Smitherman, 1994). Similarly, the adjective *mad* which means crazy and angry takes on an adverbial function
to mean intensity and quantity as in *He laid some mad tracks*.[8] The hip hop
verb *floss* is an interesting example of lexical expansion, especially since its
GE verbal usage is recent.[9] *Do you want to floss with us?* has an extremely
positive meaning. It incorporates the cleanliness of the AAE expression
being clean (or *cleaner than the Board of Health*) meaning looking especially good and trend setting (e.g. Outkast's "So Fresh and So Clean").
Its focus is coolness and the attitude and intentionality of the subject.
It follows the norms of non-state verbs (e.g. floss/flossed/flossing). Once
words are introduced, whether they become stable lexical items is determined by whether they become part of the discourse of older generations
or whether they are over appropriated by the dominant culture and must
be discarded.

The process of inversion and expansion has evolved to the point that
a word can be extended from GE and then inverted once it has stabilized as an urban youth word. For example, the hip hop word *ill*, which
began as a contrast to the GE definition, has itself undergone change
in AAE. In its first hip hop stage *ill* had a negative meaning that referred to hostility and bad attitude, and was often used in relation to
its hip hop opposite – *chill* (to be cool). In its second stage of usage
its GE and AAE adjectival form was expanded to include verbal usage
and its meaning became the opposite of its original hip hop meaning

(Stavsky, Mozeson and Reyes Mozeson, 1995; Atoon, 1992–9, Fab 5 Freddy, 1992).[10] Following are examples of *ill* as both adjective and predicate.

> *Adjective*
> Who's the illest shorty alive, I confess (Jay-Z and Memphis Bleak)
> Some of the realest, illest, chillest cats you may see (Common)

> (*Predicate/Adjective*)
> I be illin, parental discretion is advised still (KRS-One)
> And bust and rushed and illed and peeled the cap (Ice Cube)
> For chillin, illin' willin' to do what I got to do (Goodie Mob)
> Big up Grand Wizard Theodore, gettin' ill (KRS-One)
> Get ill if you wanna ill, smoke if you wanna smoke. (Jay-Z and Memphis Bleak)

Finally in AAE, the noun *player* was defined as someone who exploited people (especially women), but now it is a person who has extreme and enviable success (Major, 1994; Smitherman, 1994). This meaning has led to the compound noun *player hater*, a term that refers to envious people who criticize other's success. Now in hip hop, a Ph.D. is an insult suggesting envy and refers to *Player Hater Degree*. This usage has in turn led to the phrasal verbs *hate on/hating on* to refer to envy as in *Don't be hatin' on my hair.*

Word art, trademarks and symbolism: "Word is bond"

One of the most valued and significant features of African American behavior is the attitude toward word formation and the interest in new words and generational words. Each generation of urban youth marks its presence through lexical creativity and innovations. Popular culture, the arts and humanities have thrived on *cool cats, macks, sisters and brothers that are so bad they're good!* It is not surprising that knowing the lexicon or lexical protocol guarantees an official pass through the community – though the protocol requires that the pass be constantly tested. Though these words are popularly referred to as slang, they do more than reflect the immediacy of teenage angst. They are indexical and reflect region, neighborhood and social class, help to construct social face and coolness and thereby identify insiders and outsiders. Thus these words have exchange value and are often placed in contexts where they can accrue social capital. In fact, reading and loud-talking often include this form of word art.[11] I was reminded of the important exchange value of these indexical words when a young lady in Chicago read me and challenged

my right to claim membership in Chicago's black community because I
was unaware of what she considered to be a common word.

YOUNG LADY : I don't wear bobos
MM : What's a bobo?
YOUNG LADY : Oooh! I'm gonna have to take your GHETTO PASS back!
 ((*laughing and shaking her head*)) YOU don't EVEN KNOW what BOBOS
 ARE!

She then explained that in Chicago, *bobo* is used to refer to unbelievably
cheap sneakers.[12] And when the young lady travels outside of Chicago
she will quickly have to learn the terminology for "wack" sneakers in the
next city and how to mark new boundaries and avoid being read as having
no cool.

The rules associated with these lexical norms, and the knowledge that
new words and meanings are constantly created, are shared by all social
classes in the African American community. Smitherman (1998) explains
why lexicon plays such a significant role: "the lexicon of the Black speech
community crosses boundaries – sex, age, religion, social class, region.
That is, the Black lexicon is comprised of idioms, phrases, terms and
other linguistic contributions from various sub-communities within the
larger African American community" (Smitherman, 1998: 205). Thus
the generation of new lexicon contributes to the ecology of the community
and is a form of representation.

Linguists have long observed that AAE attaches a variety of meanings to
GE lexical items (Dalby, 1972; Dillard, 1977; McDavid and McDavid,
1951) and there are several dictionaries on the subject (Dillard, 1977;
Fab 5 Freddy, 1992; Major, 1970, 1994; Smitherman, 1994). In fact rap
and hip hop culture would not exist were it not for the unending referential capacity and possibility of lexical creativity. An artist is expected
to introduce new words with recordings as the group Outkast does consistently with titles like: "Southernplaylisticadillacmuzik," "Stankonia,"
"Aquemini" and "Atliens." In fact, when Raekwon of Wu Tang was interviewed and asked whether he had any new words coming out for his
solo release he replied "Yeah, *poly* to represent politics and politicking.
You know, taking care of the business, money and so on."[13] (See reduced words below.) Yet the focus on words in hip hop is not only at the
artistic level. It is an attempt to mark what is considered routine activity
in African American communities. One aspect of these activities is the
consumption of objects in public and popular culture and the reclaiming
of the object once it is made "black." Word art then is the transforming of
words to represent youth and artistic beliefs and practices by exploiting
the referential and linguistic norms of the dominant society.

Perhaps the focus on shifting lexical references is best represented in an excerpt from the late rapper Big L where he interprets both old and new lexicon in his song titled "Ebonics."[14]

"Speak with criminal slang" – (Nas)
That's just the way that I talk, yo
"Vocabulary spills, I'm ill" – (Nas)

The iron horse is the train and Champaign is bubbly
A deuce is a honey that's ugly
If your girl is fine, she's a dime
A suit is a fine, jewelry is shine
If you in love, that mean you blind
Genuine is real, a face card is a hundred dollar bill
A very hard, long stare is a grill
If you sneakin' to go see a girl, that mean you creepin'
Smilin' is cheesin', bleedin' is leakin'
Beggin is bummin, if you nuttin you comin
Takin' orders is sunnin', an ounce of coke is a onion
A hotel's a telly, a cell phone's a celly
Jealous is jelly, your food box is your belly
To guerrilla mean to use physical force
You took a L, you took a loss
To show off mean floss, uh
I know you like the way I'm freakin' it
I talk with slang and I'ma never stop speakin' it

Since new terms are introduced on a regular basis, only those who live in urban areas or have access can keep track of the lexical changes. Because of this, words function as tools and mediate interaction with others (cf. Rossi-Landi, 1983; Duranti, 1997).

Spelling reform[15]

The increase of hip hop fans and websites has resulted in an increased importance in the orthographic representation of words. It is another way to index a language ideology that contrasts AAE and GE. The artists included in this analysis introduced over 200 new spellings of words. New hip hop spellings follow English – consonant – vowel – format, often accompany a shift in word meaning or reference and reflect AAE and hip hop pronunciation, linguistic skill and knowledge of subversion of GE spelling rules and alphabet symbol ideology. For instance, when writing about America's negative treatment of urban youth, it is common to find America spelled as Ameri*kkk*a, using the initials of the white supremacist group the Ku Klux Klan (KKK). Similarly, the spelling convention associated with the racial insult term *nigger* is *niggah* and *nigga* (plural *niggas* or *niggaz*). Youth argue that the GE spelling is a racial insult exclusively, while the other spellings refer to social relationships ranging from friend to enemy.

New spellings also focus on English irregular spelling rules. So to give a compliment about an activity or object one might say that it is *phat* (pronounced *fat*). There are several general spelling principles that signal urban youth cultural identity. For example, nearly every word that ends with the *-er* suffix and exceeds two syllables is vocalized and spelled *-a* , *-uh* or *-ah* as in *brothah* (brother), *sucka* (sucker). Similarly, words ending in *-ing* are written as *-in/-un* as in *sumthin* (something) and *thumpun* (thumping). In contrast, one-syllable words with *-ing* reflect their intended pronunciation (*king/kang*). Spelling also reflects syllable reduction and vowel assimilation with rhotics and semi-vowels. Thus *all right* is spelled *aight*.

Reading again: fantasizing and grammaticalizing

In the case of urban youth grammar, reading dialect includes both the contrast between AAE and GE and the manipulation of the rules of either system. This process can result in what youth consider to be urban-generated words and meanings. This analysis explores the use of AAE features and the type of innovation in terms of source of word and grammatical category. In order for an item to be counted as an urban youth word (not necessarily new word), it had to meet at least two of three usage criteria. First a word had to be used by other artists in recordings, interviews, or conversations in other hip hop venues. These artists could be members of the same crew. Secondly, the terminology had to be used by LTs. The final criterion focuses on new inventions that may not be directly derived from existing words. Rather, it recognizes words that focus on language ideology that explores stylistic phrasing, syllabification, compounding and/or morphophonemics that could also be applied to other similar words. For the purpose of this discussion, there is a distinction between urban innovations and hip hop language ideology.

Urban youth words can be those not directly derived from free morphemes. They may also reflect a change in meaning, usage and/or grammatical category of a word previously occurring in GE or AAE.[16] For example, *dis* (discussed above) is not only a bound morpheme but a new word that means to reject, ignore and embarrass (see also Smitherman, 1994). Hip hop language ideology also favors adding bound morphemes (affixes and suffixes) to highlight an already established meaning or change in meaning. Other favored bound morphemes include *-est, -ous/-ious, -er, -ic* and *-un/-in*. Though the words *mack* and *mack daddy* fit within urban hip hop language style, they exist in AAE with the same meaning of someone who exploits or hustles for sexual favors (Major, 1994; Smitherman, 1994).

Likewise though *I got my mack on* is used by LTs, it is really not a new usage since the grammatical category remains a noun and the meaning of hustler is retained. However *mackadocious* and *mackness* would be considered urban innovations since they have strictly adjectival function, are used to refer to having power to control rather than just hustling for sex, and were repeated by LTs during the time of their circulation. Using these criteria, *beautifullest* is considered an urban term, though not a new one, since it retains its GE meaning. The adjectival category is the same as *beautiful*, the addition of the suffix fits hip hop language ideology and the imitation among LTs is in reference to suffixation (e.g. *He's the most particularest, realest, thoroughest, wickedest*). Aceyalone, in his recording *All Balls Don't Bounce* demonstrates the importance of bound morphemes on "Arhythamaticulas."

> oh yes welcome to hiphology please open up your workbooks to page
> and break out your pads and pens and your calculators
> for the first lesson of today is –
>
> arhythamatic, arhythamaticulas
> this rhythm is sick this rhythm's ridiculous.
> arhythamatic arhythamaticulas
> this rhythm is sick this rhythm's ridiculous Aceyalone (1995)

In "Arhythamaticulas," Aceyalone compounds and rhymes using variations on the following formula: *a+rhythm+(atic/culas/culous/culas)*.[17]

Reclaimed words have archaic English usage or were previously used in AAE. These seem to make up the smallest category of urban hip hop words and the single most used words are *mack* and *gat*.[18] The main exception is *gaffled* used by Ice Cube: *I was hassled and gaffled in the back seat*. According to *The Rap Dictionary* (Atoon, 1992–9), *gaffle* refers to harassment by the police while its earlier usage was in reference to an ordeal.

A change of word class often reflects potential grammaticalized forms of words that have a high frequency of usage. That is, the words become more grammatical over time (Hopper and Traugott, 1993). As with *ill* described above, many words listed share more than one grammatical category in hip hop but are used as one category in GE. Though one may say *I ain't mad at ya'* it is also common during rhymes to hear an Mc say

I drop madd rhymes. In this case *mad* is both a quantifier and an adjective that means crazy, intense, exceptional and extreme.

Another word that has experienced a shift in meaning and class is the hip hop word *loc*. Smitherman (1994) and Atoon (1992–9) include the following meanings and grammatical categories for this term.

1. (n) Term used for local person.
2. (n) Lock or locks, as in *Jheri-curls*, but always pronounced with the long *o* as in *go*.
3. (adj) Crazy one, from the Spanish *loco*, often used for friends or locals in a positive way [usually pronounced *loke*].
4. (adj) To get high. "We was in the park gettin' loc-ed."
5. (v) To *go loc* means to get ready for a drive-by or to shoot someone. This means putting on dark glasses, skullies, caps and generally getting hard to identify.

Thus Jay-Z and Memphis Bleak rhyme:

> Bounce if you wanna bounce, ball if you wanna ball
> Play if you wanna play, floss if you wanna floss
> . . .
> Get ill if you wanna ill, smoke if you wanna smoke
> Get ill if you wanna ill, smoke if you wanna smoke
> Kill if you wanna kill, loc if you wanna loc.[19]

Unsurprisingly, the most common urban word formation occurs through simplifications in pronunciation (also recognized in spelling). They are often morphophonemic and focus on the suffix *-ing* and contracted negation. Thus *didn't* is written *didin* or *did'n* to represent its syllabic character (West Coast) and the glottalization of voiceless stops before nasals (East Coast). As reported in Rickford (1999) and elsewhere, *I'm gonna/ I'm going to* is written *Ima* reflecting the deletion of *g*. However, *Ima* does not only refer to future action, but also implies intention and agency of the speaker.

Reduced words:

> Figg murder, crosses burnin' in my front yard
> KKK throwin up rallies but not no more in these parts
> *[(We) figure murder, crosses burning in my front yard. Klu Klux Klan*
> *having rallies but no more in these parts.]*   (Goodie Mob)

> Steada treated, we get tricked
> Steada kisses, we get kicked
> It's the hard knock life!!
> *[Instead of being treated, we get tricked. Instead of getting kisses, we get*
>   *kicked.]*   (Jay-Z)

Table 6 *Percentage usage of got(s)/ta and have to*

	Ice Cube	Outkast	KRS-One	Goodie Mob	Common	Aceyalone
had to	2	3	13	13	11	0
have to	2	10	4	22	17	11
has to	0	3	2	0	0	0
has got	4	3	6	0	0	11
got(s)/ta	92	81	75	65	72	78
Total	56	38	56	23	47	9

Ima:

> Ima try my best, and if you real like I real (Jay-Z)
>
> I don't know, but Ima be on, for eons, and eons (Aceyalone)

One urban word change that has grammatical implications concerns the contrast between *got* and *have*. As table 6 indicates, *gots'ta* (gots to) and *gotta* (got to) are frequently used in place of *have* and *have got to*. This usage is nearly categorical and highlights the agency and intention of the speaker. *Gotta* often implies urgency, logical necessity, obligation and compulsion (e.g. must) along with the speaker's attitude regarding injustice, power empowerment.[20]

> I just gots to say that, actin large I don't play that (KRS-One)
> I gots to live (Ice Cube)

When lexical expansions have grammatical consequences, it becomes important to distinguish stabilizing grammatical forms from words that are temporary targets of the counterlanguage routine. As the examples above reveal, grammatical classes and meaning are routinely shifted, but only a few achieve real stability. For example, the verb *converse* has been replaced with the verb *conversate*, including its non-finite form *conversating* (e.g. *conversate/conversated/conversating*): *They just be conversating with me all the time* (Smitherman, 1994).[21]

In addition to the grammatical norms described above, American working-class phonological features like consonant simplification and vowel length are used to distinguish regional differences. Thus the shortening of vowels, increase in glottal stops and the reduction of consonants marks the East Coast. In contrast, vowel lengthening marks the West Coast. The different use of vowels in the West and consonants in the East is related to musical influences as well as social class allegiances. Thus the word *didn't* and *ghetto* are often pronounced /d *i'n*/ and /ge'o/ on the East

Table 7 *Copula absence in hip hop*

	Noun Phrase	Locative	Adjective	Vb/*gonna*	Other	Total
West (51)						
Ice Cube	29	2	45	21	2	38
Aceyalone	8	15	23	54	0	13
South (146)						
Goodie Mob	26	12	25	37	0	57
Outkast	13	4	32	51	0	89
East (184)						
KRS	22	7	19	52	0	58
Jay-Z	19	6	40	35	0	69
Wu	10	19	25	46	0	57

Coast and /*di:n*/ and /*ge:do*/ on the West. Both the East and West coasts are heavily influenced by a variety of musical styles, though fast-paced Jamaican dance hall music is central to East Coast rap and funk rhythms are central to the West Coast.

Being and time

While hip hop may use lexicon and semantic inversion and extension to highlight regional identities and alliances, copula absence and deletion exists as a rule. Yet the importance of its use in grammatical contexts is remarkable in that it can sharply identify regional affiliations.

For example, in table 7, West Coast artists do not align in their use of copula deletion when the following grammatical environment is considered. Instead, Aceyalone favors verb *gonna* (54 percent) and Ice Cube favors adjectives (45 percent) for deletion of the copula. While in the South, the percentage of deletions for each category varies widely and the Goodie Mob and Outkast follow the same pattern of favored environments. For East Coast artists, however, there is close alignment of favored environments for deletion, with verb *gonna* being the most preferred for all groups except Jay-Z who slightly favors deletion followed by adjectives. This strong favoring of deletion environment among East Coast artists can therefore mark the urban youth identity of the region.

The preceding sections have shown how youth identity is constructed around and within an ideology that representations and references (signs and symbols) are indexical and create institutional practices. Words are powerful signs and references that imprint youth's existence in relation to their peers and in opposition to communities with which they are in

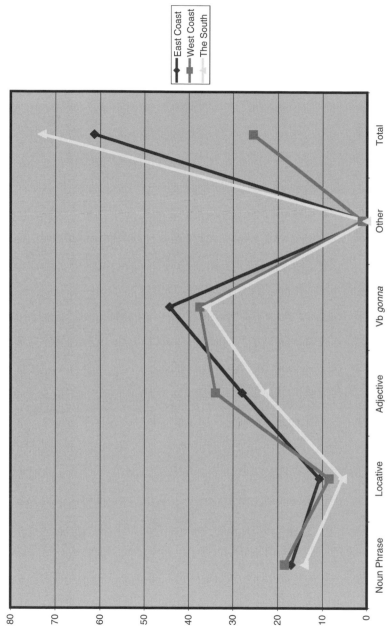

Figure 3 Copula absence and identity in hip hop

conflict. Of course the linguistic knowledge portrayed by urban youth in expressing their social identity could be applied in formal educational settings as well. They obviously value language knowledge and are willing to learn the orthographic, grammatical, lexical and phonological rules of both AAE and GE. And these rules become the grist of their power discourse. Yet, educators routinely consider African American youth's powerful knowledge of language to be in conflict with formal learning and educational goals. This is a tragedy not only for youth whose identity is often attacked through language, but for society at large, who treat black youth's identification with their community as a national problem.

6   Language, discourse and power: outing schools

While conducting fieldwork in Los Angeles, I observed a family working together to enroll a young child in a pre-school program. I visited the Cousin family regularly because one of the children, Mark, was a hip hop deejay.[1] When I first met Mark, I was fascinated with his resourcefulness in procuring old vinyl recordings and updating his mixing equipment. Originally, I paid little attention to the rest of Mark's family, except to note that he lived at his grandmother's home more often than he did at his parents'. His mixing equipment and thousands of records were in his grandmother's basement – and he preferred to sleep with his records. Everything about him – and his parents and grandmother – was middle class. It was only after his nephew Rob began his campaign to enter school early that I paid attention to Mark's sister, who regularly visited their grandmother.

Mark's nineteen-year-old sister Dina had a four-year-old son named Rob who desperately wanted to go to school. When asked if he wanted to go to daycare Rob would reply, "Not day care! School!" All of Rob's aunts and great aunts and uncles, his mother, grandmother and great grandmother thought Rob was special – an old soul. They use to say "He been here before!" And getting him into school was an elaborate undertaking that included the entire family. As I watched them work to fulfill Rob's dream I found myself repeatedly thinking "Just a typical black family in America. They'll make it." But that didn't seem good enough to me. And it definitely didn't seem good enough to them.

If I had begun my research by focusing on Dina, I might have thought the family was part of the urban poor. She was a teenage mother who had not completed high school and was unemployed. Whenever I visited she seemed to be in the background – never a part of anything. But as everyone worked to help Rob, I slowly came to realize that she was much more than a teenage mother to her family. I saw the family's version of Carol Stack's "bonds of obligation, alliance, and dependence" (1975: 66) as they conspired to get Rob into school.

132

Rob's mom taught him how to write his name, but she didn't like to read to him and would say, "I don't like the way I sound when I read." And nobody could convince her otherwise, so other relatives read to him and they bought him books. But Dina wanted her son to go to school and fulfill his dream. So Dina's grandmother asked her granddaughter (a teacher), her other two daughters (a lawyer and a nurse) and her son (a fireman) to help Rob. Actually, saying she asked them is stretching the truth a bit. She just kept saying for all to hear "Seems to me that with *all* you suppose to know, you should know how to help that boy get into school. He really wants to go to school *bad*!"

The family got to work. As I watched them over a period of two months, I noticed that everything was arranged and discussed through Dina's grandmother, though Dina watched closely as things unfolded. One by one, members of the family assumed some responsibility for Rob's education. The fireman kept saying "All the boy really needs is some good stories!" And he told him tales that terrorized me but fascinated Rob. When he finished his stories, the uncle/fireman would ask a series of "comprehension" questions like "So why did the monster bite off his hand again?" And Rob loved every minute of it.

The lawyer (Dina's mother) bought books from the *New York Times* bestseller list and Eso Won, the black bookstore. The nurse read to him and worked with him on drawing and printing. And the teacher gave regular updates on testing, Rob's progress, the educational bureaucracy and what she called "the conspiracy against black boys."

As the relatives unleashed their collective educated wisdom and resources on the task at hand, Dina quietly watched and smiled. At first I thought they considered her to be a clueless teenage mother and didn't bother to include her in Rob's education. As I watched, I realized that they weren't ignoring her; they knew she was watching what they were doing. As they worked with Rob, they would often say to him "Your mother will help you with this when I leave." Later Dina confided in me that she listened to everything carefully so that she could really teach him later when she went home and things were calm. She said, " They get carried away because they love him and he's easy to love – but my son needs time to think."

The education of Rob seemed like a choreographed dance, with everyone knowing their well-rehearsed parts and not colliding with approaches and prescribed ways of doing things. Rob was among the highest scorers and got into the program – but only after the aunt/teacher threatened the school that she would send the mother/lawyer if they didn't let him in. When it was over I asked Rob's grandmother what she thought about the way things were handled and she said, "Why are you asking me? Ask his mother, she knows what that boy needs."

Language education 101

"Black people *believe* in education – it's the *one* thing we believe in." The young woman shook her head and laughed as she uttered this statement. During my fieldwork I've heard this statement over and over again. This is not a statement of the obvious. It more than hints of incredulity and acknowledges that even though much of the cultural activity, creativity and intelligence described in the earlier chapters have been ignored or denigrated within school systems, black people believe that education is the key to success. If education is the answer, then there are at least two questions that need to be asked. First, how does the education system understand and address African American language and cultural practices? Second, why do some scholars consistently insist that black students oppose formal education (e.g. Fordham and Ogbu, 1986; Fordham, 1996) and what, if anything, does this have to do with language?

As the earlier chapters have demonstrated, from hip hop artists to university professors, the language ideology of the African American speech community values facility in both AAE and GE. The ideology also recognizes that language reflects social class, region, urban area, gender, generation, education, age, cultural background and speech community. Because language use reflects all of these things, interactions include shifts and switches that are often seamless, sometimes abrupt and awkward but always a reflection of social context, social standing and social face. Sometimes a speaker is made aware of the language choice he or she has made when it is highlighted and challenged or the social context is one where code switching is common. But irrespective of how speakers come to learn that dominant culture often considers AAE a problem, especially for young speakers, they must endure the aftermath of that revelation.

The consequences of highlighting and supporting AAE and its young speakers were demonstrated on December 18, 1996, when the Oakland, California, Unified School District Board of Education approved a language education policy for speakers of African American English (Ebonics) that, they argued, affirmed Standard English language development for all children. The media responded with an eruption of dialect language jokes and Ebonics renditions of classics like "The Night Before Christmas" and soliloquies from Shakespeare's plays that ranged from hysterical to bigoted. As Patricia Williams observed in the *New York Times*: "there is no greater talisman of lower or underclass accent status than the black accent ... Whether in *The Dartmouth Review* or *The Lion King*, black English is the perpetual symbolic code for ignorance, evil and jest, the lingo of the hep cats and hyenas" (Williams, 1996).[2]

Though the speech of African Americans was the subject of public ridicule throughout this period, in the midst of the hoopla two critically different views emerged regarding language and literacy education. One view was that black people speak AAE because they don't want to participate in American society in the same way as whites. This perspective considers AAE to be a language variety that children consciously choose to speak rather than reflecting culture, historical contact, social class, etc. The educational policy articulated with this view is that children should be taught basic, "no frills skills" that will prepare them for what amounts to non-career employment. For black children, preparation for a non-career employment track includes the requirement that they speak middle-class varieties of American English (cf. Morgan, 1997; Williams, 1996). The opposing view that emerged during the debate was that black people speak AAE for cultural and historical reasons and because of race and class discrimination. Proponents of this view argued that literacy education should include basic skills as well as other areas in order to prepare individuals to choose any employment path they desire.

The nearly exclusive association of public school education with low-level employment opportunities rather than careers or higher education persisted even though the majority of the students targeted by the resolution, as well as those shown in the media, were young children. This is particularly alarming because black children value education precisely because they believe it might lead to lucrative careers (see below). At the same time, there were fundamental political and ideological differences based on racial and class lines about the nature of social dialects in general and AAE in particular. Perhaps it was predictable that in the midst of the public debate an ideological split developed among educators and linguists over the utility of language education theories and programs that began in the 1970s (e.g. Tolliver-Weddington, 1979; Williams, 1975). The conflict among linguists and educators has persisted since the advent of public education and is particularly problematic because it foregrounds the mismatch between literacy goals and education for the working class in general and African Americans in particular. This split concerns the purpose of education for minority and working-class children and how language education programs address overall social class and minority issues.[3]

Since its beginning, public schooling has been viewed as a key socializing agent and resource for individual improvement and economic equality (Dewey, 1900). Schooling was part of a policy agenda to increase equitable distribution of life chances irrespective of social class. As the need for a trained labor force increased, public education began preparing the working class to meet the growing and changing needs of business and industry (cf. Bidwell and Friedkin, 1988; Bowles and Gintis, 1976; Durkheim, 1961 [1925]; Sorokin, 1927). In spite of these needs, literacy education in particular was not solely developed to prepare workers to read job manuals and follow instructions. Rather, it also included middle-class designs to increase writing skills, introduce literature, creativity, etc. (cf. Heath, 1983). The result was two conflicting positions on the goals of schooling: educating to know and learn and educating to do and work. Despite public education's egalitarian origins, originally African Americans were systematically excluded from public education and the system has yet to treat students equitably irrespective of race or social class (Bond, 1969 [1939]; West, 1972; Wharton, 1947). In many respects, today's call for middle-class language usage for black students coupled with cries for "just the basics" reflects a contradiction over the purpose of education for African American children in particular.

The two positions of educating to know and learn, and educating to do and work continue to have an uneasy coexistence in language education planning today, and are often a source of conflict when social dialects are considered. The split, often presented as a battle over "traditional" values, is essentially a policy argument over whether a fully developed literacy education is for the economically privileged alone or includes the working class. This split affects the extent and nature of educational policies, attitudes toward parental and community involvement, and overall implementation in schools. Thus for the public, as well as in educational circles, the Oakland resolution created a fracas over language and literacy education for all American children. That is, it created a context in which to air views about the importance of literacy education in the US and attitudes toward racial groups and social class in language and education planning.

Once the media began its "spin" on the Oakland resolution, debates and opinions about the value of African American speech patterns and Ebonics circulated throughout the country. In the black community, these discussions eventually gave way to near-unanimous agreement that all children should speak "good English" in order to improve career opportunities. This trend was repeated in black-oriented publications and other media throughout the country. In all reports and television interviews, those claiming to represent the African American community focused on the importance of white middle-class varieties of English in achieving academic and later financial success. Only after the necessity of Standard English was clearly articulated did African Americans discuss AAE's cultural value.[4] Moreover, many community leaders argued for the teaching of code switching or style shifting – processes that they maintained are not made available to some adolescents and working-class students.

In contrast, with few exceptions, non-African American communities responded to the Oakland proposal with charges of "going too far" in order to achieve political correctness and special privileges. On talk radio programs and many Internet sites, little or no attention was paid to cultural, political, historical or social differences and the idea that African American children do not have equal chances in life. As one caller said to me when I was a guest on a radio show, "Why can't you people just be like us and stop complaining? You've gotten enough!"

Though many linguists who research African American dialects attempted to address the media coverage and draw relationships between white working-class dialects and other situations in the world, for the most part the arguments fell on deaf ears.[5] To make matters worse, the public debate was well into its second week before linguists were able to introduce theories about language norms, standards and dialects into public debate. Thus a racist "genetic" argument that black people do not master educated English norms because they are biologically incapable of it and because African Americans want to receive special treatment was circulated without effective rebuttal for nearly a week.

This striking polarization by African American and non-African American communities of popular interpretations of what actually happened and what it was about reflects and is partially due to social psychological theories about literacy, race and social class in research and educational policy.

Psychological models

Since the forced integration of public schools in the 1960s, numerous psychological theories about the school performance of African American children have surfaced.[6] In the 1960s, one influential psychological theory purported to explain differences in educational achievement between black working-class and white middle-class children holds that black children suffer from genetic or cognitive deficiencies (e.g. Bereiter and Engelman, 1966; Jensen, 1969). These deficit theories ignore social class and racial inequality, arguing that inherent characteristics are the true culprit.[7] As recently as 1994, Hernstein and Murray attempted to resurrect these theories. Educational psychologists have also explained black children's poor performance through social pathology theories. These theories attack the cultural and social environment of African American children (cf. Deutsch, Katz and Jensen, 1968). Deprivation theories are repeatedly given credence by other sociological theories that consider middle-class family values and childhood experiences to be normative (Brodkin, 1994). Middle-class life is then compared to the social life of those from different racial groups and social classes. But, as Fischer et al. write in their convincing debunking of Hernstein and Murray: "Research has shown that 'nature' determines neither the level of inequality in America nor which Americans in particular will be privileged or disprivileged; social conditions and national policies do. Inequality is in that sense designed" (Fischer et al., 1996: xi).

The response of linguistic scholars to the deficit and deprivation approaches of social psychologists has been aggressive and thorough. Detailed descriptions of language and verbal style and the system and structure of AAE have been conducted (e.g. Baratz, 1973; Baugh, 1983a,b; Brooks, 1985; Kochman, 1972b; Labov, 1972a; Mitchell-Kernan, 1972a; Morgan, 1994a; Smitherman, 1977; Stewart, 1969; Wolfram, 1969). Many linguists and education theorists have directly addressed this particular issue by detailing working-class and African American working-class varieties and the plight of African Americans within public education (e.g. Baugh, 1981; Labov, 1982; Morgan, 1994b; Ogbu, 1978; Rickford and Rickford, 1995; Smitherman, 1981a,b). In addition, linguists and language educators have been consistent if not always united in their recognition of the necessity to contribute to educators' understanding of AAE. Some linguists and communication specialists developed language programs that were designed to use the child's home language as a vehicle to learn school specific activities, and middle-class varieties of English.

Standard English as a Second Dialect (SESD)

Language education plans specifically designed to address the needs of African American children began in the early 1970s under the name Standard English as a Second Dialect (SESD) instruction. SESD was introduced into the school curriculum of most major metropolitan areas including Los Angeles, Chicago, Washington, DC, Detroit, Gary, Indiana, and Brooklyn.[8] These programs emerged at the height of the Black Power, civil rights, and African liberation support movements. This period was an extremely creative, intense and fluid time when identity was being redefined throughout the black community. In fact, many Black Power advocates argued that African Americans should speak both Standard English and Swahili! Some proponents of these beliefs began an alternative school movement that focused on African history, African languages and attacked the public educational system. It was also a period when community representatives focused on the rights of African Americans to the same quality education afforded middle-class whites.

Within this climate, the mission of SESD programs was to improve the life chances of African American children by introducing Standard English norms into their verbal repertoire, while respecting the child's home dialect. Criticism of these programs evolved around what was considered respecting the home dialect and how parents perceived the function of literacy education.

The SESD approach focused on structural language learning methods and communicative competence models. J. Dillard, who wrote a comprehensive review of bi-dialectal education programs, describes the SESD approach as one which teaches the relationship between AAE and school talk "enabling the child to use a second type of 'everyday talk'" (1978: 300). Both linguists and educators involved in the 1970s effort focused on the need for equality and justice, viewing the school as the equalizing and socializing agent.[9]

It was felt, moreover, that there should be incorporated some of the sociological knowledge which led many practitioners of the newly developed sociolinguistics to believe that "Your Language is Good Language," while a noble slogan, did not take sufficiently into account the social problems which might be encountered by one holding to the first language variety which he happened to have learned as a child. (Dillard, 1978: 300)

Yet Dillard's own discussion of language education programs and issues illustrates the difficulty of reconciling how schooling works in America with linguistic and educational policy making and the rights and interests of African American parents and their children. While using terminology like "the language of the classroom" and "the language of the community," few theorists actually studied the discourse about language in either the classroom or community. There was no development of an assessment instrument to determine whether a student's knowledge of AAE caused problems with learning and whether he or she could benefit from the program. What's more, administrators of SESD programs did little to explain these programs to parents and inform them about the dialect materials and how they would be used in the teaching of standard literacy. Nor did they train teachers about stereotypes, racism and the relationship between language and culture, historical and language loyalty issues. This failure to inform both parents and teachers had dire effects on all SESD programs.

For example, African American parents reproached one program conducted in Florida that included dialect reading material about a young black boy who repeatedly skipped school. In his article "Teaching Blacks to Read Against their Will" William Stewart (1975) condemned the parents for rejecting the program and, ironically, charged them with having middle-class values. He argued that they suffered from self-hate because they didn't want their children to bring home "realistic" reading material written in AAE grammatical style (Morgan, 1994a). Though his assessment is clearly offensive, it also reveals the depth of the belief among linguists that African American homes do not contain families who care about their children's literacy education and can participate in it. Unsurprisingly, Stewart's program was not the only one to be rejected. Nearly every city that had an AAE program saw it rejected by parents, and its proponents were accused of attempting to miseducate black children.

This was also the fate of one of the most innovative programs to emerge during this SESD period. The Bridge Program (Simpkins, Holt and Simpkins, 1977) was designed for students in grades 7–12 and differed from many other programs in that it incorporated grammatical, verbal play and discourse styles into the body of literature read by the children (Rickford and Rickford, 1995). It includes African American folk tales and experiences with transitional grammatical exercises, and is written in a variety of AAE and standard school grammar. Because Bridge incorporated culturally relevant materials that included respect for oral traditions and that made dialect shifting logical as opposed to a simple structural exercise, many thought it would have great success (e.g. Smitherman, 1977). Yet it ran into problems similar to other SESD approaches which could be attributed to parental resistance to dialect readers in the school. That is, though effective at every level of educational assessment, parents and many students did not accept the argument that it was the best way to attain GE literacy. As one community college teacher, who was unsuccessful in using it in junior high, told me, Bridge is "fantastic for older students" who understand what the texts are teaching and who don't have to explain their assignments to parents.

Yet closer examination reveals two key factors that actually shaped the controversy during the 1970s. First, parental complaints focused on cultural attitudes toward literacy, literacy standards, social status and formal education. That is, the questions parents raised about the SESD approach were not whether AAE existed, but the cultural and political implications of programs that did not highlight the social functions of literacy (Baugh, 1981; Gee, 1996; Gilyard, 1996; Rickford and Rickford, 1995; Wolfram, 1991). Their questions were about the nature and purpose of education for all children and their children in particular. For example, in at least two programs (Chicago and Florida) parents could see the following types of materials their children brought home: (a) dialect stories and folk tales, some developed for the purpose of SESD exercises; (b) grammatical exercises that reviewed AAE structure exclusively; (c) grammatical exercises that tested GE structure exclusively; and (d) contrastive exercises that included both forms.

It is not surprising that reaction to SESD was overwhelmingly hostile, in spite of numerous studies showing the success of dialect readers (Rickford and Rickford, 1995; Simpkins and Simpkins, 1981).[10] But these readers were an innovation that actually contradicted everything that the community – and most Americans – expected to happen in a classroom. No one had been socialized around dialect readers and with the notion that a quality education included them – especially when integrated educational institutions had worked so hard to exclude black children culturally. So even during the Black Power movement, dialect readers were a problem in the hands of children and their families who viewed public schooling as a socializing agent in preparation for an equal chance and careers for their children too. It is not difficult to imagine what parents must have thought as their children shared their materials, practiced AAE grammar and read to them dialect versions of schoolbooks and classics!

Language and culture: ebony and ivory?

Around 1975, a group of linguists and communications professionals met to promote a definition of African American English that represented an ideology focusing on the importance of culture and language and African retentions (Williams, 1975). The development of Ebonics[11] was a direct response to the failure of SESD programs and what was perceived as a lack of commitment to and understanding of the education and needs of black children and their community. Specifically, it was an attempt to incorporate African American historical, cultural and political realities within the language education of black children. This approach does not compare African American English to American English standards, but considers it to be unique among varieties in the US (Morgan, 1994b). For these educators, AAE is a social and cultural product that began in Africa, and is a result of resistance to slavery, and should now be valued because of its origins. Thus those promoting Ebonics philosophy describe AAE's historical ancestry primarily in terms of African languages (see chapter 3). They argue that African American culture and language are part of a larger non-American tradition and should be taught as such (e.g. Hale-Benson, 1982; Kunjufu, 1989; Smith, 1997).

These language scholars draw direct links to specific features of African language systems and their views are seldom represented in traditional linguistic scholarship.

The result of the omission of Ebonics scholarship in some academic circles is that many linguists are detached from the range of views about African American language use that the community regularly considers. This is particularly problematic because Ebonics theorists have long valued commitment to the education of black children, and they educate teachers and community residents regarding their beliefs about the structure and history of AAE. Few linguists are prepared to participate in educational debates with members of the African American speech community and scholars from diverse backgrounds that challenge them according to African American speech community rules. Thus while Ebonics theorists educate teachers in community schools, organizational meetings, job preparation programs and so on, linguists appear in the media purporting to understand and represent the complex views of the African American community.

The lack of publicly diverse scholarly representation concerning AAE – that nevertheless supports and respects black children and culture – cannot be overstated. One outcome is the erasure of discussion on social class and cultural differences in styles of education that are ignored by the school.

Language education and social dialect

Though the controversy concerning the use of non-prestige dialects in literacy education is rife with misinformation and prejudice, it is not about racial prejudice alone. Disputes over educational practices include social class differences and values about the function and style of home literacy appropriate for a child's preparation for school literacy.[12] Both Martha Ward (1971) and Shirley Brice Heath (1983) conducted ethnographic studies of language learning in poor and working-class African American homes. Heath's (1983) study of a black and white community in the Piedmont Carolinas revealed that attitudes toward the value of home reading differ, though the amount of reading and writing and the motivations are similar. In the black community of Trackton, Heath describes reading as a public group affair and writes that for young people "reading alone . . . marks an individual as someone who cannot make it socially" (1983: 191). Consequently, quiet reading time, a process valued in middle-class education, is not always made available to working-class children. Instead, for African American children, reading activities that facilitate social action or that are instrumental are encouraged.

Heath's findings support Labov's (1972a) earlier work in New York City where he identified those who pursued education as lames. Heath's work suggests that the middle-class homework practices of most schools may be disruptive to working-class households because they are child centered, focusing on the value of the individual child rather than all members of the family.

Contrasts with the white working-class community are significant not in outcome, but in the overall attitude toward literacy activities associated with schooling. In the white working-class community of Roadville, reading is "a frequently praised ideal" (Heath, 1983: 231). In spite of this, it usually occurs in order to complete a task. It should be noted that for working-class families, children often have household responsibilities that take precedence over reading for pleasure. Similarly, in my observations of young people from working-class families in urban areas, private time is allowed for writing among peers, though parents are not as supportive of writing as a private activity at home.[13] Yet, it is clear that, irrespective of the nature of these literacy activities, "Neither community's ways with the written word prepares it for the school's ways" (Heath, 1983: 235). It is within this problematic construction of the working-class household as semi-literate and uncaring that social psychological theories about literacy and race have taken shape.

Unfortunately, since working-class children's home literacy practices are not ideally suited to the middle-class language education norms, working-class parents are regularly viewed as bad parents and indifferent toward education. Consequently, the school often conducts literacy education with the assumption that parents either will not or cannot be involved because of ignorance. Yet this mismatch is not benign but a reflection of an education system that does not support diverse views of the importance and function of literacy education, or does so uneasily. It is the unspoken dirty secret of public education: to receive a middle class education you must criticize working-class and African American cultural practices. This creates a crisis of identity and loyalty for students who want to excel academically without sacrificing membership in their community. In order to avoid a crisis, they must concentrate on creating a balance in order to maintain a positive social face and avoid becoming the most tragic character described by the African American community. That is what Carter G. Woodson calls educated blacks who "have the attitude of contempt toward their own people." Or "an educated fool playing by educated rules."

Avoiding the educated fool

In his 1933 bestseller the *Mis-Education of the Negro*, Carter G. Woodson describes the African American notion of the educated fool as one whose education has made him or her ashamed of African American history and culture.

When you control a man's thinking you do not have to worry about his actions. You do not have to tell him not to stand here or go yonder. He will find his "proper place" and will stay in it. You do not need to send him to the back door. He will go without being told. In fact, if there is no back door, he will cut one for his special benefit. His education makes it necessary. (p. xiii)

The "educated Negroes" have the attitude of contempt toward their own people because in there as well as in their mixed schools Negroes are taught to admire Hebrew, the Greek, the Latin and the Teuton and to despise the African. (p.1)

Woodson goes on to suggest that the most confident and successful African Americans achieve that success because they are not affected by the values of higher education and have avoided becoming educated fools. Woodson is referring to the maintenance of a cool social face that assumes African Americans are intelligent. This is the same sentiment articulated by hip hop artist Ice Cube (O'Shea Jackson) in his acknowledgments on *The Predator* album (1992) and virtually every hip hop artist who talks about education. Ice Cube sarcastically chides the institutions he believes miseducate and destroy urban youth and led to the rise of his hip hop persona:

Ice Cube wishes to acknowledge the failure of the public school system to teach all of its students about the major contributions made by our African American scientists, inventors, artists, scholars and leaders ... Without its role in the conspiracy, the Predator album might not have been made.

Ice Cube wishes to acknowledge America's cops for their systemic and brutal killings of brothers all over the country. (Most of their stories never made it to the camera.) These actions committed by the police have provided me with some of the material for this album.

To sum it all up, thanks for nothin! White America needs to thank all black people for still talkin' to them 'cause you know what happens when we stop. You say Ice Cube is a problem – well you're right, he's two people in the same body, one African, one American. I see myself through the eyes of Africa and I will continue to speak as an African. I will become an African American when America gives up oppression of my people. KEEP RAP LEGAL!

Ice Cube links police racial stereotyping and education as co-conspirators against black youth. But even more damning is the eerie similarity between Ice Cube's and Carter G. Woodson's description of educational attitudes toward African American language use. "In the study of language in school pupils were made to scoff at the Negro dialect as some peculiar possession of the Negro which they should despise rather than directed to study the background of this language...in short to understand their own linguistic history" (1933: 19).

These accusations are harsh, but timely. Some educated African Americans believe that AAE harms the black community and should no longer be a part of the African American experience. This group inadvertently supports the psychological and cultural deprivation theorists described above. A devastating example of the black middle class supporting theories that AAE inhibits thinking was the "Speak Out Against Ebonics" newspaper advertisement that listed the National Head Start Organization (NHSO) as its sponsor (see figure 4). It was actually created by Ketchum Advertising for Atlanta's black professionals who believed in the "importance of slang and colloquialism" but thought support of AAE meant a lack of support for "proper English." As the ad's creator explained: "What if Martin Luther King had not spoken as eloquently as he did?" St. James asks. "His credibility would have been diminished" (Newspaper Association of America).

While Mr. St. James admitted that the initial response from the black community was mixed, he maintained that that quickly changed as he received hugs, smiles and sheepish grins of support. He argued, "It's not about black or white. It's about credibility and freedom."[14] After the ad won a $100,000 grand prize from the Newspaper Association of America, the *New York Times* decided to run it free of charge in its national edition on October 9, 1998. Soon after it appeared in the *New York Times*, a group called the Concerned Linguists and Educators (CLE), headed by Professor Geneva Smitherman of Michigan State University, contacted the NHSO to provide information about AAE and to determine who initiated the ad. There was great concern that the NHSO was demeaning the language of many of the children they claim to represent. On its web page (https://www.nhsa.org/about/index.htm) the NHSO describes itself as.

a private not-for profit membership organization representing the 835,000 children, upwards of 170,000 staff and 2,051 Head Start programs in America. It is governed by a 49-member Board of Directors composed of a director, staff, parent and friend representative from each of the 12 federal regions and the immediate past president. NHSO provides a national forum for the continued enhancement of Head Start services for poor children ages 0 to five, and their families. It is the only national organization dedicated exclusively to the concerns of the Head Start community.

Figure 4 "Speak Out Against Ebonics," Ketchum Advertising

Does this bother you? It should. We've spent over 400 years fighting for the right to have a voice. Is this how we'll use it? More importantly, is this how we'll teach our children to use it? If we expect more of them, we must not throw our hands in the air and agree with those who say our children cannot be taught. By now, you've probably heard about Ebonics (aka black [sic] English). And if you think it's become a controversy because white America doesn't want us messing with their precious language, don't. White America couldn't care less what we do to segregate ourselves.

The fact is, language is power. And we can't take that power away from our children with Ebonics. Would Dr. Martin Luther King, Malcolm X, and all others who paid the price of obtaining our voice with the currency of their lives embrace this? If you haven't used your voice lately, consider this an invitation. **SPEAK OUT AGAINST EBONICS,** The National Head Start Association, 1651 Princeton Street, Alexandria, VA 22314, *New York Times*, October 9, 1998, A19 [National Edition]

After receiving numerous calls and faxes from CLE, the NHSO issued a statement saying that they did not endorse the ad. But the confusion continued once it was learned that the ad's creators donated some of the prize money to the NHSO and the deputy director actually saw the ad. Still the NHSO insisted that the board of directors was not consulted and did not approve the use of the organization's name in the ad.[15] What's more, the *New York Times* did not check with the NHSO to confirm their support of the ad before printing it. The Atlanta group that initiated the ad continued to defend their position saying that members wanted to stress that AAE is appropriately used at home, but in the workforce and out in the world, there needs to be a common language.

But the image of Dr. Martin Luther King Jr. turning his back on speakers of AAE was too much for the CLE. The CLE wrote a letter to the *New York Times* asking them to print the Linguistic Society of America's (LSA) position on Ebonics free of charge. The newspaper denied that it ever prints free ads – though it had in this case – and flatly refused. But the notion that a group of educated African Americans would support an effort that produced a powerful criticism of the speech of black children, that it was printed free of charge in the *New York Times*, and that the ad was circulated throughout the country without any mention of support of the children's identity is a shameful example of the level of disdain some have for the speech of black children.

Considering the above, it is odd that the sentiments of both Woodson and Ice Cube have been misinterpreted to mean that black children resist education because they associate education and GE with whiteness. But the value of education to African Americans had never been questioned until integration. As table 8 shows, until the 1960s, virtually every sociological survey of African Americans found that education was a prestige indicator in African American communities (Glenn, 1963). So it is too simplistic to think that the problems over education are mainly about avoiding whiteness. It is much more likely that education itself is not a problem to young African Americans.

Cool education 101: knowledge rules

The promise of American education cannot be achieved through the education of its white students alone – it has proved it can do that – but if it successfully educates a group it has heretofore systematically excluded – its black students (Steele, 1990). One persistent argument concerning the differences in educational and job mobility for African Americans is that there are cultural attitudes toward achievement that are at odds with established norms (Anderson, 1994; Hannerz, 1969; Lewis, 1969;

Table 8 *Major criteria of prestige discovered in sixteen empirical studies*

Study and date of publication or completion	Major criteria
DuBois: *Negroes in Philadelphia's Seventh Ward*, 1899	Respectability, income, occupation, style of life, education, general social efficiency
Daniels: *Boston Negroes*, 1914	Occupation, wealth, education, refinement
LaGrone: *Negroes in Marshall, Texas*, 1932	Education, cultural similarity to whites (especially with respect to morals)
Burke: *Tulsa Negroes*, 1936	Education, wealth, occupation
Dollard: *A Small Town in the Deep South*, 1937	Property ownership, occupation, white ancestry, education, morality
Powdermaker: *A Small Town in the Deep South* (same community studied by Dollard), 1939	Sex morality and stable family life, education, occupation, forms of religious worship
Frazier: *Louisville Negroes*, 1940	Wealth, family background, skin color, occupation
Warner: *New Haven, Connecticut, Negroes*, 1940	Morality, refinement, education, income, occupation
Davis, Gardner and Gardner: *A Small Town in the Deep South*, 1941	Education, occupation, manners and refinement, skin color, morality, status of employer
Johnson: *Rural Negroes in Eight Southern Counties*, 1941	Family social heritage, education, occupation, income, property ownership, stability of residence, cultural standards
Drake and Cayton: *The Chicago Black Belt*, 1945	Education, wealth, occupation, standards of behavior, organizational affiliations, skin color
Hill: *A Small all-Negro Community in Oklahoma*, 1946	Cultural pattern, wealth, education, family status, leadership
Jones: *Negroes in a Small Virginia Town*, 1946	Education, wealth, occupation, family tradition
King: *Negroes in a Southern City*, 1953	Education, occupation, source of income
Lewis: *Negroes in a Southern Piedmont Community*, 1955	Respectability, education, occupation
Rohrer and Edmonson: *New Orleans Negroes*, 1960	Occupation, education, income

Liebow, 1987; Solomon, 1991). Signithia Fordham and John Ogbu have explored cultural attitudes regarding schooling and argue that black students develop an oppositional culture that undervalues formal education and overvalues other forms of learning (Fordham and Ogbu, 1986; Fordham, 1996).

In her ethnography of an urban high school, Fordham (1996) explores what she considers to be black students' resistance of school-sanctioned learning. She is also interested in what differentiates adolescents who do well in school from their less successful peers and the costs associated with school success for adolescents. Fordham addresses these questions through her theory that student resistance occurs in the forms of both conformity and avoidance. Conformity is described as the active participation in education and the unqualified acceptance of claims of the larger society that blacks are not as smart as whites.

By contrast, avoidance occurs because the educational system is perceived as hostile to black cultural affirmation and familial values – even when black people are involved. She concludes that youth intentionally underachieve in order to protect their black identity. Moreover, while both high achievers and underachievers vary in their beliefs about why blacks do poorly in school, underachievers internalize stereotypes about blacks. Fordham believes that all of those attending Capital High are either aware of or believe this stereotype.

While Fordham's findings are provocative, both Claude Steele and Prudence Carter would argue that they provide a woefully incomplete picture of the student's experience. As Steele (1999) has demonstrated, high-achieving students are the most affected by "stereotype threat" – the threat of being viewed through the lens of a negative stereotype, or the fear of doing something that would inadvertently confirm that stereotype. The problem is that negative stereotypes apply in many situations and there are many stress-reducing strategies. According to Jennifer Crocker and Brenda Major (1991), one strategic response to being on the receiving end of negative stereotypes is "attributional ambiguity," where the student disidentifies or behaves as though he or she cares less about the situation. However, according to Carter (1999), this withdrawal is from the individuals who are the source of pain, it is not a withdrawal from a desire to be educated, though the loss of formal education may be an outcome. As numerous black comedians have exclaimed in pleading tragicomic incredulity and exuberance in response to the question whether blacks want an education, "I WANT TO REEEEAD!!!" But we have to ask, who really doesn't? Where does this question come from?

In fact, Carter (in press) challenges the oppositional culture and resistance to the "acting white" explanation of disidentification and supports the language ideology and social face literature presented in the previous chapters. Carter argues that African American and Latino students in her study maintained high academic achievement goals but refused to adhere to certain styles and preferences around (a) speech, (b) dress, (c) white-dominant peer networks, and (d) social acts that invoke superiority and subjugation.

Carter interviewed and surveyed sixty-eight low-income youth over a ten-month period in 1997–8 from Yonkers, New York. She found that the youth did not have a developed notion of acting white, but they did have a clear notion of the social and cultural values of being black and Spanish. She considered "Acting 'black,' 'Spanish' and 'white' as cultural forms encompassed both those explicit and symbolic individual and collective acts and meanings, including beliefs, art forms, language, gossip, dress, stories and rituals in daily life..." (p. 12). In fact neither survey nor interview data supported the theory that the youth would have low values about education. What's more, although 77 percent of the youth believed structural barriers existed, they did not believe it thwarted their chances to succeed. Likewise, though black parents, especially those with higher education, believe that job discrimination exists (Colins, 1990; Feagin, 1991; Hochschild, 1995), their children aspire to have better jobs. Thus neither racism nor class elitism cause youth to reject their education and associate it with whiteness.

African Americans in all academic areas may too often pay the price of stereotyping and discrimination. But in high school, when peer groups are most influential, how one handles stereotype is how one handles social face. And, of course, students have knowledge of the counterlanguage to maintain this social face while confronting paralyzing racism. In fact, Carter's research suggests that black students maintain a positive social face through the use of AAE and GE, musical choice and avoidance of nerdiness labels. Students resist using only GE and consider the exclusive use, irrespective of context, as not culturally black. For youth, it is important to minimize GE as a sign of oppression and condensation by finding opportunities and contexts where varieties of AAE are appropriate. And it is important for adults to guide and support them in that search.

Though Carter is not conducting a linguistic analysis, it would be crucial to see how educational and social context and topic influence the preference for AAE and GE usage and code switching. It would also be important to determine whether language facility influences other social and cultural values or how language, music and style combine to form coolness and a positive social face.

In his famous 1963 speech "I Have a Dream," Martin Luther King Jr. longed for the day when African Americans would be judged not "by the color of their skin but by the content of their character." This statement does not address a simplistic argument against discrimination that assumes that if black children only discarded AAE and studied really hard, everything would be okay. Instead, it focuses on the social construction and realities of racial discrimination that include institutions and cultural beliefs and practices. To be colorblind, especially in the millennium, is not an asset since those who fail to recognize racism can neither envision nor understand the dimensions, depth and nuances of the lives of others. As Americans of all races daydream about the eradication of racism, they should be struck by the drama that unfolds when African American language and culture is discussed as though there were nothing at stake beyond a scholarly analysis or public critique.

This book has incorporated ethnographic, linguistic and multidisciplinary research that analyzes and identifies the system of African American culture and language. I have presented examples and analyses that reflect what I have found in my field research. While there are diverse social class, generational, gender and regional voices, most African Americans are involved in similar discursive and linguistic practices for the same reasons.

African American culture is based on acquiring and mediating knowledge – both local and general. This challenge is inherent in the counter-language, discourse styles, language socialization and contrast between General American English and African American English. All speech communities show some variation of language use and beliefs about what is socially and culturally acceptable and grammatical. While most social scientists accept this fact, language use within the African American speech communities is often interpreted according to social and political interests. Consequently, we cannot study AAE without engaging the politics surrounding it – whether we know it or not. And within the political realities of the US, the African American speech community recognizes AAE as a symbol of their culture, as resistance to and celebration of the political history of America that it represents – whether we like it or not.

In this sense, AAE is much more than the dialect and language of a culture; it is the evidence of what happened to the people who speak it proudly. The question that arises is whether African Americans want to be like the very people who seem to want to eradicate their language and culture, and whether refusing to be like them will result in exclusion from the resources and rewards deemed necessary to survive in the United States.

The urgency, complexity and resolution of these questions are reflected in the title track of Lauryn Hill's 1998 album *The Miseducation of Lauryn Hill*. In referring to Carter G. Woodson's classic tome, Lauryn Hill recalls the intellectual betrayal that she and her generation endure. She knows that to turn away is not an option. She remembers the first time – and all we have to do.

> My world it moves so fast today
> The past it seems so far away
> And life squeezes so tight that I can't breathe
> And every time I try to be, what someone else has thought of me
> So caught up, I wasn't able to achieve
>
> But deep in my heart, the answer it was in me
> And I made up my mind to define my own destiny   (Hill, 1998)

Notes

INTRODUCTION

1 This story of Mrs. Jackson (a fictitious name) actually covers two similar events I experienced as a child. One was with my family and the other occurred at a friend's house with her family. When I decided to write about Mrs. Jackson, I was concerned that this might be an experience unique to my neighborhood. I found that over twenty individuals I consulted who grew up in black urban communities prior to 1960 confirmed that someone like Mrs. Jackson taught them or friends African American history.

2 Questions of who speaks AAE in reference to age, gender, socioeconomic status, social context and so on abound. Discussion of this topic and the difficulty of discerning cultural norms from racial and social class stereotyping can be found in Morgan (1994a,b), Mufwene et al. (1998), Labov (1998), Spears (1988), Rickford (1997) and more.

3 When used in this way, it can be a signifying expression that compliments the receiver and critiques white supremacy.

4 Grace Holt (1972) refers to the case where a word or sign can have opposite referential meaning as inversion.

1 THE AFRICAN AMERICAN SPEECH COMMUNITY: CULTURE, LANGUAGE IDEOLOGY AND SOCIAL FACE

1 A. Leon Higginbotham (1996) analyzes and describes the legal process and steps involved in developing the precept of black inferiority and white superiority. The steps include: establish white superiority and black inferiority and enforce the notions publicly and through theology.

2 James Weldon Johnson is a significant figure in African American literature, music and history. He wrote what is sometimes called the black national anthem "Lift Every Voice" as well as his classic short novel about racial passing, *The Autobiography of an Ex-Coloured Man*, first published in 1912, when he was a student at Columbia University.

3 Also see Mufwene for discussion of European contact during US slavery and Rickford (1999) for discussion of Hiberno influence.

4 According to the 1790 federal census, of the 757,000 blacks who resided in the US, 700,000 were slaves.

5 Mannix and Cowley (1962) report that 86 percent of slaves brought to Virginia and 60 percent brought to South Carolina did not stop in the West Indies.
6 The majority of captives were simply listed as Africans.
7 Turner (1949/1973) and other linguists of pidgin and creole languages (e.g. Rickford, 1999; Mufwene, 1994) have provided lexical and other linguistic evidence of African language influence.
8 It is not always clear that those who recorded this information knew where an African originally came from and how he or she ended up as a slave. I do not mean to suggest that families remained intact; rather, familial roles were created whenever possible.
9 Carole Marks (1989) argues that a majority of the migrants were urban laborers and not share croppers.
10 Speakers, therefore, were rarely viewed as innocent in terms of intent; and what a speaker may argue is a *misunderstanding*, is largely viewed as the hearer's *understanding* of what the speaker really means (cf. Morgan 1989, 1991).
11 They were collected by interviewers who were familiar with the speaker and/or aspects and issues associated with black life in the South and/or early migration North. The aims of the ethnographic fieldwork were, primarily, to improve health outcomes related to high blood pressure and to include African American contributions in the history of a county in Mississippi. Both of the narrators were born in the Southern United States.
12 Throughout this book African American will refer to those in the African diaspora who reside in the US rather than other nations in the Americas.
13 This narrative was told to Sherman James, a psychologist and epidemiologist. It appears in its entirety in James (in press).
14 Indeed, the life story of John Henry Martin (James, in press) was the catalyst for the studies by James and colleagues on John Henryism. The latter refers to the nineteenth-century black, folk hero, John Henry, the famous steel-driver (see Johnson, 1929; Levine, 1977), and explores both the positive and negative consequences of engaging in hard work in the face of difficult, if not insurmountable, odds. Viewed in this sense, John Henryism is not only a discourse about physical toil but also about African American labor as physical and symbolic capital.
15 In fact there is considerable disagreement over what actually happened. Some say he called her baby, others that he whistled. It was also reported that he had a lisp and probably did not whistle. See Whitfield (1988).
16 Mr. West's narrative was collected in 1990 in Holmes County, Mississippi. It was part of fieldwork for children who were involved in an after-school program on the African American history and culture of Lexington, Mississippi. The video project was organized by Marshall High Students through the Rural Organizing and Cultural Center (ROCC). The project, "The History of Holmes County," included group meetings and interviews.
17 The gin referred to in the narrative is probably in reference to alcoholic liquor.
18 Most of the older Southerners that I've interviewed use formal address terms for adults, even if they are friends. "That's the way we got it – chopped him up" refers to the public rationalization for the lynching. Very often, though

not in the case of Mr. West, acerbic descriptions like "chopped him up" are followed by short laughter. I would like to suggest that this laughter, which is often mistaken for humor, is actually a sign of recognition of the insanity of the excess of power unleashed in life events (see chapter 3).

19 Also notice how this further explains Mr. Martin's anxiety about owning his own farm after his sister's husband owned his. He was clearly concerned with the possibility.

20 Mr. West believes that he is still a victim of racial discrimination. He is referring to the civil rights struggles of the late 1950s and early 1970s that fought for citizenship rights for African Americans.

2 FORMS OF SPEECH: VERBAL STYLES, DISCOURSE AND INTERACTION

1 Little Milton recorded this song "Grits Ain't Groceries" in 1968. Another popular song that was endlessly quoted was Lou Rawls' rendition of "If I could, I would, I should of."

2 See Geertz (1983) for discussion of the importance of local knowledge and Lee (1993) for prior knowledge in African American communities.

3 Linguistic ideologies should not be confused with linguistic determinism, often associated with Sapir (1949) and Whorf (1956) or even relativism.

4 Recently Lakoff and Johnson (1999) and others have critiqued the Cartesian notion of the separation of mind, body and society.

5 Linguistic homogeneity was employed during the development of the autonomous states of Europe under a strategy that can be described as one named language for one people. Anderson (1983) also discusses the importance of language unification in the formation of a European state. Duranti (1993, 1994, 1997) provides further cultural examples of heteroglossia.

6 This does not include children, who are taught to be active but silent hearers when among adults.

7 All of these terms have been in use for over two decades (Major, 1994; Smitherman, 1994) though their meanings have shifted over time. The definitions included here are those of urban youth and rap fans (Fab 5 Freddy, 1992; Jones, 1994).

8 For example, African American coolness is similar to the Akan notion of dry speech as clear, precise, witty and having integrity. This contrasts with Akan wet or un-cool speech which is viewed as immature, dull and slurred (cf. Yankah 1991a: 47–54)

9 Don Lee's (Haki Madhabuti) poem: "But He Was Cool or: he even stopped for green lights" ends with the following verse: "cool-cool- so cool / he didn't know, / after detroit, newark, chicago &c.,/ that/ to be black/is/to be/very-hot."

10 I'm not referring to the frequent use of *fool* to refer to individuals who are intentionally comical.

11 Kool Aid is a commercial drink powder that comes in flavors (or colors) and is mixed with water and sugar (if not pre-sweetened). It is one of the most common drinks given to kids in urban areas.

12 But see Amina Mama (1995) for a critique of black psychology's interpretation of double consciousness.

13 This table concentrates on examples from West Africa. The Akan references are from Yankah (Yankah, 1991b, 1995); the Wolof references are from Irvine (1990, 1993, 1998), the Ewe references are from Rosenthal (1995) and the Yoruba references are from Gates (1988).

14 The term indirectness is used to refer to the ethnopragmatic act (cf. Duranti, 1994) rather than those that exclusively refer to language practices.

15 See Geertz (1983) for importance of local knowledge in interpreting culture.

16 During fieldwork in Chicago, I saw a man expelled from a middle-class gathering (at the host's mother's request) because he told his friend's mother that her son didn't have to worry about his job because her son could trust him to take care of things. The mother became agitated and said, "I never asked him anything. If he has to say it, it isn't true."

17 This song was constantly played in the homes I visited in Chicago and at parties given by women over the age of twenty-five.

18 The discussion presented here is based on my fieldwork and participation in communities of African descent in Chicago, Mississippi, Los Angeles, Philadelphia and Boston.

19 This should not be confused with those cases where targeted audiences make literal interpretations that artists insist were not intended. This argument has been widely reported in popular culture when Jamaican dance hall and hip hop artists defend interpretations of their words and lyrics.

20 These definitions are an expansion of Morgan (1989, 1993).

21 Adolescents, who are not fully socialized into the discourse style, often respond as though it is baited indirection. Pointed indirection assumes that all participants evaluate other hearers and work to maintain a positive social face.

22 Her friend the interviewer did not recognize that the story was about how Mr. Walker could pass for white.

23 Because of pressure from police unions and others regarding the song "Cop Killer," Ice T lost his recording contract with Warner Brothers.

24 This form of directed discourse is also called "throwing shade."

25 Some people will use the term reading to mean "telling someone off." Since this cannot be confirmed (no audience), it is not always considered proof that reading occurred.

26 Dr. Dre produced Eminem, a white rapper, in 1999 and included a song about violence that referred to the incident.

27 This term includes an assessment that a person wants to have another identity that is not and never will be socially corroborated.

28 It is important to consider context and social standing, since some young women appropriate, what they report to be, male language styles during play to demonstrate their notion of hard-core cultural membership.

29 Of course I'm representing adolescent notions. As such, I'm clueless regarding criteria for most of these insults.

30 In fact, this is becoming a recurring issue within African American culture because when signifying occurs without any cultural context, especially when performed by adults, it appears perverse, and a form of self-loathing.

31 The obsessive interest in these categories seems to reflect the extent and limitation of adolescent male humor and imagination.

32 This analysis is preliminary and based on hundreds of "mother" statements, many of which have the same content. Most of the statements were produced by adolescent boys, who originate them, share them, or memorize them from joke books, magazines and records. Though this analysis focuses on the comparative nature of these constructions, *so* could also be viewed as functioning mainly as a quantifier (cf. Labov, 1972c). The grammatical norms for playing the dozens seem to rely on copula full forms rather than contractions. With the exception of full form *is*, professional comedians tend to use AAE grammar categorically (e.g. lack of verbal or plural *s*), though this may be because they consider "mother" statements stereotypical or stylized.

3 LANGUAGE NORMS AND PRACTICES

1 Not all trainers were like Lou, but he stormed throughout the factory bellowing – for all to hear – his threat to fire Jesse.

2 The distinction here is similar to Labov's (1998) comparison of African American and General English components. Here, AAE includes usage across social class and other interactions and discourses where speakers use both dialects. GE refers to prestige and not white working-class usage unless otherwise indicated.

3 See also Wolfram (1969).

4 Smitherman (1991) provides a very useful discussion of this notion in her article on the significance of the name African American. Of course Berger and Luckman (1966) in their text on language as a construction of social reality discuss language as representing subjective and inter-subjective worlds.

5 American advertising uses AAE linguistic and verbal expressions to represent urban sophistication as well as all social classes.

6 The terms "good English," "talking white," "talking proper" and "talking good" are widely reported in literature on the African American speech community (Mitchell-Kernan, 1972; Spears, 1988). More recently, these terms were used interchangeably during a lively talk-show discussion/debate under the topic of Black English (Winfrey, 1987).

7 An entire issue of the *Journal of Black Studies* (1979) was devoted to African American English and *The Black Scholar* devoted two issues to the topic in 1997. In addition, African American linguists have debated which name (e.g. Ebonics) best reflects both its African origin and development in the US (cf. Mufwene, 1992a).

8 McClendon is concerned that words should not be used or pronounced incorrectly in job interviews. Yet criteria and descriptions of pronunciation are not clear. His problem word pronunciation list includes "ambulance" and the misuse list includes words like "anxious."

9 While this is similar to the AAE and GE contrasts described above it is actually significantly different. The problem is that scholars and educators did not interpret AAE usage among educated African Americans and simply considered

them to be weak. See Baugh (1999) and chapter 6 for more discussion of this point.

10 Keith Gilyard (1991) provides a particularly critical portrayal of the interplay of race and class in relation to Labov's (1972a) chapter "The Linguistic Consequences of Being a Lame." Gilyard futilely insists on concrete proof that to be educated means that he is not a member of the African American speech community and concludes: "Labov . . . still can't tell us how he knows who specifically is or is not a lame" (1991: 119).

11 In fact a special conference on black and white dialects resulted in heated and provocative arguments about the relation between dialect, social class and race. See *American Speech* (1987), Butters (1989) and Sankoff et al. (1986).

12 See chapter 6 for Glenn's later argument on the importance of education in determining status in African American communities.

13 These thoughts are confirmed by the personal biographies of Jill Nelson and Ellis Cose.

14 This is an expansion of Gumperz (1982: 59).

15 When reading occurs in formal contexts, it is usually considered inappropriate.

16 This occurred on the black situation comedy *Living Single* when the character Khadijah, played by Queen Latifah, commented on a writer's work.

17 My two assistants or I interviewed all participants. All researchers had linguistic training and were trained in ethnographic methodology as well. All interviewers were familiar to the participants prior to the interview. The examples included here were collected at the end of the program. The short stories were excerpts from "Salvation" by Langston Hughes and "To Hell With Dying" by Toni Cade-Bambara.

18 Some studies (e.g. Myhill and Harris, 1986; Vaughn-Cooke, 1987) suggest a decrease in /r/-lessness within the lifetime of older African American speakers and that in some formal contexts some AAE speakers actually self-monitor their use of /r/ (Baugh, 1983). Chapter 5 discusses this variable and found that youth tended toward *r*-lessness while older adults tended to use fewer of the features categorically overall.

19 Among youth there is nearly a categorical absence of verbal -*s* in subject–verb agreement (Labov, 1980; Rickford, 154). The occurrence of /s/, where the form can represent pluralization, possession and subject–verb agreement, can also depend on the speech event (Baugh, 1983). Baugh (1983: 96) reports that third-person singular -*s* is the least likely form to occur, followed by possessive and plural respectively, while Mufwene (1994) suggests third-person singular -*s* is also a part of the realis tense system. On a different note, Butters (1989) argues that the form's only importance is that it can occasionally lead to misunderstandings between AAE and GE speakers.

20 For the alveolar stops /t,d/, Labov (1972a) suggests a rule where deletion applies in monomorphemic words such as *past* and less often in polymorphemic words such as *passed*. Some creolists argue that unmarked verbs in AAE are typical of Caribbean Creoles where the tense system is not verbally marked (Baratz, 1973; Dillard, 1972; Mufwene, 1994; Stewart, 1967, 1968) so that, for example, *walk* and *walked* are both produced as *walk*.

21 Mispronunciations were common throughout the word list and the readings. They ranged from words with high usage to those that were unfamiliar to the reader.

22 In line 22 *She cook and clean* is ambiguous regarding tense.

23 See the above note. Line 22 may be past or present.

4 WHEN WOMEN SPEAK: HOW AND WHY WE ENTER

1 This heading is from two major texts on black women, race and feminism: Gloria Hull, Patricia Bell Scott and Barbara Smith (1982), *All The Women Are White, All The Blacks Are Men, But Some of Us Are Brave* and Paula Giddings (1984), *When and Where I Enter: The Impact of Black Women on Race and Sex in America.*

2 There are notable exceptions. Walter Wolfram's (1969) study of Detroit speech was an attempt to get at a cross-section of African Americans.

3 In a later work Abrahams seemed to reverse himself and described African American women as restrained in their talk, less loud, less public and much less abandoned compared to men (1974: 242). Finally, in his examination of the representation of women's speech styles in literature, he suggested that women might have the same expressive acuity as men (Abrahams, 1975).

4 Fortunately, the scholarship on women's language use in their communities is growing. Current research critiques the prevailing literature on African American women and girls' speech (e.g. Ball, 1992; Etter-Lewis, 1991, 1993; Etter-Lewis and Foster, 1996; Foster, 1995; Goodwin, 1980, 1982, 1985, 1988, 1990; Morgan, 1989, 1991, 1993). Similarly, much of John Rickford's work and his collaborations with colleagues (Rickford, 1986; Rickford, Ball, Blake, Jackson and Martin, 1991; Rickford and McNair-Knox, 1993) on variation and style shifting in AAE is based on long-term interviews with a young female community participant.

5 The narratives and interviews included here are based on long-term ethnographic fieldwork with black women residing in Los Angeles, Chicago and Mississippi. All of the names are fictitious and some of the locations and details have been changed to protect the identity of the speaker.

6 In fact what seems to be significant is that it is perceived that everyone is talking about a person because someone else told something. The point is that since it was told, people will exploit the situation.

7 This is a prime example of the expression reported in chapter 2: "It's an A and B conversation so C your way out."

8 This expression means confront or fight.

9 Although this is a reported story, I have other recordings of teenagers engaged in actual instigating. Sete (1997) has videotaped similar episodes involving these elements. I have helped mediate the pre-confrontation stage of these episodes, but with only minor success.

10 In fact, as young women become adults, it is common to hear them say "I don't play" to signal that they no longer instigate and will not participate in a conversation.

11 This general rule only holds true for generation groups and for people that are not mere acquaintances. Parents and others often talk about children and young adults when they are not present.

12 I initially thought Judy thought the voice on the recorder was Hazel's.

13 In fact, when I was thinking of moving back to Chicago an affluent friend warned that if I moved to the north side she'd never visit me!

14 Men also use this laugh, but within the culture it seems to occur more frequently among women without additional comment.

15 The Chicago riot occurred between July 27 and August 2, 1919. According to the 1922 publication by the Chicago Commission on Race Relations, thirty-eight people were killed, 537 were injured and a thousand were rendered homeless. Both blacks and whites were killed and injured.

16 This is especially true of women in the South. Because they were willing to discuss the lynching of Emmett Till, I thought all women would talk about institutional and other recurring forms of racism directly. I was surprised to find that only young women in their late teens and twenties discussed racism and bigotry directly with any frequency.

17 Drake and Cayton (1945: 66) refer to this as the 29th Street beach but everyone who described the incident referred to it as the 31st.

5 URBAN YOUTH LANGUAGE: BLACK BY POPULAR DEMAND

1 There are too many organizations to mention here. Some can be found in Davey D's website (*http://www.daveyd.com/*), Ards (1999). Hip hop has become so instrumental in organizing youth that Lorene Cary, founder of the culture and performance venue Art Sanctuary in Philadelphia, insisted that hip hop be among visual and performance arts along with classical music, jazz, ballet, literature and so on.

2 Tagging refers to the writing of names and is not always associated with good graffiti writing and art. Graffiti writing is practiced in notebooks known as "piece books" (often leather). For more detail see: the movies *Wild Style* (1983; dir. Charlie Ahearn, First Run Features) and *Graffiti Verité* (1995; dir. Boo Bryan, Bryan World Productions) and Ferrell (1996).

3 www.Ohhla.com is a hip hop archive website. Fans of an artist submit lyrics and update various versions of a song. This site is significant since it represents what the audience actually believes an artist is saying as well as loyalty from the audience or crews that relate to particular artists.

4 These were the two women artists most frequently mentioned at the time of the survey, though they had both moved into other areas of entertainment and did not have current recordings. Because of this, I do not discuss them as individual artists here and include them within the East Coast grouping.

5 It was further stigmatized when jokes were made of rapper/producer Puff Daddy's recording where he says "Lord give me the skrength to..." In subsequent interviews and performances, he pronounced the word as *strength*.

6 American regional urban Spanish refers to Spanish spoken by youth in urban areas. This form of Spanish often includes code switching with English. The

point here is that youth from Spanish-language communities incorporate their language practices within the general urban youth experience.

7 Semantics is the term widely used by youth to refer to this type of lexical activity though this discussion focuses mainly on pragmatic functions.

8 This means an artist recorded or arranged exceptionally good sound and lyrics.

9 My Webster's dictionary lists its entry as 1974.

10 Its hip hop meaning has evolved and it has been inverted as illustrated by Chris Rock's excited promotion of his upcoming comedy special, *It's gon be ill y'all!* The evolution to predicate adjective occurred with the inverted positive meaning of the word, though in many cases the focus is ambiguous. There are also forms such as *illified* (Stavsky et al., 1995) and *Illtown* which refers to Orange, New Jersey.

11 The lexical terms included here represent those widely used by urban youth at the time of writing.

12 Many urban areas seem to have a term for cheap sneakers without brand names that are found at discount stores and supermarkets.

13 This was on Black Entertainment Television's program *Rap City* November 29, 1999.

14 Big L Album, *The Big Picture Song: Ebonics*, typed by shinyo@geocities.com.

15 The regularizing of spelling conventions is impressive considering the various literacy histories of some of the writers and fans. There is often a move toward iconicity in spelling, though, except in cases like *Amerikkka*, in-depth local knowledge is necessary to locate the sound/letter/symbol relationship.

16 Several dictionaries were consulted in this process. Those referring to AAE include Major (1994) and Smitherman (1994). Those referring to hip hop include *The Unofficial Rap Dictionary*, and several earlier sources (e.g. Fab 5 Freddy's *Rap Dictionary*, *The Source* magazine glossary) were used, though the most common method for current usage was to ask LTs and observe usage in context.

17 Spelling symbolism is discussed below. Aceyalone uses *culas* as a bound morpheme though the spelling may be derived from *calculus* as part of a word play on *arithmetic*.

18 Reclaimed words also include archaic racial insults like *jiggaboo*, *handkerchief head* and so on.

19 *Bounce* means leave and *ball* is in reference to someone who has an enviable life.

20 Note the difference in Leech (1971).

21 I have collected over twenty cases of this usage among black and white working-class youth. I have also noted seven cases of its use among the black and white middle class.

6 LANGUAGE, DISCOURSE AND POWER: OUTING SCHOOLS

1 Names and some details have been changed.

2 For example, Jay Leno, the popular host of the late-night program *The Tonight Show*, introduced a comedy routine titled "The Ebonics Plague," a local Los Angeles radio station introduced a skit modeled after a reading program ("Hooked on Phonics") and named theirs "Hooked on Ebonics."

3 In fact, some accused proponents of Standard English on a Second Dialect (SESD) of avoiding and often exacerbating failures in language education programs (e.g. Smith, 1997).

4 This included community leaders like Jesse Jackson who eventually modified his comments.

5 Linguists' support of the spirit of the resolution was overwhelming. In addition to appearing on television and radio news programs and writing op-ed pieces, the Linguistic Society of America, the American Association of Applied Linguists, the Committee of Linguists of African Descent and others produced resolutions in support of Oakland's efforts.

6 I have yet to discover any study that looked at the effects of racism on black children's performance that was pervasive at the beginning of integration. Only recently has the effect of stereotyping in schools been taken seriously (e.g. Steele, 1998).

7 In fact, it was partly the infamy of deficit theories that jeopardized the Oakland proposal, which included an argument that there are genetic links between African languages and AAE. Many interpreted the argument as a purely biological one where pronunciation of English is determined by racial features or recessive genes.

8 For further reference see Dillard (1968, 1972), Fasold and Shuy (1970), Lin (1965).

9 Many significant works and collections appeared during this period, including Fasold and Shuy (1970), Baratz and Shuy (1969).

10 McWhorter (1997) presents evidence that SESD instruction has not been effective. However, his review of studies reporting on dialect readers does not include details of the nature of the programs or assessments of the actual evaluations.

11 This term is not widely used among youth with whom I work. In fact, it is mainly used when joking about someone's speech.

12 Though there have been numerous studies on the verbal style and interaction of African American youth, few extensive works have been published on literacy activities in working-class African American homes (Heath, 1983 is one exception). Some Head Start programs have attempted to address these issues (Snow, 1987, 1993).

13 Ward (1971) also found that children were more vocal with peers, though she did not report an increase in literacy activities. There are some practical reasons why working-class parents are less than enthusiastic about reading and writing that is not directly related to school. Often older children must be available to help with other children or household activities. Reading and writing in the home is probably high for working-class families who have an Afrocentric focus and for those youth interested in writing rap music and graffiti. In the first case, children's books, literature and home education in general are very important. In the case of hip hop, writing skills are individually practiced, and all writers must learn some aspect of history and social science as well as politics.

14 Fortunately, I had the opportunity to correspond with Lee St. James, the creator of the "Speak Out Against Ebonics" advertisement. Following, in his own words, is a description of his intentions and concerns regarding the ad.

"My belief and those shared by the organization that we were representing –
Atlanta's Black Professionals – was and remains that Ebonics aka Black
English has been vital to the social fabric of the African American community
and as such should be used inside that community to unite people. I do not
however recognize it as a language that should be taught in lieu of or as an
adjunct to Standard English. We should arm African-American youth and all
youth with the tools they need to succeed in the world. Therefore, Standard
English should be taught as a primary focus of American schools, not to
the exclusion of any other language, but certainly to the fore of any other
language. Is the ad shocking? Yes. Attention grabbing? Certainly. But most
importantly, the ad was intended to be honest, even-handed, and supportive
of all black children everywhere in America."

15 The NHSO was never shown a copy that included their name in the ad. The
donation to the NHSO was from someone involved in the competition and
who had benefited from the Headstart program.

References

Abrahams, Roger (1962). Playing the Dozens. *Journal of American Folklore* 75: 209–18.

(1970). *Deep Down in the Jungle.* Chicago: Aldine Publishing Co.

(1976). *Talking Black.* Rowley, MA: Newbury Press.

Abrahams, Roger. D., and R. C. Troike (1972). *Language and Cultural Diversity in American Education.* Englewood Cliffs, NJ: Prentice Hall.

Adero, M. Malaika (ed.) (1993). *Up South: Stories, Studies and Letters of African American Migrations.* New York: The New Press.

Adler, B. (1991). *Rap: Portraits and Lyrics of a Generation of Black Rockers.* New York: St. Martin's Press.

Alleyne, Mervyn (1980). *Comparative Afro-American: An Historical-Comparative Study of English-Based Afro-American Dialects of the New World.* Ann Arbor: Karoma Press.

(1989). *Roots of Jamaican Culture.* London: Pluto Press.

American Speech (1987). Are Black and White Dialects Diverging? Papers from the NWAVE-XVI Panel Discussion. 62: 3–80.

Anderson, Benedict (1983). *Imagined Communities: Reflections on the Origins and Spread of Nationalism.* New York: Schocken Press.

Anderson, Elijah (1994). The Code of the Streets. *Atlantic Monthly* 273: 80–90.

Anderson, James D. (1995). Literacy and Education in the African-American Experience. In Vivian Gadsden and Daniel A. Wagner (eds.), *Literacy among African-American Youth,* pp. 19–38. Cresskill, NJ: Hampton Press, Inc.

Ards, Angela (1999). Rhyme and Resist: Organizing the Hip-Hop Generation. *The Nation.*

Atoon, P. (1992–9). *The Rap Dictionary.* www.rapdict.org.

Austin, John L. (1962). *How to Do Things with Words.* Oxford: Oxford University Press.

Bailey, Beryl (1965). Toward a New Perspective in Negro English Dialectology. *American Speech* 40: 171–7.

Bailey, Guy, and Natalie Maynor (1987). Decreolization? *Language in Society* 16: 449–73.

Bakhtin, Mikhail M. (1981a). *The Dialogic Imagination: Four Essays,* ed. M. Holquist. Austin: University of Texas Press.

(1981b). Discourse in the Novel. In M. Holquist (ed.), *The Dialogic Imagination: Four Essays,* pp. 259–422. Austin: University of Texas Press.

Ball, Arnetha (1992). Cultural Preference and the Expository Writing of African-American Adolescents. *Written Communication* 9(4): 501–32.

164

Baratz, Joan (1973). Language Abilities of Black Americans. In M. Dreger (ed.), *Comparative Studies of Blacks and Whites in the United States*, pp. 125–83. New York: Seminar Press.

Baratz, Joan, and Roger Shuy (eds.) (1969). *Teaching Black Children to Read*. Washington, DC: Center for Applied Linguistics.

Baugh, John (1980). A Re-examination of the Black English Copula. In W. Labov (ed.), *Locating Language in Time and Space*. Philadelphia: University of Pennsylvania Press.

   (1981). Design and Implementation of Language Arts Programs for Speakers of Nonstandard English: Perspectives for a National Neighborhood Literacy Program. In B. Cronell (ed.), *The Linguistic Needs of Linguistically Different Children*, pp. 17–43. Los Alamitos, CA: South West Regional Laboratory (SWRL).

   (1983a). A Survey of Afro-American English. *Annual Review of Anthropology* 12: 335–54.

   (1983b). *Black Street Speech: Its History, Structure and Survival*. Austin: University of Texas Press.

   (1984). Steady: Progressive Aspect in Black English. *American Speech* 50: 3–12.

   (1988). Discourse Function for *Come* in Black English Vernacular. *Texas Linguistics Forum* 31: 42–9.

   (1992). Hypocorrection: Mistakes in Production of Vernacular African American English as a Second Dialect. *Language and Communication* 12(3/4): 317–26.

   (1999). *Out of the Mouths of Slaves*. Austin: University of Texas Press.

Bauman, Richard (1986). *Story, Performance and Event: Contextual Studies of Oral Narrative*. Cambridge: Cambridge University Press.

Bender, John, and David E. Wellbery (eds.) (1991). *Chronotypes: The Construction on Time*. Stanford, CA: Stanford University Press.

Benedict, Ruth (1940/1959). *Race: Science and Politics*. New York: Viking.

   (1934/1959). *Patterns of Culture*. New York: American Library, Mentor Books.

Bereiter, C., and S. Engelman (1966). *Teaching Disadvantaged Children in the Preschool*. Englewood Cliffs, NJ: Prentice Hall.

Berry, Mary F., and John Blassingame (1982). *Long Memory: The Black Experience in America*. Oxford: Oxford University Press.

Bezilla, R. (ed.) (1993). *America's Youth in the 1990s*. Princeton, NJ: George H. Gallup International Institute.

Bidwell, C. E., and N. E. Friedkin (1988). The Sociology of Education. In N. J. Smelser (ed.), *Handbook of Sociology*, pp. 449–71. Newbury Park, CA: Sage Publications.

Boas, Franz (1945). Commencement Address at Atlanta University. In E. P. Boas (ed.), *Race and Democratic Society*. New York: Augustin.

   (1963/1945). *The Mind of Primitive Man*. New York: Macmillan.

Bobo, Lawrence (1997). The Color Line, the Dilemma, and the Dream: Race Relations in America at the Close of the Twentieth Century. In J. Higham (ed.), *Civil Rights and Social Wrongs*, pp. 31–58. University Park, PA: Pennsylvania State University Press.

   (1998). *Mapping Racial Attitudes at the Century's End: Has The Color Line Vanished or Merely Reconfigured?* New York: Aspen Institute.

Bond, Horace M. (1969). *Negro Education in Alabama: A Study in Cotton and Steel*. New York: Atheneum.

Bourdieu, Pierre (1977/1991). *Language and Symbolic Power*. Cambridge, MA: Harvard University Press.

Bowles, Samuel, and Herbert Gintis (1976). *Schooling in Capitalist America: Educational Reform and the Contradictions of Economic Life*. New York: Basic Books.

Brenneis, Donald, and Fred Myers (1984). *Dangerous Words: Language and Politics in the Pacific*. Prospect Heights, IL: Waveland Press.

Brent, Linda, and H. Jacob (1973). *Incidents in the Life of a Slave Girl*. New York: Harcourt, Brace, Jovanovich.

Brodkin, Karen (1998). *How Jews Became White Folks and What that Says about Race in America*. New Brunswick, NJ: Rutgers University Press.

Brooks, C. K. (ed.) (1985). *Tapping Potential: English and Language Arts for the Black Learner*. Urbana, IL: National Council of Teachers of English.

Bryce-Laporte, Roy S. (1971). The Slave Plantation: Background to Present Conditions of Urban Blacks. In P. Orleans and W. R. Ellis Jr. (eds.), *Race Change and Urban Society*, pp. 257–84. Beverly Hills: Sage.

Burgest, D. R. (September 1973). The Racist Use of the English Language. *Black Scholar* 37(41).

Burling, R. (1973). *English in Black and White*. New York: Holt, Rinehart and Winston.

Butler, Judith (1995). Collected and Fractured: Response to Identities. In Anthony Appiah and Henry Louis Gates Jr. (eds.), *Identities*, pp. 439–47. Chicago: University of Chicago Press.

Butters, Ronald (1989). *The Death of Black English: Divergence and Convergence in Black and White Vernaculars*. Frankfurt: Lang.

Carter, Prudence (1999). Balancing "Acts": Issues of Identity and Cultural Resistance in the Social and Educational Behaviors of Minority Youth. Ph.D. Dissertation, Department of Sociology, Columbia University, New York, NY.

(in press). Low-Income Black and Latino Youths' Orientation to Mobility: Why School Success is not Perceived as "Acting White." *American Sociological Review*.

Chadwick, B. A., and T. B. Heaton (1996). *Statistical Handbook on Adolescents in America*. Phoenix, AZ: Oryx Press.

Chodorow, N. (1978). *The Reproduction of Mothering: Psychoanalysis and the Sociology of Gender*. Berkeley: University of California Press.

Clark, Kenneth (1965). *The Dark Ghetto*. New York: Harper and Row.

Collins, Sharon M. (1997). *Black Corporate Executives: The Making and Breaking of a Black Middle Class*. Philadelphia, PA: Temple University Press.

Connor, M. (1995). *What is Cool? Understanding Black Manhood in America*. New York: Crown Publishers.

Coombe, Rosemary (1996). Embodied Trademarks. Mimesis and Alterity on American Commercial Frontiers. *Cultural Anthropology* 11: 202–24.

Crenshaw, Kimberle (1992). Whose Story Is It Anyway? Feminist and Antiracist Appropriations of Anita Hill. In T. Morrison (ed.), *Race-ing Justice, Engendering Power: Essays on Anita Hill, Clarence Thomas, and the Construction of Social Reality*, pp. 402–40. New York: Pantheon Books.

(1998). Demarginalizing the Intersection of Race and Gender in Antidiscrimination Law, Feminist Theory, and Antiracist Politics. In Anne Phillips (ed.), *Feminism and Politics*. New York: Oxford University Press.

Crocker, J., K. Voelkl, M. Testa and B. Major (1991). Social Stigma: The Affective Consequences of Attributional Ambiguity. *Journal of Personality and Social Psychology* 60: 218–28.

Cross, W. (1991). *Shades of Black: Diversity in African American Identity.* Philadelphia: Temple University Press.

Dalby, David (1969). *Black Through White: Patterns of Communication in Africa and the New World.* Bloomington: Indiana University Press.

(1972). The African Element in American English. In Kochman, 1972a: 170–86.

Dandy, E. (1991). *Black Communications: Breaking Down the Barriers.* Chicago: African American Images.

De Genova, N. (1995). Gangster Rap and Nihilism in Black America. *Social Text* 43: 89–132.

DeBerry, S. (1995). Gender Noise: Community Formation, Identity and Gender Analysis in Rap Music. MS.

DeBose, C., and N. Faraclas (1993). An Africanist Approach to the Linguistic Study of Black English: Getting to the Roots of the Tense-Aspect-Modality and Copula Systems in Afro-American. In S. Mufwene (ed.), *Africanisms in Afro-American Language Varieties*, pp. 364–87. Athens, GA: University of Georgia Press.

DeFrantz, A. (1979). A Critique of the Literature on Ebonics. *Journal of Black Studies* 9(4): 383–96.

Deutsch, M., I. Katz and A. Jensen (eds.) (1968). *Social Class, Race, and Psychological Development.* New York: Holt, Rinehart and Winston.

Dewese, M. (1991). *How Kool Can One Blackman Be. On Kool Moe Dee: Funke Funke Wisdom.*

Dewey, John (1900). *The School and Society.* Chicago: University of Chicago Press.

Dillard, J. L. (1968). Nonstandard Negro Dialects: Convergence or Divergence? *Florida Reporter* 6: 9–12.

(1972). *Black English: Its History and Usage in the United States.* New York: Random House.

(1977). *Lexicon of Black English.* New York: Seabury Press.

(1978). Bidialectal Education: Black English and Standard English in the United States. In D. Spolsky and R. L. Cooper (eds.), *Case Studies in Bilingual Education*, pp. 293–311. Rowley, MA: Newbury House.

Dillingham, G. (1981). The Emerging Black Middle Class: Class Conscious or Race Conscious? *Ethnic Racial Studies* 4(4): 432–51.

Dollard, J. (1939/1973). The Dozens: Dialectic of Insult. In A. Dundes (ed.), *Motherwit from the Laughing Barrel*, pp. 277–94. Jackson, MS: University of Mississippi Press.

Drake, St. Claire, and Horace Cayton (1962/1945). *Black Metropolis.* New York: Harcourt, Brace.

DuBois, W. E. B. (1903). *The Souls of Black Folk.* Chicago: A. C. McClurg.

Dunbar, Paul Lawrence (1893). *Oak and Ivy.* Dayton, OH: Brethren.

(1940). *The Complete Poems of Paul Lawrence Dunbar.* New York: Dodd, Mead, and Co.

Duranti, Alessandro (1993). Truth and Intentionality: An Ethnographic Critique. *Culture Anthropology* 8(2): 214–45.

(1994). *From Grammar to Politics: Linguistic Anthropology in a Western Samoan Village.* Berkeley: University of California Press.

(1997). *Linguistic Anthropology.* Cambridge: Cambridge University Press.

Durkheim, E. (1925/1961). *Moral Education.* Glencoe, IL: Free Press.

Dylan, Bob (1963/1968). *The Death of Emmett Till.* Warner Bros. Inc. Renewed 1991 Special Rider Music.

Early, Gerald (1993). *Lure and Loathing: Twenty Black Intellectuals Address W.E.B. DuBois's Dilemma of the Double-Consciousness of African Americans.* New York: Penguin Books.

Etter-Lewis, G. (1991). Standing Up and Speaking Out: African American Women's Narrative Legacy. *Discovering Society* 2: 425–37.

(1993). *My Soul Is My Own: Oral Narratives of African American Women in the Professions.* New York: Routledge.

Etter-Lewis, Gwendolyn, and Michele Foster (1996). *Unrelated Kin: Race and Gender in Women's Personal Narratives.* New York: Routledge.

Fab 5 Freddy (1992). *Fresh Fly Flavor: Words and Phrases of the Hip-Hop Generation.* Stamford, CT: Longmeadow Press.

Fabian, J. (1990). *Power and Performance.* Madison: University of Wisconsin Press.

Fanon, Frantz (1963). *The Wretched of the Earth.* New York: Grove Press.

Fasold, R. (1972). *Tense Marking in Black English: A Linguistic and Social Analysis.* Arlington, VA: Center for Applied Linguistics.

Fasold, R., and R. Shuy (eds.) 1970. *Teaching Standard English in the Inner City.* Washington, DC: Center for Applied Linguistics.

Feagin, Joe, and Melvin P. Sykes (1994). *Living with Racism: The Black Middle-Class Experience.* Boston: Beacon Press.

Ferguson, C., and S. Heath (eds.) (1981). *Language in the USA.* Cambridge: Cambridge University Press.

Ferrell, Jeff (1996). *Crimes of Style: Urban Graffiti and the Politics of Criminality.* Boston: Northeastern University Press.

Fields, B. J. (1985). *Slavery and Freedom on the Middle Ground: Maryland During the Nineteenth Century.* New Haven, CT: Yale University Press.

Fischer, C., M. Hout, M. S. Jankowksi, A. Swidler and S. R. Lucas (1996). *Inequality By Design: Cracking the Bell Curve Myth.* Princeton: Princeton University Press.

Fisher, L. (1976). Dropping Remarks and the Barbadian Audience. *American Ethnologist* 3(2): 227–42.

Fordham, Signithia (1996). *Black Out: Dilemmas of Race, Identity and Success at Capital High.* Chicago: University of Chicago Press.

Fordham, Signithia, and John Ogbu (1986). Black Students' School Success: Coping with the Burden of Acting White. *Urban Review* 18:176–206.

Foster, M. (1994). Are You with Me? Power, Solidarity and Community in the Discourse of African American Women. In K. Hall, M. Bucholtz and B. Moonwomon (eds.), *Locating Power: Proceedings of the Second Berkeley*

Women and Language Conference, pp. 132–43. Berkeley: Berkeley Woman and Language Group.

Foucault, Michel (1973). *The Order of Things: An Archaeology of Human Sciences.* New York: Vintage Books.

(1980). *Power/Knowledge: Selected Interviews and Other Writings 1972–1977.* New York: Pantheon.

Fox, Derrick (1992, July). Punchline. *The Source*, p. 20.

Franklin, John Hope and Alfred A. Moss Jr. (1947/1988). *From Slavery to Freedom: A History of Negro Americans.* New York: Alfred A. Knopf.

Frazier, E. Franklin (1934). Traditions and Patterns of Negro Family Life in the United States. In E. B. Reuter (ed.), *Race and Culture Contacts*, pp. 191–201. New York: MacGraw-Hill.

(1939/1966). *The Negro Family in the United States.* Chicago: University of Chicago Press.

(1968). *On Race Relations.* Chicago: University of Chicago Press.

Frege, Gottlob (1977). *Translations from the Philosophical Writings*, ed. and trans. P. T. Geach and Max Black. Oxford: Basil Blackwell.

Garner, T. (1983). Playing the Dozens: Playing the Dozens as Strategies for Living. *Quarterly Journal of Speech* 69: 47–57.

Gates Jr., Henry Louis (1988). *The Signifying Monkey: A Theory of African-American Literary Criticism.* Oxford: Oxford University Press.

Gee, J. P. (1996). *Social Linguistics and Literacies: Ideology in Discourses.* London: Taylor and Francis.

Geertz, C. (1983). *Local Knowledge: Further Essays in Interpretive Anthropology.* New York: Basic Books.

George, Nelson (1992). *Buppies, B-Boys, Baps and Bohos: Notes on Post-Soul Black Culture.* New York: Harper Collins.

Giddings, Paula (1984). *When and Where I Enter: The Impact of Black Women on Race and Sex in America.* New York: William Morrow.

Gilligan, C. (1982). *In A Different Voice: Psychological Theory and Women's Development.* Cambridge, MA: Harvard University Press.

Gilroy, Paul (1993a). *Small Acts: Thoughts on the Politics of Black Cultures.* London: Serpent's Tail.

(1993b). *The Black Atlantic: Modernity and Double Consciousness.* Cambridge, MA: Harvard University Press.

(1994). After the Love Has Gone: Biopolitics and Ethnopoetics in the black public sphere. *Public culture* 7: 49–76.

Gilyard, Keith (1991). *Voices of the Self: A Study of Language Competence.* Detroit: Wayne State University Press.

(1996). *Let's Flip the Script: An African American Discourse on Language, Literature and Learning.* Detroit: Wayne State University Press.

Ginsberg, E. (1967). *The Middle Class Negro in a White Man's World.* New York: Columbia University Press.

Glazer, Nathan, and Daniel P. Moynihan (1963). *Beyond the Melting Pot.* Cambridge, MA: MIT Press/Harvard University Press.

Glenn, Norval (1963). Negro Prestige Criteria: A Case Study in the Base of Prestige. *American Journal of Sociology* 68(6): 645–57.

Goffman, Erving (1961). *Asylums: Essays on the Social Situation of Mental Patients and Other Inmates.* New York: Anchor Books.

(1967). *Interaction Ritual: Essays in Face to Face Behavior.* Garden City, NY: Doubleday.

(1974). *Frame Analysis.* New York: Harper Collins.

(1981). *Forms of Talk.* Oxford: Basil Blackwell.

(1997). *The Goffman Reader*, ed. Charles Lemert and Ann Branaman. Oxford: Basil Blackwell.

Goodwin, M. H. (1982). "Instigating": Storytelling as a Social Process. *American Ethnologist* 9: 76–96.

(1985). The Serious Side of Jump Rope: Conversational Practices and Social Organization in the Frame of Play. *Journal of American Folklore* 98: 315–30.

(1988). Cooperation and Competition Across Girls' Play Activities. In S. Fisher and A. Todd (eds.), *Gender and Discourse: The Power of Talk*, pp. 55–94. Norwood, NJ: Ablex.

(1990). *He-Said-She-Said: Talk As Social Organization Among Black Children.* Bloomington: Indiana University Press.

(1992). Orchestrating Participation in Events: Powerful Talk Among African American Girls. In K. Hall, M. Bucholtz and B. Moonwomon (eds.), *Locating Power: Proceedings of the 1992 Berkeley Women and Language Group*, pp. 182–296. Berkeley: Berkeley Woman and Language Group, Linguistics Dept.

Grier, W., and P. Cobbs (1968). *Black Rage.* New York: Bantam Books.

Griffin, Farah J. (1995). *"Who Set You Flowin'?": The African American Migration Narrative.* Oxford: Oxford University Press.

Gwaltney, John (1981). *Drylongso: A Self-Portrait of Black American.* New York: Vintage Books.

Hale-Benson, J. (1982). *Black Children: Their Roots, Culture and Learning Styles.* Baltimore, MD: Johns Hopkins University Press.

Hall, Stuart, David Held, Don Hubert, and Kenneth Thompson (eds.) (1996). *Modernity: An Introduction to Modern Societies.* Oxford: Blackwell.

Hall, Kira, and Mary Bucholtz (1995). *Gender Articulated: Language and the Socially Constructed Self.* London: Routledge.

Halliday, Michael K. (1978). *Language as Social Semiotic: The Social Interaction of Language and Meaning.* London: Edward Arnold.

Hannerz, Ulf (1969). *Soulside: Inquiries into Ghetto Culture and Community.* New York: Columbia University Press.

Harris, C. I. (1996). Finding Sojourner's Truth: Race, Gender and the Institution of Property. *Cardozo Law Review* 18: 309–409.

Haskins, J., and H. F. Butts (1973). *The Psychology of Black Language.* New York: Hippocrene Books.

Heath, Shirley B. (1983). *Ways With Words: Language, Life and Work in Communities and Classrooms.* Cambridge: Cambridge University Press.

Heller, Monica (1993). Code-Switching and the Politics of Language. In L. Milroy and P. Muysken (eds.), *One Speaker, Two Languages: Cross-linguistic Perspectives on Code-Switching*, pp. 158–74. Cambridge: Cambridge University Press.

Hernstein, R., and C. Murray (1994). *The Bell Curve: Intelligence and Class Structure in American Life*. New York: Free Press.

Herskovits, Melville (1925). The Negro's Americanism. In A. Locke (ed.), *The New Negro 1974*, pp. 353–60. New York: Atheneum.

(1935). What Has Africa Given America? *New Republic* 84(1083): 92–6.

(1941). *The Myth of the Negro Past*. Boston: Beacon Press.

Higginbotham Jr., A. Leon (1996). *Shades of Freedom: Racial Politics and Presumptions of the American Legal Process*. Oxford: Oxford University Press.

Hill, L. (1998). *The Miseducation of Lauryn Hill*. New York: Ruffhouse Records.

Hine, D. C. (1991). Black Migration to the Urban Midwest: The Gender Dimension, 1915–1945. In Joe William Trotter Jr. (ed.), *The Great Migration in Historical Perspective: New Dimensions of Race, Class and Gender*, pp. 127–46. Bloomington, IN: Indiana University Press.

Hochschild, J. (1995). *Facing up to the American Dream: Race, Class and the Soul of the Nation*. Princeton: Princeton University Press.

Holt, G. S. (1972). "Inversion" in Black Communication. In Kochman, 1972a: 152–9.

hooks, b. (1990). *Yearning: Race, Gender, and Cultural Politics*. Boston: South End Press.

(1992). *Race and Representation*. Boston: South End Press.

Hopper, P. J., and E. C. Traugott (1993). *Grammaticalization*. Cambridge: Cambridge University Press.

Horton, J. (1972). Time and Cool People. In Kochman, 1972a: 19–31.

Hughes, L. (1957). *Simple Stakes a Claim*. New York: Rinehart.

Hull, G., B. Scott and B. Smith (1982). *All the Women Are White, All the Blacks Are Men, But Some of Us Are Brave*. Old Westbury, NY: The Feminist Press.

Hunter, L. (1982). Silence is Also Language: Hausa Attitudes about Speech and Language. *Anthropological Linguistics* 24(4): 389–95.

Hurston, Zora Neale (1935/1993). *Mules and Men*. Philadelphia: Lippincott.

Hutcherson, W. (1993). Dr. Hutcherson's Guide to Mother Jokes. *Source* 4: 52.

Ice T, and H. Siegmund (1994). *The Ice Opinion*. New York: St. Martin's Press.

Irvine, Judith (1974). Strategies of Status Manipulation in the Wolof Greeting. In R. Bauman and J. Sherzer (eds.), *Exploration in the Ethnography of Speaking*, pp. 167–9. Cambridge: Cambridge University Press.

(1982). Language and Affect: Some Cross-Cultural Issues. In H. Byrnes (ed.), *Georgetown University Roundtable on Language and Linguistics*. Washington, DC: Georgetown University Press.

(1990). Registering Affect: Heteroglossia in the Linguistic Expression of Emotion. In C. Lutz and L. Abu-Lughod (eds.), *Language and the Politics of Emotion*, pp. 126–61. Cambridge: Cambridge University Press.

(1993). Insult and Responsibility: Verbal Abuse in a Wolof Village. In J. H. Hill and J. T. Irvine (eds.), *Responsibility and Evidence in Oral Discourse*. Cambridge: Cambridge University Press.

(1998). Ideologies of Honorific Languages. In B. Schieffelin, Kathryn Woollard and Paul V. Kroskrity (ed.), *Language Ideologies: Practice and Theory*, pp. 51–67. Oxford: Oxford University Press.

(1989). When Talk Isn't Cheap: Language and Political Economy. *American Ethnologist* 19(2): 248–68.

Isaacs, H. (1963). *The New World of Negro Americans*. New York: John Day.

Jacobs-Huey, L. (1999). *Becoming Cosmetologists: Language Socialization in an African American Beauty College*. University of California, Los Angeles.

James Sherman, A. (1994). John Henryism and the Health of African-Americans. *Culture, Medicine and Psychiatry* 18:163–82.

Jensen, A. (1969). How Much Can We Boost IQ and Scholastic Achievement? *Harvard Educational Review* 39(1): 1–123.

Johnson, Charles (1982). *Oxherding Tales*. New York: Grove Weidenfeld.

Johnson, Daniel, and Rex Campbell (1981). *Black Migration in America*. Durham, NC: Duke University Press.

Johnson, James Weldon (1922). *The Book of American Negro Poetry*. New York: Harcourt, Brace.

Jones, D. (1988). Towards a Native Anthropology. In J. Cole (ed.), *Anthropology for the Nineties*, pp. 30–41. New York: Free Press.

Jones, K. M. (1994). *The Story of Rap Music*. Brookfield, CT: Millbrook Press.

King, B. B. (1978). *Midnight Believer*. Universal City, CA: MCA Records, Inc.

Kochman, Thomas (ed.) (1972a). *Rappin' and Stylin' Out: Communication in Urban Black America*. Urbana, IL: University of Illinois Press.

(1972b). Toward an Ethnography of Black American Speech Behavior. In Kochman, 1972a: 241–64.

(1973). Review of *Language Behavior in a Black Urban Community* by Claudia Mitchell-Kernan. *Language* 49(4): 967–83.

(1981). *Black and White Styles in Conflict*. Chicago: University of Chicago Press.

(1983). The Boundary Between Play and Nonplay in Black Verbal Dueling. *Language and Society* 12(3): 329–37.

(1986). Strategic Ambiguity in Black Speech Genres: Cross-Cultural Interference in Participant-Observation Research. *Text* 6(2): 153–70.

Kondo, Dorinne (1997). *About Face: Performing Race in Fashion and Theater*. London: Routledge.

Krapp, George (1924). The English of the Negro. *American Mercury* 2: 190–5.

Kronus, S. (1970). Some Neglected Aspects of Negro Class Comparison. *Phylon* 31(4): 359–71.

Kunjufu, J. (1986). *Countering the Conspiracy to Destroy Black Boys* (vols. I and II). Chicago: African American Images.

(1989). *Critical Issues in Educating African American Youth*. Chicago: African American Images.

Kurath, H. (1928). The Origin of Dialectal Differences in Spoken American English. *Modern Philology* 25: 285–95.

Labov, William (1966). *The Social Stratification of English in New York City*. Washington, DC: Center for Applied Linguistics.

(1969). Contraction and Deletion and Inherent Variability of the English Copula. *Language* 45: 715–62.

(1972a). *Language in the Inner City: Studies in the Black English Vernacular*. Philadelphia: University of Pennsylvania Press.

(1972b). *Sociolinguistic Patterns*. Philadelphia: University of Pennsylvania Press.

(1972c). Rules for Ritual Insults. In Kochman 1972a: 265–314.

(1982). Objectivity and Commitment in Linguistic Science: The Case of the Black English Trial in Ann Arbor. *Language in Society* 11: 165–202.

(1985). The Increasing Divergence of Black and White Vernaculars, *The Influence of Urban Minorities on Linguistic Change*.

(1998). Co-existent Systems in African-American Vernacular English. In Mufwene et al., 1998: 110–53.

Labov, William, and Wendell A. Harris (1986). De Facto Segregation of Black and White Vernaculars. In Sankoff, 1986: 45–58.

Lakoff, George, and Mark Johnson (1999). *Philosophy in the Flesh: The Embodied Mind and its Challenge to Western Thought*. New York: Basic Books.

Lee, Carol (1993). *Signifying as a Scaffold for Literary Interpretation: The Pedagogical Implications of an African American Discourse Genre*. Urbana, Illinois: NCTE.

Lee, D. L. (1969). But He Was Cool or: He Even Stopped for Green Lights, *Don't Cry, Scream*. Detroit: Broadside Press.

Leech, Geoffrey N. (1971). *Meaning and the English Verb*. London: Longman.

Leech, Geoffrey N., and Jan Svartvik (1975). *A Communicative Grammar of English*. London: Longman.

Levine, Lawrence (1977). *Black Culture and Black Consciousness: Afro-American Folk Thought from Slavery to Freedom*. Oxford: Oxford University Press.

Levinson, S. (1983). *Pragmatics*. Cambridge: Cambridge University Press.

Lewis, Oscar (1969). The Culture of Poverty. In Daniel P. Moynihan (ed.), *On Understanding Poverty*. New York: Basic Books.

Liebow, Elliott (1967). *Tally's Corner: A study of Negro Streetcorner Men*. Boston: Little Brown.

Lin, San-Su C. (1965). *Pattern Practice in the Teaching of Standard English to Students with a Non-Standard Dialect*. New York: Teachers' College, Columbia University.

Lindstrom, L. (1992). Context Contests: Debatable Truth Statements on Tanna (Vanuatu). In A. Duranti and C. Goodwin (eds.), *Rethinking Context: Language as an Interactive Phenomenon*, pp. 101–24. Cambridge: Cambridge University Press.

Locke, Alain (ed.) (1974). *The New Negro*. New York: Atheneum.

Luelsdorff, P. (ed.) (1975). *Linguistic Perspectives on Black English*. Regensburg, Germany: Verlag Hans Carl.

Major, Clarence (1970). *Dictionary of Afro-American Slang*. New York: International Publishers.

(1994). *Juba to Jive: A Dictionary of African-American Slang*. New York: Penguin Books.

Majors, R., and J. M. Billson (1992). *Cool Pose: The Dilemmas of Black Manhood in America*. New York: Lexington Books.

Males, M. A. (1996). *The Scapegoat Generation: America's War on Adolescents*. Monroe, ME: Common Courage Press.

Mama, A. (1995). *Beyond the Masks: Race, Gender and Subjectivity*. London: Routledge.

Mannix, Daniel and Malcolm Cowley (1962). *Black Cargoes: A History of the Atlantic Slave Trade*. New York: Viking Press.

Marks, Carole (1989). *Farewell – We're Good and Gone: The Great Black Migration*. Bloomington: Indiana University Press.

Massey, D. S., and N. A. Denton (1993). *American Apartheid: Segregation and the Making of the Underclass*. Cambridge MA/ London: Harvard University Press.

McClendon, G. O. (1993). *The African-American Guide to Better English*. Culver, IN: Hampton Academic Press.

McDavid, Raven (ed.) (1963). *The American Language by H. L. Mencken (with the assistance of D. W. Maurer)*. New York: Knopf.

McDavid, Raven, and Virginia McDavid (1951). The Relationship of the Speech of the American Negroes to the Speech of Whites. *American Speech* 26: 3–17.

McWhorter, John (1997). Wasting Energy on an Illusion: Six Months Later. *Black Scholar* 27(2): 2–5.

Meier, A. (1963). *Negro Thought in America, 1800–1915: Racial Ideologies in the Age of Booker T. Washington*. Ann Arbor: University of Michigan Press.

Mencken, H. L. (1977). *The American Language: An Inquiry Into the Development of English in the United States*. New York: Knopf.

Mercer, K. (1994). *Welcome to the Jungle: New Positions in Black Cultural Studies*. New York / London: Routledge.

Miller, J. B. (1976). *Toward a New Psychology of Women*. Boston: Beacon Press.

Mintz, Sidney (1970). Foreword. In N. Whitten and J. Szwed (eds.), *Afro-American Anthropology: Contemporary Perspectives*, pp. 1–15. New York: Free Press.

Mintz, Sidney, and Richard Price (1992). *The Birth of African-American Culture: An Anthropological Perspective*. Boston: Beacon Press.

Mitchell-Kernan, Claudia (1971). *Language Behavior in a Black Urban Community* (Working Paper 23). Berkeley, CA: Language Behavior Research Laboratory.

(1972a). On the Status of Black English for Native Speakers: An Assessment of Attitudes and Values. In C. Cazden, V. P. John and D. Hymes (eds.), *Functions of Language in the Classroom*. New York: Teachers' College Press.

(1972b). Signifying, Loud-talking, and Marking. In Kochman, 1972a: 315–35.

(1973). Signifying. In A. Dundes (ed.), *Mother Wit from the Laughing Barrel*, pp. 310–28. New York: Garland Publishing.

Morgan, K. (1980). *Children of Strangers: The Stories of a Black Family*. Philadelphia: Temple University Press.

Morgan, Marcyliena (1989). *From Down South to up South: The Language Behavior of Three generations of Black Women Residing in Chicago*. University of Pennsylvania.

(1991). Indirectness and Interpretation in African American Women's Discourse. *Pragmatics* 1(4): 421–51.

(1993). The Africanness of Counterlanguage among Afro-Americans. In S. Mufwene (ed.), *Africanisms in Afro-American Language Varieties*, pp. 423–35. Athens, GA: University of Georgia Press.

(ed.) (1994a). *Language and the Construction of Identity in Creole Situations*. Los Angeles: UCLA Center for Afro-American Studies.

(1994b). The African American Speech Community: Reality and Sociolinguistics. In Morgan, 1994a: 121–48.

(1996). Conversational Signifying: Grammar and Indirectness Among African American Women. In E. Ochs, E. Schegloff and S. Thompson (eds.), *Interaction and Grammar*, pp. 405–33. Cambridge: Cambridge University Press.

(1997). Editorial. *UCLA Today*.

(1998). More Than a Mood or an Attitude: Discourse and Verbal Genres in African-American Culture. In Mufwene et al., 1998: 251–81.

Morrison, Toni (1987). *Beloved*. New York: Knopf.

(1994). *The Nobel Lecture in Literature, 1993*. New York: Knopf.

Mudimbe, V. Y. (1988). *The Invention of African: Gnosis, Philosophy, and the Order of Knowledge*. Bloomington, IN: Indiana University Press.

(1994). *The Idea of Africa*. Bloomington, IN: Indiana University Press.

Mufwene, Salikoko (1992a). Ideology and Facts on African American English. *Pragmatics* 2(2): 141–68.

(1992b). Why Grammars are not Monolithic. In D. Brentari, G. Larsen and L. A. MacLeod (eds.), *The Joy of Grammar: A Festschrift in Honor of James D. McCawley*, pp. 225–50. Amsterdam: John Benjamins.

(1994). African-American English. In J. Algeo (ed.), *The Cambridge History of the English Language*, Vol. 6. Cambridge: Cambridge University Press.

Mufwene, Salikoko, John Rickford, Guy Bailey and John Baugh (eds.) (1998). *African-American English: Structure, History, and Use*. London / New York: Routledge.

Myrdal, Gunnar (1944). *An American Dilemma: The Negro Problem and Modern Democracy*. New York: Harper and Row.

Nelson, Jill (1993). *Volunteer Slavery: My Authentic Negro Experience*. Chicago: Noble.

Ochs, Elinor, and Lisa Capps (1996). Narrating the Self. *Annual Review of Anthropology* 25: 19–43.

Ochs, Elinor, and Bambi Schieffelin (1984). Language Acquisition and Socialization: Three Developmental Stories. In *Emotion*, pp. 276–320. Cambridge: Cambridge University Press.

Ogbu, J. (1978). *Minority Education and Caste*. Orlando, FL: Academic Press.

Oliver, M. L., and T. M. Shapiro (1997). *Black Wealth/White Wealth: A New Perspective on Racial Inequality*. New York: Routledge.

Painter, N. (1977). *The Exodusters*. New York: Alfred A. Knopf.

(1994). Representing Truth: Sojourner Truth's Knowing and Becoming Known. *Journal of American History* 81(2): 461–92.

Peirce, Charles S. (1960). *Collected Papers of Charles Sanders Peirce*. Cambridge, MA: Harvard University Press.

Percelay, J., I. Monteria and S. Dweck (1994). *Snaps*. New York: Quill.

Perkins, W. E. (ed.) (1996). *Droppin' Science: Critical Essays on Rap Music and Hip Hop Culture*. Philadelphia: Temple University Press.

Phillips, U. (1918). *American Negro Slavery: A Survey of the Supply, Employment and Control of Negro Labor as Determined by the Plantation Regime*. New York: D. Appleton.

Polanyi, L. (1989). *Telling the American Story*. Cambridge, MA: MIT Press.

Pomerantz, A. (1984). Agreeing and Disagreeing with Assessments: Some Features of Preferred/Dispreferred Turn Shapes. In J. M. Atkinson and

J. Heritage (eds.), *Structures of Social Action*, pp. 57–101. Cambridge: Cambridge University Press.

Pratt, Mary Louise (1992). *Imperial Eyes: Travel Writing and Transculturation*. London: Routledge.

Price, Richard (1983). *First-Time: The Historical Vision of an Afro-American People*. Baltimore: Johns Hopkins University Press.

Quirk, R., G. L. Greenbaum and J. Svartvik (1972). *A Grammar of Contemporary English*. London: Longman.

Rauch, E. N. (1991). Paul Lawrence Dunbar 1872–1906. In V. Smith (ed.), *African American Writers*, pp. 87–102. New York: Scribners.

Reed, Adolph L. (1997). *W. E. B. DuBois and American Political Thought: Fabianism and the Color Line*. New York: Oxford University Press.

Reisman, K. (1974). Contrapuntal Conversations in an Antiguan Village. In Richard Bauman and J. Sherzer (eds.), *Explorations in the Ethnography of Speaking*, pp. 110–24. Cambridge: Cambridge University Press.

Rickford, John (1975). Carrying the New Wave into Syntax: The Case of Black English *Bin*. In R. W. Fasold and R. W. Shuy (eds.), *Analyzing Variation in Language*, pp. 162–83. Washington, DC: Georgetown University Press.

(1977). The Question of Prior Creolization of Black English. In A. Valdman (ed.), *Pidgin and Creole Linguistics*, pp. 190–221. Bloomington: Indiana University Press.

(1986). The Need for New Approaches to Social Class Analysis in Sociolinguistics. *Language and Communication* 6(3): 215–21.

(1997). Unequal Partnership: Sociolinguistics and the African American Speech Community. *Language and Society* 26: 161–97.

(1999). *African American Vernacular English: Features, Evolution, Educational Implications*. Oxford: Basil Blackwell.

Rickford, John, Arnetha Ball, Renée Blake, Raina Jackson and Nomi Martin (1991). Rappin on the Copula Coffin: Theoretical and Methodological Issues in the Analysis of Copula Variation in African American Vernacular. *Language Variation and Change* 3: 103–32.

Rickford, John, and Faye McNair-Knox (1993). Addressee and Topic-influenced Style Shift: A Quantitative Sociolinguistic study. In *Perspectives on Register: Situation Register Variation Within Sociolinguistics*, ed. D. Biber and E. Finegan. Oxford: Oxford University Press.

Rickford, John, and Angela Rickford (1976). Cut-Eye and Suck Teeth: African Words and Gestures in New World Guise. *Journal of American Folklore* 89(353): 194–309.

(1995). Dialect Readers Revisited. *Linguistics and Education* 7: 107–28.

Rose, Tricia (1994). *Black Noise: Rap Music and Black Culture in Contemporary America*. Hanover, NH: Wesleyan University Press.

Rosenthal, Judy (1995). The Signifying Crab. *Cultural Anthropology* 10(4): 581–6.

Rossi-Landi, F. (1983). *Language as Work and Trade: A Semiotic Homology for Linguistics and Economics*. South Hadley, MA: Bergin and Garvey Publishers, Inc.

Saah, K. (1984). Language Use and Attitudes in Ghana. *Anthropological Linguistics* 28(3): 367–77.

Sacks, Harvey, Emmanuel Schegloff and Gail Jefferson (1974). A Simplest Systematics for the Organization for Turn-Taking in Conversation. *Language* 50(4): 696–735.

Sager, M. (1990). Cube: The Word According to Amerikka's Most Wanted Rapper. *Rolling Stone* 10.

Sampson, W., and V. Milan (1975). The Interracial Attitudes of the Black Middle-Class: Have They Changed? *Social Problems* 23(2): 151–65.

Sankoff, David (ed.) (1986). *Diversity and Diachrony*. Amsterdam: Benjamins.

Sapir, Edward (1949 [1929]). The Status of Linguistics as a Science. In D. Mandelbaum (ed.), *Selected Writings of Edward Sapir in Language, Culture and Personality*, pp. 160–6. Berkeley and Los Angeles: University of California Press.

Schieffelin, B., and E. Ochs (1986). *Language Socialization Across Cultures*. Cambridge: Cambridge University Press.

Schneider, E. (1989). *American Earlier Black English*. Tuscaloosa: University of Alabama Press.

Scott, David (1991). That Event, this Memory: Notes on the Anthropology of African Diasporas in the New World. *Diaspora* 1(3): 261–84.

Sebba, Mark (1997). *Contact Languages: Pidgins and Creoles*. New York: St. Martin's Press.

Silverstein, Michael (1979). Language Structure and Linguistic Ideology. In P. R. Clyne, W. F. Hanks and C. L. Hofbauer (eds.), *The Elements: A Parasession on Linguistic Units and Levels*, pp. 193 247. Chicago: Chicago Linguistic Society.

 (1993). Metapragmatic Discourse and Metapragmatic Function. In J. Lucy (ed.), *Reflexive Language*, pp. 33–58. New York: Cambridge University Press.

 (1998). The Uses and Utility of Ideology: A Commentary. In Bambi Schieffelin and Kathryn Woolard (eds.), *Language Ideologies Practice and Theory*, pp. 123–45. Oxford: Oxford University Press.

Simonsen, T. (1986). *You May Plow Here: The Narrative of Sara Brooks*. New York: Simon and Schuster, Inc.

Simpkins, G., and C. Simpkins (1981). Cross Cultural Approach to Curriculum Development. In Smitherman, 1981a: 221–40.

Simpkins, G. A., G. Holt and C. Simpkins (1977). *Bridge: A Cross-Cultural Reading Program*. Boston, MA: Houghton Mifflin.

Slaughter, Diane (1983). *Early Intervention and its Effects on Maternal and Child Development*. Chicago: University of Chicago Press.

Smith, E. (1997). *The Historical Development of African-American Language: The Transformationalist Theory*. San Francisco: Aspire Books.

Smith, Valerie (1987). *Self-Discovery and Authority in Afro-American Narrative*. Cambridge, MA: Harvard University Press.

Smitherman, Geneva (1977). *Talkin and Testifyin: The Language of Black America*. Boston: Houghton Mifflin.

 (ed.) (1981a). *Black English and the Education of Black Children and Youth: Proceedings of the National Invitational Symposium on the King Decision*. Detroit: Harpo Press.

(1981b). What Go Round Come Round: King in Perspective. *Harvard Educational Review* 1: 40–56.

(1991). What Is Africa to Me? Language, Ideology and African American. *American Speech* 66: 115–32.

(1994). *Black Talk: Words and Phrases from the Hood to the Amen Corner*. New York: Houghton Mifflin.

(1998). Word from the Hood: The Lexicon of African American English. In Mufwene et al., 1998: 203–25.

Snow, Catherine (1987). Factors Influencing Vocabulary and Reading Achievement in Low Income Children. In R. Apple (ed.), *Toegepaste tallwetenschap in artikelen*, pp. 124–8. Amsterdam, The Netherlands: ANELA.

(1993). Families as Social Contexts for Literacy Development. In C. Daiut (ed.), *The Development of Literacy Through Social Interaction*, pp. 11–24. San Francisco: Jossey-Bass.

Sorokin, P. (1927). *Social and Cultural Mobility*. New York: Harper.

Spears, A. (1982). The Semi-Auxiliary *come* in Black English Vernacular. *Language* 58: 850–72.

(1988). Black American English. In J. Cole (ed.), *Anthropology for the Nineties: Introductory Readings*, pp. 96–113. New York: Free Press.

Stack, Carol (1975). *All Our Kin: Strategies for Survival in a Black Community*. New York: Harper and Row.

Starling, M. (1981). *The Slave Narrative: Its Place in American History*. Washington, DC: Howard University Press.

Stavsky, L., I. E. Mozeson and D. Reyes Mozeson (1995). *A2Z: The Book of Rap and Hip-Hop Slang*. New York: Boulevard Books.

Steele, Claude M. (1999, August). Thin Ice: "Stereotype Threat" and Black College Students. *The Atlantic Monthly* 284(2): 44–7, 50–4.

Stepto, Robert (1991[1979]). *From Behind the Veil: A Study of Afro-American Narrative*. Chicago and Urbana: University of Illinois Press.

Stevenson, Brenda (1997). *Life in Black and White: Family and Community in the Slave South*. Oxford: Oxford University Press.

Stewart, W. (1967). Sociolinguistic Factors in the History of American Negro Dialects. *Florida FL Reporter* 6: 14–16, 18.

(1969). Historical and Structural Bases for the Recognition of Negro Dialect. In J. Alatis (ed.), *School of Languages and Linguistics Monogr. Ser. No. 22*, pp. 215–25. Washington, DC: Georgetown University Press.

(1975). Teaching Blacks to Read Against Their Will. In Luelsdorff, 1975: 107–32.

Stonequist, E. V. (1965). *Race Relations and the Great Society*. Saratoga Springs, NY: Skidmore Faculty Research Lecture.

Stuckey, Sterling (1971). Twilights of Our Past: Reflections on the Origins of Black History. In J. A. Williams and C. F. Harris (eds.), *Amistad 2*, pp. 261–95. New York: Vintage.

(1987). *Slave Culture: Nationalist Theory and the Foundation of Black America*. Oxford: Oxford University Press.

Szwed, John (1974). An American Anthropological Dilemma: The Politics of African-American Culture. In D. Hymes (ed.), *Reinventing Anthropology*, pp. 153–81. New York: Vintage.

Tolliver-Weddington, Gloria (1979). Introduction: Ebonics (Black English): Implications for Education. *Journal of Black Studies* 9(4): 364–6.

Toop, David (1991). *Rap Attack 2: African Rap to Global Hip Hop*. London: Pluto Press.

Turner, Lorenzo D. (1949/1973). *Africanisms in the Gullah Dialect*. Ann Arbor: University of Michigan Press.

Turner, Patricia (1993). *I Heard It Through the Grapevine: Rumor in African American Culture*. Berkeley: University of California Press.

van Keulen, J., G. Tolliver-Weddington and C. E. DeBose (eds.) (1998). *Speech, Language, Learning, and the African American Child*. Boston: Allyn and Bacon.

Visweswaran, K. (1994). *Fictions of Feminist Ethnography*. London: University of Minnesota Press.

Volosinov, V. N. (1930/1973). *Marxism and the Philosophy of Language*. Trans. Ladislav Metajka and I. R. Titunik. New York: Seminar Press.

Walker, Alice (1982). *The Color Purple*. New York: Harcourt Brace Jovanovich.

Ward, Martha C. (1971). *Them Children*. New York: Holt, Rinehart and Winston.

West, Cornel (1993). *Race Matters*. Boston: Beacon Press.

West, E. H. (1972). *The Black American and Education*. Columbus, OH: Charles E. Merrill.

Wharton, V. L. (1947). *The Negro in Mississippi, 1865–1890*. New York: Harper Torchbooks.

Wheeler, E. (1992). "Most of My Heroes Don't Appear on No Stamps": The Dialogics of Rap Music. *Black Music Research Journal* 11(2): 193–216.

Whitfield, S. (1988). *A Death in the Delta: The Story of Emmett Till*. Baltimore: Johns Hopkins University Press.

Whorf, B. (1956). *Language, Thought and Reality*. Cambridge, MA: MIT Press.

Williams, Patricia (1996, December 29). Op-Ed. *The New York Times*.

Williams, R. (ed.) (1975). *Ebonics: The True Language of Black Folks*. St. Louis: Institute of Black Studies.

Williams, Shirley Ann (1986). *Dessa Rose*. New York: Berkeley Books.

Williamson, Juanita (1970). Selected Features of Speech: Black and White. *Colloquial Language Association Journal* 13(4): 420–3.

(1971). A Look at Black English. *Crisis* 78: 169–73.

Willis, William (1970). Anthropology and Negroes on the Southern Colonial Frontier. In J. C. Curtis and L. L. Gould (eds.), *The Black Experience in America*. Austin: University of Texas Press.

Wilson, W. J. (1978). *The Declining Significance of Race*. Chicago: University of Chicago Press.

(1987). *The Truly Disadvantaged*. Chicago: University of Chicago Press.

(1996). *When Work Disappears: The World of the New Urban Poor*. New York: Knopf.

Winford, D. (1992). Another Look at the Copula in Black English and Caribbean Creoles. *American Speech* 67(1): 21–60.

Winfrey, O. (1987). *Standard and "Black" English* (transcript no. W309). Chicago: WLS TV.

Wiredu, K. Wasi (1992). Formulating Modern Thought in African Languages: Some Theoretical Considerations. In V. Y. Mudimbe (ed.), *The Surreptitious*

Speech: Presence Africaine and the Politics of Otherness 1947–1987. Chicago: University of Chicago Press.

Wolfram, Walt (1969). *A Sociolinguistic Description of Detroit Negro Speech*. Washington, DC: Center for Applied Linguistics.

(1991). *Dialects and American English*. Englewood Cliffs, NJ: Prentice Hall and Center for Applied Linguistics.

Wolfram, Walt, and Natalie Schilling-Estes (1998). *American English*. Oxford: Blackwell Publishers.

Woodson, Carter G. (1930). *The Rural Negro*. Washington, DC: Association for the Study of Negro Life and History.

(1933/1990). *The Mis-Education of the Negro*. Trenton, NJ: Africa World Press, Inc.

Woolard, K. (1998). Introduction: Language Ideology as a Field of Inquiry. In B. Schieffelin, K. Woolard, and P. Kroskrity (eds.), *Language Ideologies: Practice and Theory*, pp. 3–47. New York: Oxford University Press.

Woolard, Kathryn and Bambi Schieffelin (1994). Language Ideology. *Annual Review of Anthropology* 23: 55–82.

Wright, Richard (1957). *White Man Listen!* New York: Doubleday.

Yankah, Kwesi (1991a). Power and the Circuit of Formal Talk. *Journal of Folklore Research* 28(1): 1–22.

(1991b). Oratory in Akan Society. *Discourse and Society* 2.1: 47–64.

(1995). *Speaking for the Chief: Okyeame and the Politics of Akan Royal Oratory*. Bloomington: Indiana University Press.

Zentella, A. C. (1997). *Growing Up Bilingual: Puerto Rican Children in New York*. Malden, MA: Blackwell Publishers.

Index

Studies in the Social and Cultural Foundations of Language

Editors
JUDITH T. IRVINE
BAMBI SCHIEFFELIN